OFFICE HOURS

ACTIVISM and CHANGE in the ACADEMY

Cary Nelson and Stephen Watt

ROUTLEDGE
NEW YORK AND LONDON

Published in 2004 by
Routledge
270 Madison Avenue
New York, NY 10016
www.routledge-ny.com

Published in Great Britain by
Routledge
2 Park Square
Milton Park, Abingdon
Oxon OX14 4RN U.K.
www.routledge.co.uk

Library of Congress Cataloging-in-Publication Data

Nelson, Cary.
    Office hours : activism and change in the academy / Cary Nelson &
Stephen Watt.
        p. cm.
    Includes bibliographical references.
    ISBN 0-415-97185-3 (hb : alk. paper)—ISBN 0-415-97186-1 (pb : alk. paper)
1. College teachers—United States—Political activity. 2. Universities and colleges—
United States—Sociological aspects. 3. College teachers' unions—United States.
I. Watt, Stephen, 1951– II. Title.
    LB2331.72.N43 2004
    378.1'2--dc22
                                                                    2004013127

About *Office Hours*:

"Straightforward, unpretentious, immensely readable, and on matters of extreme urgency to a very wide potential readership."

—Bruce Robbins, Columbia University

"*Office Hours* is always pointed, often poetic and amusing, and never dull. Nelson and Watt accurately diagnose the serious malady that threatens American higher education, and then suggest the cure. Do read this book — it's a tonic."

—Jane Buck, President, American

Association of University Professors

"With the same acumen, energy, and urgency that they displayed in *Academic Keywords*, Professors Nelson and Watt here address the crises, plural, facing higher education today, including the downsizing and part-timing of the professoriate; the corporatization of the university from 'Citadel of Reason' into 'Campus Sweatshop'; the failure of many graduate programs to develop ethical standards for the treatment of their student-employees; and the mounting threats to academic freedom in the wake of 9-11. A spirited call to action, *Office Hours* is must reading for everyone interested in preserving and improving the best, most vital features of the academy."

—Patrick Brantlinger, Indiana University

Contents

Preface

Within a very few years, higher education as we have known it may largely cease to exist. Economic, demographic, and political forces, combined with faculty passivity, have led to a serious decline in research that seeks to advance knowledge rather than generate profits. Meanwhile the professoriate has seen its intellectual independence and institutional influence deteriorate. While most academics have looked exclusively to external forces to explain this crisis, we place a significant part of the blame on the professoriate itself. At the same time we look to the professoriate and graduate student activists as potential sources of resistance and reform.

The first half of the book details the current state of higher education—emphasizing the most imperiled disciplines—while the second half of the book offers a series of routes out of the present crisis. These alternative futures take the form of case studies, covering unionization, instruction, academic organizations, public outreach through the Internet, and campus organizing as means to secure a better future for higher education.

Office Hours: Activism and Change in the Academy deals not only with the current crisis but also with a series of emerging ones—the risks to academic freedom inherent in future terrorist attacks, the increasing impact of globalization, the trend toward surveillance of research content. Its solutions are numerous, but they also have one common thread: the need for collective action on every front.

Introduction

It Might as Well Be a Conspiracy

HIGHER EDUCATION AS WE HAVE KNOWN IT for nearly half a century is in the process of unravelling. Few of the forces shaping its future are easy to welcome. Most will be destructive, especially to the most profession-ally vulnerable employees and the most financially vulnerable arts and humanities disciplines. The linchpin of our vulnerability is higher education's increasing reliance on contingent labor. It diminishes our ability to do creative work and undermines our capacity to serve our students, while simultaneously undercutting our independence, our dig-nity, and our potential to have any critical impact on American culture. As we point out in chapter 3, a department can drift into dependence on contingent labor without ever intending to do so. The collapse of state budgets from 2002 to 2004 means there will be steady pressure to in-crease reliance on part-time and non-tenure track instruction over the next several years. To the extent that administrators are responsible for meeting needs within reduced budgets, they are not the allies of the fac-ulty in this matter. Many administrators, answerable to governing boards dominated by business executives, see no choice but to increase the ex-pendable instructional workforce. At the same time, they pursue more corporate partnerships despite the loss of independence and shift in mission they entail. As a result, arts and humanities faculty in particular may come to feel increasingly less common cause with their administra-tions. This could hardly be otherwise, considering how many provosts now seem interested only in disciplines likely to produce wealthy alumni.

Confronted by this dual crisis in the status of the professoriate and the fundamental goals of higher education, many faculty opt for denial

1

or fall prey to delusion. Accustomed to a lifetime of privilege, faculty at prestige institutions continue to dig for fool's gold in their imaginations and predict the return of good times. At disadvantaged schools, co-opted faculty may resort to the alternative lure of alienated sacrifice in which to ground their self-esteem. Reduced health care coverage apparently only purifies the mission of the academic priesthood. There is, we argue, but one way to resist all the forces at work to disempower and degrade the professoriate and instrumentalize education—collective action, though, as we shall demonstrate, collective action takes many forms, from efforts to reform academic disciplines (chapter 7) to projects aiming to reform the curriculum (chapter 10) and collaborative outreach projects (chapter 11), from short-term ad hoc organizing around critical local issues (chapter 8) to strikes over wages and working conditions (chapter 9).

Every other benighted proposal we and others have put forward—writing a note to the Pope, sending a valentine to your local legislator, forwarding plaintive emails to the President, handing out your offprints on street corners—will be of no avail. There are less absurd versions of these burlesqued suggestions, from efforts to sound a moral warning to the public about higher education's potential decline to efforts to reach out to politicians. They will not suffice. It is now too late to tell your grocer about the virtues of your research. That is not to say that some long-term cultural persuasion should not also be initiated on many fronts; it is just to say that such efforts will not meet our needs over the next decade.

Well endowed and high prestige private universities will be able to sustain the status quo if they choose, and some private liberal arts colleges will continue to deliver education that is both intimate and challenging. The pedagogical innovations we have seen since the 1950s, like the expanded canon in literary studies (chapter 11), are in significant ways national in character, though if they lose much of their local funding they will be unable to develop and adapt. The intellectual growth of disciplines is altogether collective, made up of ongoing work by groups and individuals that is mutually reinforcing, competitive, and transformative. If the system loses much of its arts and humanities research capacity, the intellectual caliber of the relevant disciplines will rapidly decline. That means their critical purchase on contemporary culture will diminish, a development some will welcome. It is just what the political right has worked for since the heyday of McCarthyism, and, more recently, the culture wars of the 1980s.

The increasing threat to humanities research and writing has not been well recognized. Nor have we seen how many economic and political forces bear on this crisis, let alone how the country may change as a result. Examples of a chain of consequences are simple enough to describe. As we show in chapter 10, you cannot reform the curriculum, either at Miami Dade Community College or at Yale University, without new textbooks embodying the principles of transformed disciplines. You cannot conceive of the new textbook without the disciplinary research that makes it necessary and possible. Much of that intellectual work inevitably takes place on campuses whose faculties have the time and resources to do it. Even dedicated part-time faculty, however overworked and underpaid, do innovative intellectual work, but not enough to sustain the vitality of their disciplines. There is both trickle down and trickle up in academic research, but the system as a whole requires a significant amount of dedicated leisure to function. In public higher education that dedicated leisure is imperiled at every level and in every location. In private higher education it is imperiled at many financially challenged institutions. Increased class sizes, increased teaching loads, decreased library resources, decreased research funding, declining real salaries in less entrepreneurial disciplines, increasingly centralized curricular control, steadily increasing reliance on contingent labor, decreasing job security, increasing political threats to academic freedom, challenges to cultural diversity on campus, the specter of repressive surveillance of research, segmentation and fragmentation of faculty labor, increasing corporate pressure to focus education on job training, decreasing political support for higher education funding, increasing student demand for services—all these and more do not bode well for disciplines unable to generate their own revenue.

The fixation on revenue generation can penetrate every element of the university's mission, sometimes producing humiliating results for the losing disciplines. At Indiana University a scenario common to research universities played itself out in 2002–2003. Under programs with cheerful umbrella terms like "Strategic Planning" or "Commitment to Excellence" faculty are given the opportunity to submit proposals competing for new funding. As in Bloomington, the deadlines are always tight, but unit heads are advised to "think big" and come up with "new ideas," all old ideas presumably being unsupportable. Like rats in a maze, humanities faculty scurry about calling meetings and producing documents. The results are usually predictable, since the real aim is to support revenue-generating programs: the sciences get 80–90% of the funds.

Not all threats, happily, materialize. Distance learning, now flatter than a new computer screen, has largely failed its promise to transform higher education, though its promotion has eroded the intellectual property rights of faculty members and increased administrative control over the curriculum. The assault on affirmative action is a work in progress and still a subject of cultural struggle. The possibility that Institutional Review Boards will intervene widely in humanities research, addressed in chapter 5, remains just that: a possibility. The international effort to make job training, foreign investment, and revenue generation the primary focus of higher education, while defunding humanities based cultural critique (chapter 6), remains in its early stages and can be stopped. Other fundamental changes await events whose likelihood we can gauge but cannot precisely predict.

Foremost among such probable but unspecifiable events, in the wake of September 11, 2001, is the possibility of further terrorist attacks within the United States. American academics work today in the aftermath of a defining moment of violence, rupture, and loss. Spreading out from that center of horror—from an experience simultaneously rich and hollow, meaningful and unspeakable—are multiple possible futures whose relative probability we cannot reliably assess. We will surely contemplate in detail the character of events that will never come to pass. And events we never imagined, like the events of September 11th, will surely overtake us and displace our wisdom, our fears, and our best professional knowledge. We cannot remember another time when the future seemed so decisively unreadable, outside our control, even while it fills our imaginations with spectacular eruptions of deadly reality. As subjects supposed to know, academics now are merely ignorant like everyone else. Yet one small segment of our national future—the future of higher education—is taking shape with greater clarity. Unfortunately, it is a weakened professoriate that confronts the aftermath of September 11th.

Meanwhile we will continue to be haunted by images without precedent in our experience. The dissolving towers of the World Trade Center, unfurling outward in a wind of dust and flesh, scissored with falling beams of steel, exceed the possibilities for description or analysis. One of us visited the site at the end of October 2001. The pile of rubble was still smoking, a doorway to hell opened up in the middle of the metropolis. Fifty and a hundred feet in the air, steel beams from the twin towers remained driven into the sides of surrounding buildings. Area shops were still closed, their goods coated with thick gray dust. There and throughout the city people continued to gather at makeshift memorials for the dead and the lost. The simultaneous presence of incomprehensible mass numbers with all too comprehensible individual accounts pull us in opposite directions. And the academic Left in particular struggles to find consensus narratives that can sustain political community in the midst of grief. The need for interpretation in depth calls all of us in ways we could not have anticipated.

Yet we are called. Consider this scenario: several more terrorist attacks take place in the United States, perhaps low tech episodes like suicide bombings. The U.S. Attorney General expands still further the practice of extra-legal detention. Protests mount on American campuses. In several small-town colleges part-time faculty write letters to local newspapers attacking the Attorney General and the president. They read the letters to their classes, whose subject matter has little to do with contemporary politics. The campus chapters of the Young Republicans join local business leaders in demanding they be fired. Talk radio hosts take up the cause. And a Republican congressman adds his voice to the rising clamor. Donors threaten to withdraw funding. Now multiply this story by dozens. Factor in September 11 plus one, plus two, plus . . . which of us can pretend to know? What happens to academic freedom in this context? At the very least we can predict that political speech could carry an increased risk of employment insecurity, not only in industry but also for teachers without the protection of tenure. Collective local action and a high degree of local solidarity would be essential both to protect individual speech and to sustain university-based political critique.

It is not clear, unfortunately, that the American Association of University Professor's (AAUP) current definition of academic freedom would provide teachers with the protections they would need in this sort of crisis. Across the world, academic freedom needs to embrace the right not only to question the legitimacy of a particular government but also to ask whether the nation itself has the moral and legal legitimacy to exist. Teachers—not just tenured faculty but also graduate student employees and part-time faculty—need the right to make such statements not only about other countries but also about their own. And they need to be free to debate such issues not only in the community and in public campus spaces but also in the classroom.

Just over thirty years ago, one of our friends was a student in a chemistry class at Wesleyan. The day after Martin Luther King, Jr. was killed, the faculty member teaching the class felt himself unable to talk about chemistry. He spoke instead about King and his legacy. The AAUP's famous 1940 "Statement of Principles on Academic Freedom and Tenure" includes the following warning: "Teachers are entitled to freedom in the classroom in discussing their subject, but they should be careful not to introduce into their teaching controversial matter which has no relation to their subject." A later footnote adds this qualification: "The intent of this statement is not to discourage what is `controversial.' Controversy is at the heart of the free academic inquiry which the entire statement is designed to foster. The passage serves to underscore the need for teachers to avoid persistently intruding material which has no relation to their subject." For many of us King was a transcendent heroic figure, but in 1968 he was also controversial. Presumably, the footnote would cover the single day's departure from chemistry, even in the American South of the day. But what if the faculty member decided to return to the subject later in the semester? What if students, having time to think about the matter, brought it up a week later? When does activity cross the line to become "persistent?" Do you want any given administrator to decide that question?

A faculty member who teaches political poetry every year, including poetry about war, as one of us does, is well positioned to deal with controversial political topics. Even if he or she confines lectures to, say, poetry about World War I, the students are likely to introduce comparisons and questions about any controversial current war. Should they be silenced? If not, can the faculty member reintroduce the comparisons later in the semester? Is the faculty member required to wait for the students to make comparisons between past and present events?

Consider this: following further terrorist violence, the FBI expands its questioning and detention of foreign students. A student from a Middle Eastern country disappears from a physics class. Do AAUP guidelines permit the faculty member to address the issue in detail? What if the student detained—without access to an attorney—is enrolled across campus or across the country? What if such actions recur throughout the semester? Must the foreign country at issue develop a nuclear weapons program to justify discussing the matter in a physics class? Does the faculty member teaching a class on constitutional law have more warrant to discuss the detentions than one teaching a class on religious philosophy? Academic freedom should mean that each individual faculty member has the right to decide such issues.

Already there have been glimmers of what could happen under the right pressures, among them the aborted February 2004 attempt by a U.S. attorney to investigate antiwar activism at Drake University in Iowa. Such assaults on academic freedom might begin at schools with less faculty autonomy. In 2002 a dean at Middletown Community College questioned whether a faculty member had the right to discuss the events of September 11 in a sociology class. After all, September 11 was not listed in the course description as one of the anticipated topics. Plus this was the semester *after* September 11. The slack cut for our Wesleyan University professor or other instant responses might not apply. In Spring 2003 the academic vice-president at Irvine Valley College in California warned faculty members they should not discuss the war in Iraq "unless it can be demonstrated, to the satisfaction of this office, that such discussions are directly related to the approved instructional requirements and materials associated with those classes." After a faculty protest, the administration said it did not want to ban such discussions but rather to "define the proper context" for them. Whatever that means, it is clear the ambiguous space opened up between the AAUP's 1940 statement and its clarifying footnote leaves too much room for both administrative and peer restrictions on and punishment of faculty speech. Some faculty might feel their resolve to exercise their free speech rights strengthened by such incidents, especially if they have tenure. Others, especially part-timers, might experience the notorious "chilling effect." They might be well advised to react in just that way.

We have previously urged faculty to address the campus workplace in class every semester—regardless of what they are teaching—because the salaries, benefits, and working conditions of teachers and other employees are part of the structure that makes every class possible. They are part of the hidden subject matter of every course. So are principles of academic freedom, as are emerging restrictions on international student access to American education.

Teachers should also be free to see their role not simply as one of covering declared subject matter but also as one of modeling responsible and politically engaged citizenship. They need to make it absolutely clear that no student will be penalized for holding different opinions, but they need also need to be able to express their own opinions on controversial subjects freely if they choose. Casting this solely as a question of "advocacy" demeans the complex social implications of the intellectual life.

Despite all the good work it has done, the AAUP's 1940 statement has too narrow and constipated a view of appropriate classroom speech, one that fetishizes subject matter and creates a classroom that is a bizarre, contradictory site of permission and prohibition. A broader notion of academic freedom in the classroom would be most needed in a time of national crisis, precisely when it would be most difficult to win support for it. That is why it is time to redefine academic freedom now. For if more repressive government actions followed more terrorist violence on American soil, university classrooms might be among the last places where people could speak freely.

The AAUP's principled and courageous investigative report on the University of South Florida in Tampa—produced after the university put tenured faculty member Sami Al-Arion on paid leave and denied him due process after he exercised his First Amendment rights *outside* the classroom—shows that the organization stands firmly behind faculty political speech in the public sphere. And the organization will continue to insist that controversial classroom speech *on topic* is fully protected. Biology teachers can advocate the theory of evolution *almost* anywhere in the country. But no one should be deluded into thinking there are clear guidelines from the organization on political speech off topic in the classroom. There is but a high tension guide wire strung between opposing poles, and even experienced high fliers sometimes plummet to their deaths.

Meanwhile, economic inducements are falling in place to prepare us instead for the new political conformity. Throughout their long history, universities have always been willing to follow the money. In cultures where the lines between church and state have been blurred or nonexistent, higher education too often is paid to become the higher indoctrination. We have seen over the last twenty years how a shift from government to corporate funding has begun to reshape research missions and priorities. But new federal funding is beginning to flow from the emerging post-September 11th national security state. As administrators scramble to cash in on homeland security, how many will seek to incorporate political and cultural commentary and critique in their plans? And how long will it be before the federal government becomes less eager to send money to campuses that give equal time to the loyal opposition? Factor in September 11 plus one, plus two, plus . . . which of us can pretend to know? Once again, we will need universities as sites of principled opposition.

Principled, alas, is precisely what higher education no longer is, if indeed it ever was. As the university Citadel of Reason has gradually evolved into the Campus Sweat Shop, an instrumentalized view of human beings has become ever more prevalent in higher education. Universities increasingly employ people without health care, without job security, without fundamental rights to due process, and at salaries below a living wage. Administrators increasingly view many of their employees as expendable. And they readily accept millions of dollars from corporations that treat many of their employees the same way. As universities behave more and more like our most ruthlessly exploitive employers, they steadily lose any moral authority they might wield in world culture.

To say, for example, that top university administrators are acting like greedy CEOs is no longer news. They are CEOs. When Indiana University President Myles Brand resigned to become head of the National Collegiate Athletic Association (NCAA)—at an estimated annual salary package of $763,000 (*The Indianapolis Star*, 27 February 2004: A1)—he stood to lose some $300,000 of deferred compensation he would have received had he stayed at Indiana until age sixty-five. As a faculty member he would have been out of luck; faculty are lucky to get a year's unpaid leave if they take another job. The university sets that limit precisely to avoid paying deferred compensation. Brand needed six years' leave to stay on the employee list long enough to get his golden parachute. The Indiana Board of Trustees happily gave him the six years, one trustee declaring it the "right" thing to do. Greed at the top inevitably shapes the public perception of the entire enterprise. Commenting on Brand's salary at the NCAA, Murray Sperber challenged the organization's statement that college sports is not a business, but part of education: "It seems to me that for him to be making that kind of salary, the only justification is that he has to sit down with guys in Armani suits from the [television] networks and deal with them" (*Star* 2004, A9). The salary was justified by NCAA Executive Committee chair Carol Cartwright, president of Kent State University, where non-tenure eligible instructors in English, some of them doctoral recipients from Kent State, teach eight courses or more per year for barely a living wage.

Perhaps it would not matter if we did not need both the university's moral and intellectual authority. But we do. Over the last half century, higher education has become the home of many of the country's critical intellectuals. They cannot speak with authority if their institutional homes are rightly perceived as honoring few if any of the principles they claim to espouse. These include commitment to justice, fairness, decency, humanity, and community responsibility—not only as values to be taught in the classroom but also to be practiced on campus.

Yet it will not be easy to reform higher education to meet these standards. We could point to several forces working against doing so, among them the corporate values that university administrators and governing boards increasingly espouse. It is now regularly the case that faculty committed to making the university a fair, even a model, workplace, are fundamentally at odds with senior administrators, who are often devoted to the corporate model of extracting labor at its lowest possible cost. But the regrettable truth is that many tenured faculty are apparently perfectly happy to sustain their own salaries and benefits through the exploitation of other campus workers. And indeed many, if not most, tenured faculty are comfortably unreflective about the economic and human practices that undergird their own privileges. We begin to analyze how this has come to pass in chapter 2.

It is not, however, as if there was a plot afoot to transform higher education in multiple ways, or rather, there *are* one or two plots, but no plan and no agency encompass all the developments we list above. Perhaps it would be better if there were a conspiracy with an antagonist to fight, a Saddam Hussein we could blame for a complicated state of affairs we have ourselves helped to create. As we point out in chapters 5, 6, 8, and 9, there is certainly a consensus among some that faculty power needs to be curtailed, but there is not an organized campaign to do so. Moreover, as we argue above and in chapter 2, faculty themselves are also substantially to blame for higher education's difficulties. It was not a plot, moreover, that produced growing numbers of high school graduates seeking higher education. It wasn't quite a plot, though it was certainly an ideology, that led some Americans to believe prisons, rather than schools and colleges, were the best solution to crime and unemployment. It will, however, partly be plotters who will take advantage of a more vulnerable professoriate to stifle dissent in the wake of a new series of terrorist attacks. Not only political figures but also cultural conservatives in non-governmental organizations will seek every advantage they can gain from further violence on American soil. While we would not want to suggest that conservatives would welcome the murder of more Americans, we are confident they are already planning how to take advantage of such events should they occur.

We badly need cohesive campus-wide organizations capable of advocacy and resistance in advance of such occurrences. We need organizations that can defend individual faculty and that can apply credible force when reason alone is of no use. Such an organization has to be grounded in solidarity, common purpose, shared understandings, willingness to act, strength of will, and mutual respect across disciplines. We are certainly not describing a faculty senate. The description more accurately fits a union.

In many ways our present situation represents a failure of this and other forms of collectivity—a failure to negotiate collective forms of identity, a failure of collective institutional self-analysis, and a failure of collective action on all levels of the profession. Yet there have been successes as well. We offer in *Office Hours: Activism and Change in the Academy* strategic case studies of both failure and success. Since it is failure that has brought us to where we are, we begin there in Part One. The second section of the book mines recent successes in search of partial blueprints for the future. We specify our failure to address the human cost of our graduate programs in chapters 3 and 4, then offer some alternatives in chapter 12. We rely frequently on our own experience, not because it has been so central but rather because we know it best and because, for better or worse, it has frequently been representative.

Indeed little happens to anyone in higher education that is unique, no matter how singularly miraculous or disastrous it seems at the time. Academics most often view their own experiences as distinctive because they have not recognized who their brothers and sisters in similar situations are, or because they cannot identify the institutional forces that have shaped events in their lives. Academics are trained to think otherwise, trained to treasure their personal achievements and to blame irrational injustice for their problems. They are trained as well to be suspicious of collective analysis and collective action. We learned to think of them as extremes of right and left politics. And we learned to trust in our ability to locate ourselves elsewhere, away from group cohesion or dispersal.

The effort to repair these conceptual failures, to substitute collectivity for the lure of unencumbered individuality, is fraught with multiple difficulties. Error is inevitable. Events sweep aside what seemed moments earlier to be reliable analyses. And everywhere the blindness of institutions and their subjects offer resistance to change. Such problems pervade both halves of our book. In chapter 7 we sketch collective reform efforts within the largest humanities professional organization, reform driven by the discontent of the association's most exploited members, and recount the strategies its elite forces have used to derail every such initiative. We have both been involved in efforts to help reform and update the curriculum by editing anthologies. In chapter 10 we show how the short-term greed of corporate publishers who own reprint rights has nearly made such efforts financially impossible. In contrast, chapter 8 tells the remarkable story of how local organizing saved a nature preserve threatened with destruction, and chapter 9 tells the story of the solidarity a campus strike generated and sustained.

In none of these instances, we should be clear, are we attempting to provide a comprehensive survey of all comparable activist efforts. The full story of campus union activism would occupy several books, not one chapter. Reform efforts in other academic disciplines will, we hope, be described by those who have participated in them. Local organizing like that around Indiana's failed country club initiative often remains unknown outside the campus where events occurred. Our purpose here is to disseminate telling and instructive examples, examples readers can learn from and apply to their own situations when the occasion arises. We have given the book a title that reflects both the current inequities in higher education and the faculty activities we need to rethink. All of us keep office hours but not all of us have offices. We would like to see some of those hours devoted to activism. If our book inspires others to tell their stories and join comparable efforts for change it will have done its work.

Part One

Where We Are and How We Got There

1. Cohorts—The Diaspora of the Teachers

THE YEAR WAS 1975. Just west of Champaign-Urbana, Illinois, where one of us lives, there is a place where the freeway adapts to what counts as a local hill. On the way home one day, my car rose in the air just enough for me to see across the surrounding fields. There, atop a tractor, churning along furrows owned by the local garden supply center, was one of my former university colleagues. She was not in my department, English, but rather in Comparative Literature, where she had been turned down for tenure the previous year because she hadn't published enough. Unable to find an academic job, there she was, in the Midwest's longest-running occupation. In my mind's eye she will always be there, the dust spewing out behind her, poised in a living lesson that anything is possible, proof that the world (or at least the teaching profession's corner of it) is utterly unpredictable and surreal. Yet in actuality she was gone again in a few months, this time like a mail-order bride unwittingly betrothed to history. She had answered an ad to teach at Birzeit University on Israel's West Bank. It was neither a destination nor a culture she knew much about in advance, but she would learn. Or so her occasional letters to friends suggested. But then the letters stopped. The Israelis had closed down the Palestinians' notoriously politicized campus—it was at the very least an organizing site for the *intifada*—and she was unemployed again. This time innocence and industry combined to make a still more risky move possible. She took a job teaching in Hafez al-Assad's Syria, vanishing for a time into one of the world's notorious police states. When she resurfaced again it was to teach in Jordan.

A few months earlier, at the annual meeting of the Modern Language Association, I had run into one of my cohorts from graduate school at

15

the University of Rochester. He was making one last futile run at the nonexistent job market of the early 1970s. In a doomed effort to unify counter-culture and academia, his student years of the 1960s and his dreams about the profession of the 1970s, he had decided to write a dissertation about drugs and literature. There had been no interest in interviewing him to date, and he was more than a little cynical about himself and the game he had wagered in so badly. "I decided the way to make the dissertation different was to make it comprehensive, *really* comprehensive," he emphasized, "but my committee felt differently. As one of them put it, 'You've compiled a dismal bibliography for junkies.'" There were no takers for what he had to offer in the job wars.

I am not offering these stories as accounts of departmental misconduct or even of professional injustice, though how attentive the advising was that my fellow Rochester graduate student received I cannot say; they are simply among the innumerable individual disasters of academic life in recent decades. Among the people in my several cohorts without guarantees—fellow graduate students, fellow assistant professors, and University of Illinois graduate students who received their degrees while I was on the tenure track—who lost their jobs, for example, were two Illinois PhDs of the early 1970s; they won tenure at institutions oriented toward teaching and then lost it shortly thereafter, one to alcoholism and one to a manic-depressive illness.[1] In a different job system, recovery might have made re-entry to full-time teaching possible. Instead, they both survive now on the margins of the profession, teaching part-time on the cusp of age fifty-five.

Their marginalization has been exacerbated by an unforgiving job system. They are not alone. Several other Illinois PhDs of the 1970s have known nothing but part-time or adjunct work all their lives. They are among the thousands of PhDs in what my own institution now formally calls the "lost generation" of the 1970s and 1980s, some of whom have spent twenty years cobbling together an income of sorts at $800 or $1,000 or $1,500 a course.

Yet among the three cohorts I am concerned with here, the one that haunts my memory most decisively perhaps is my class of assistant professors at Illinois. In the fall of 1970 ten faculty members joined the English department here; it was the last year of boom hiring. The following year, 1971, saw only one appointment, a British PhD who had accepted the Illinois job while suffering from a typically British misapprehension about American geography. He had visited a colleague in

---

1. For interesting comments on a graduate student cohort, see Peter N. Carroll, *Keeping Time: Memory, Nostalgia, and the Art of History*.

London, Illinois, offer in hand, more than a little uneasy about the move. The friend spun a globe and stopped it with his finger on Illinois. "Look," he said, "you like New York, you like California; now both will be equally accessible. You don't have to choose." On a bleak day in London it seemed to make sense. The inch on either side of his friend's finger didn't seem like much of an obstacle. He would soon find out otherwise. Like other assistant professors without a partner in residence, he also found out that an isolated Midwestern campus is not a good place to be alone. His daily intake by the time he left was one hardboiled egg and a bottle of scotch. The egg, as I remember, came in and out of the fridge as he nibbled away at it during the course of the day. On sleepless nights he listened to rock music stations on the radio, entering their contests to identify band members one after another. Luckily for him, within two years he made it back to an academic job in England before the market closed down there as well. Before long, Margaret Thatcher decided universities were inherent enemies of the state and instituted a mix of cuts, job insecurity, and obscure rules for intercampus competition.

Meanwhile ten of us were teaching our six courses a year at what purported to be a research university. The survival rate for assistant professors at Illinois in those days was not impressive. We were more than expendable; we were forgettable. We would earn tenure or we would not, but the department was not about to be of any help in the matter. As casually as we were hired, it is only surprising that people were actually fired with regret. But when I went into the department to test my memory against our office records, I quickly found out that there *were* no records. My department could not tell me the names of the faculty members we hired in 1970. No one at the time was keeping lists of that sort.

We do keep records now, or at least we did for a while, having hired two first-rate administrative aides in the mid-1970s, both of whom decided on their own initiative that institutional history matters.[2] With their help, and with a few conversations with colleagues, I could piece together the ten names. In one case a trip to basement personnel files was necessary because none of us could remember when a particular assistant professor was hired or when he left. Since then, both those administrative staff members have retired; assembling additional historical details would be more challenging still. And I would not want to stake my life on the fidelity of our records of recent adjunct faculty hires.

Back then, there was little time to publish on the teaching schedules we were assigned, especially when we taught three *different* courses in a

---

2. The two administrative secretaries were Rene Wahlfeldt and Carol Severins, both of whom helped me with data for this essay.

single semester. One can only imagine what it is like for those teaching five or more courses at once. In one of the numerous ways the department found to flaunt hierarchy, assistant and associate professors taught six courses a year, while full professors taught but four.[3] Worse still, several of my young colleagues suffered from long-running writing blocks. Others were doing work that the conservative gate-keepers who then controlled the profession were not about to approve for publication. Assuming they knew both themselves and the profession well—and recognized their own strengths and limitations, a very large assumption indeed in academia—a more robust job market might have provided them with more realistic employment options, namely teaching jobs at colleges that did not expect publication. Instead they were here at Illinois, headed toward disaster.

Two of my faculty class of 1970 saw the lack of their own writing on the wall and bowed out quietly, resigning before the department made the decision for them. One had a book manuscript arguing, with a helping hand from psychoanalytic theory, that the eighteenth century was anything but the age of reason. His senior colleague in the eighteenth century couldn't decide whether this thesis was primarily comical or criminal, but he had no such doubts about the appropriate fate for someone irresponsible enough to make such an argument. He himself was notorious for teaching seminars by reciting lists of words from the week's readings he deemed unfamiliar and then sharing the dictionary definitions with the class. Another untenured colleague found his claim that Milton was actually *subverting* the genres he worked in falling on journal editors' deaf ears. These were the early 1970s, when a number of specializations were still dominated by the folks who had kept feminism, Marxism, and theory generally, along with women and minority writers, out of the profession. The young faculty members in my cohort should have fought back, trying multiple submissions and writing still more, but they did not. They let themselves be broken.

In retrospect, of course, it seems like the department made sound decisions. But success has a way of building on itself and breeding more successes, until it looks like the sweet triumph of justice, whereas failure sits stolidly and moves nowhere, merely confirming itself more thoroughly over time. We all know that early luck and good mentoring play important roles in successful careers, as does a PhD from some prestige institutions; it's just that we have no way of thinking about such things

---

3. Teaching loads were reduced to five courses a year for assistant and associate professors in English in the early 1980s at Illinois and reduced again to four courses toward the end of the decade.

institutionally.[4] Harvard considers publishing the books of its graduates—not just its faculty—*a priority*, a perk most of the rest of higher
education has never dreamed of, let alone put in place. Meanwhile, from
the late 1960s through the mid-1970s my department occasionally tenured some of the most uninspired teachers and unimaginative research
faculty I have ever known, all because they had just barely met the
university's publication requirements.[5] Those who had exceeded the requirements and done exceptionally well all went through elaborate hazing
rituals and were nearly fired. I was turned down for tenure two years in
a row, receiving it on my third nomination. The second time I was denied tenure the official reason was "insubordination," a crime I am more
than willing to claim as my own; in any case, whether I was guilty or not,
there is little chance I can persuade anyone now that I was innocent. All
in all, except for those fired outright, those who had the greatest difficulty being approved for tenure either then or later proved to be the
department's most productive scholars.

We could certainly have done better at mentoring and supporting
new faculty. Indeed we do much better now, giving new faculty rapid
access to specialized courses, guaranteeing time off for research, and
conducting annual reviews that give significant feedback. Individual senior faculty, it is true, do not all help younger colleagues individually,
but that is only partly a failure of our collective culture; it is partly a
problem of character. Whether we could have handled the review process for my cohort more effectively I still do not know. Certainly more
meaningful criteria exist—one might ask whether a candidate for tenure is in fact a committed intellectual—but negotiating issues like that
collectively is not likely to be easy.

---

4. "Luck" can include such things as whether you have a senior colleague or dissertation
director who convinces a press to send your book manuscript out for review. It can
include whether the people who choose your outside evaluators for tenure are knowledgeable and sympathetic. As late as 1996, my own department's Advisory Committee
willfully chose antifeminist outside reviewers selected to torpedo an accomplished
feminist's case.

5. Apart from their individual idiosyncrasies, this group has some common professional
characteristics. Several resisted the New Critical revolution throughout their careers,
refusing to do close readings of literary texts in the classroom. Almost all treated the rise
of theory as a "fad" that would soon pass; those still on the faculty persist in telling
students planning graduate study they need not learn anything about theory because it
will have been swept away by the time they come to write a dissertation. A few refused to
add female writers to their courses through the 1980s and 1990s, declaring that feminist
criticism felt like an attempt to "castrate" them. More recently, one complained about
the presence of Marxist theory in the curriculum and urged formal adoption of "anti-
dotes" to it. Such positions are frequently of little use in any productive professional
dialogue.

In any case, four others in my 1970 cohort of faculty stayed on and were subsequently fired. Of the ten, four received tenure and were still on the faculty nearly thirty years later. What has happened to the others? One returned to Oakland, California, to live with her parents, becoming a part-time legal secretary and eventually inheriting her parents' home. Back in Illinois her house was full of dozens of puzzles she assembled obsessively, though not realizing it until it was time to leave. Another went to work in his father-in-law's hardware store outside Chicago, inheriting that business in time. Still another landed a job working on the editorial staff of a Jacksonville, Mississpippi, newspaper. When that job ended, he edited a computer magazine for a time. Thereafter he tried free-lance writing, but the need for something more secure was apparent. Soon he was running a bed-and-breakfast establishment in North Carolina. My closest friend in the group became a property manager in the Bay Area, his considerable skills at close reading Renaissance poems now focused instead on analyzing leases and contracts. On bad days he must evict tenants from apartment buildings. His worst day ever was the one on which he had to put the equivalent of a small village of Southeast Asian refugees, all wearing black pajamas, out on the street.

Neither he nor any of the other of these people has a large income, though the property manager worked himself up to a modest small-college level professorial salary as he reached age sixty. They all have fundamentally insecure jobs with inadequate salaries. Retirement is not an option. None have careers that make use of the skills honed in years of graduate study and teaching, if indeed they can be thought to have "careers" at all. Twenty-five years after leaving academia the Miltonist turned property manager remarks, "I still resent that I know *Paradise Lost* well and cannot share the knowledge with students." None have given up talking about their Illinois tenure decision. Part of their lives is lived substantially in the aborted years of devotion to literature. They remain at some level psychologically in transit toward new identities they will never reach.

And as for the jobs they occupied so briefly? Well, most academic professional associations like to talk about tenure-track jobs as though they flow harmoniously into tenure and "lead to academic careers." That was not to be the fate of my class of 1970. Moreover, when the individuals themselves were fired, the jobs they held were cancelled. The university was downsizing its largest humanities department rapidly in the 1970s. It was partly a tactical decision by the director of the School of Humanities. The best way to secure a power base, so the reasoning appears to have gone, was to protect all the small, weak humanities departments, while hacking away remorselessly at English and History. It worked until English revolted, withdrew from the school, and celebrated the school's collapse. We never got those faculty lines back and we never will. The positions were eliminated.

As my cohort of faculty hires headed toward their confrontation with tenure, the casualties of the previous class had barely been cleared away. Five assistant professors were hired that year (1969). Two were tenured, two were fired, and one resigned in anticipation of his termination. Of the last three, only one remained in academia, finding a position in a junior college. One now works in a bank in Indiana, one found work in advertising and consulting and has not been heard from since.

Meanwhile the graduate students who finished their degrees here in those years had equally mixed fates. My first graduate student completed her PhD in the dead market year of 1973. We counted her lucky to land a tenure-track community college job in New Jersey. Twenty-five years later, thousands of composition papers assigned and graded, she chose to take early retirement. Her life has had its pleasures, but substantial parts of her "career" have not been counted among them. Articulate, well-organized, she could easily have published and to a larger degree led a life of the mind in a different sort of job. I realize she was not doomed to wander the killing fields of Cambodia. There are worse fates than hers. Now there are even ideologies available that idealize those grading tasks. But I would not trade my career for hers. And she did not need the intellectual training she received to prepare her for the job she landed.

One of the uncomfortable—and rarely acknowledged—lessons to be learned from her life and others like it is that there are some tenure-track jobs out there very possibly not worth having. A teacher of composition may easily grade 120 papers a week. It is true that one of our own graduate students specializing in rhetoric and composition told me she would rather read a set of rhetoric papers than a Jane Austen novel any day of the week, but I have decided to insist she was pulling my leg. It's like taking home a badly written 600-page novel that repeats itself every five pages. Over the course of a thirty-year career you may grade 120,000 or more composition papers.

Yet my student was among the 40 percent or so of the more than 200 PhDs produced by the University of Illinois English Department in the 1970s who eventually found some sort of college teaching job. Because our program provides immense amounts of teaching experience, our placement rate has often run relatively high. Of course, that still means more than half of our PhDs ended up in other careers. The list is varied: free-lance editor, management methods analyst, supervisor at the Internal Revenue Service, management-training consultant, librarian. Several teach high school. A few found places in higher education administration. A number have unspecified business careers. And among the hundreds of graduate students who dropped out of the program and never finished their degrees, the roles range from bartender to screen writer. One of my advisees went the bartender route, and I find myself leaving him a tip at least once a month; I have done so for twenty years.

Few of these people have the career satisfaction a faculty member can attain. For many failed PhDs or PhD wannabes must trade idealization for income. They are forced to find a way of earning a living doing something they neither love nor admire. They will no longer be paid a salary for talking about truth and beauty. The sense of deep inner division this shift causes should not be underestimated. That is partly why the promotion of "alternative careers" can produce such anger among dissertation students and unemployed PhDs. We spend years instilling an ideology of idealization in students and then expect them to abandon it cheerfully to work in an insurance agency. It is also why so many failed literary academics seem homeless, rudderless, endlessly and hopelessly self-justifying. Some, to be sure, go on to law school and do satisfying work earning a good salary in time, but many remain in career and identity limbo.

Overall, things work out best for those who leave soonest. In my cohort at Rochester, all the graduate students I knew well and most admired intellectually simply dropped out of the program, abandoning their plans for the PhD. Of those completing their Rochester PhDs in the 1970s, a tiny handful won jobs at research universities, a few others at undergraduate institutions. The others joined the lost generation. Yet the most fully shattered careers remain those of the faculty members who were denied tenure. For them, the sense of personal failure is most wounding and disabling.

In the 1970s the genteel academic world of the previous decade largely disappeared, never to return. It used to be that when an academic fell from a position of high prestige he—the appropriate pronoun, since the profession of the 1950s and 1960s was largely a boys' club—might land securely but one or two levels down and live out his career there with relative satisfaction. If an apprenticeship as a graduate student at a highly ranked department was followed by yet another apprenticeship as, say, an assistant professor at an Ivy League research university, failure to achieve tenure might lead to a job at a good liberal arts college. But by the early 1970s far fewer failed academics descended to a nearby perch. They fell instead like Milton's Lucifer. Many fell out of the profession altogether, some into nether worlds from which they were never to be heard from again. We became a profession that was unusually wasteful of its personnel.

The wastefulness starts early. Statistics have shown for decades that the national attrition rate from graduate programs runs at about 50 percent. Since 1971, only about a third of new PhDs have landed tenure track jobs. Of those, at some schools significant percentages fail to win tenure. As best as I can calculate, of the people who began to enter graduate school in the late 1960s, fewer than ten percent actually earned tenure, stayed in the profession, and had lifelong careers as college or university teachers. It is a statistic no one thinks of, but it speaks a certain brutal truth about the academic enterprise nonetheless. For some cohorts the percentage of "careers" in higher education would be nowhere near 10 percent. Battlefield survival rates are often better.

As Barbara Lovitts has shown, wasteful graduate programs are typically graduate programs that care little about their students.[6] There are always more where they came from, so indifferent departments make little effort to socialize students into the codes of the discipline. In some departments 80 percent or more of the graduate students drop out without completing their degrees. So too with departments wasteful of their new faculty members. They may actually maximize the teaching loads of faculty on the tenure-track, as mine did, or if not, they may assign assistant professors the courses (like composition) with the heaviest paper grading burden; there are always more assistant professors where they came from. Now we have a profession that is still more wasteful of its members, shifting ever more of the professoriate into part-time positions, holding on to the apprenticeship model of graduate education despite its wholesale evisceration by a job system that denies most "apprentices" full-time salaries throughout their lives.

Whatever sort of profession we can become in the future will be increasingly shaped by the sort of profession we have been over the past thirty-five years of the job crisis. Yet the full nature of that profession—and its vast human cost—remains largely invisible and unknown. How many casualties have humanities departments actually generated since the late 1960s? How could we find out not only about the sheer numbers of people abandoned or discarded at each stage of the profession, but also about what happened to them? What sort of lives did humanities

---

6. See Barbara E. Lovitts, "Leaving the Ivory Tower: A Sociological Analysis of the Causes of Departure from Doctoral Study." For a summary of her findings, see the entry on "Attrition Rates" in Cary Nelson and Stephen Watt, *Academic Keywords: A Devil's Dictionary for Higher Education.*

disciplines generate in the second half of the twentieth century? Where have all the teachers gone?

Finally, I suppose some will ask whether it matters. Did the thousands upon thousands of people who washed out of the profession belong in it? The most likely answer, one based on my own experience, is that some did and some did not. Certainly the people denied tenure at Illinois included some immensely successful teachers who would have done very well at a liberal arts college. Some were and continue to be serious readers, so they would have kept up with the field, not become the sort of popular teacher who grows steadily out of date. Perhaps these people just did not belong at a place that demanded publication. Unfortunately, the inexorable job system did not give them many choices.

In a way, the discipline of the last several decades has run simultaneously on two parallel tracks. There has been the discipline of astonishing intellectual advancement and ambition—the discipline that promoted new interpretive methods, that opened up the canon, that reached out to study new kinds of texts and objects. We might call this the discipline of the dreamers. But alongside it all the while has churned a discipline of another sort, Moloch, the devourer of souls. Moloch is the discipline that sustained its privileges and ambitions by cheapening thousands of human lives. Moloch is the disciplinary system founded on a base of cheap instruction provided by slaves deceived into thinking they are serving a higher cause. One of the rules of the game is that Moloch and the Dreamer pretend never to cast eyes on one another.

There is of course some evidence that this is changing. Since the mid-1990s both regional conferences and national disciplinary organizations have run numerous sessions on professional issues at their annual meetings, including sessions on part-time work. Sessions on "MLAlienation" have become something of an ongoing tradition in literature. Yet the conferences appear somewhat schizophrenic as a result, with sessions on literature or history or anthropology and sessions on the job crisis passing each other like ships in the night. There is no mutual interrogation of each enterprise, and MLA, the largest disciplinary organization for humanities professors, mostly keeps interpretation and professional politics in separate publications, *PMLA* and *Profession.*

The uneasy coexistence of these worlds reflects long-standing blindnesses. During the very same years we were celebrating theory we failed to recognize, or even evaluate, let alone theorize, our own relentlessly wasteful institutional practices. Theory has powerfully pervaded literary studies, history, and the foreign languages, but been little applied to the profession itself. We celebrated the new feminism while destroying women's lives. We investigated Marxism while expanding our own exploited proletariate. We democratized our annual conventions and curricula while acting like plantation overseers in our own workplaces. Now the plantation chickens have come home to roost. The rest of the world has embraced the conclusion, long inherent in our own practices, that humanities professors are of little value. And so they are increasingly employed at sweatshop wages with no job security and little time for intellectual reflection.

We believe we cannot master the forces operating on our present and shaping our future unless we confront our past. The kind of departmental self-study the Modern Language Association has appropriately called for needs to be deepened and expanded and applied in all disciplines. We need to record the myriad histories of the individuals who passed through the institutions of History and English and French and German since the 1960s. We need to recover our collective institutional history, department by department, and then we need to find a way to share that history and reflect on it as national disciplines. We offer this chapter in part to issue a call for that project to begin.

For those still in the game, we do not urge the academic equivalent of universal survivor's guilt, though we do think survivor's awareness and reflection are essential. Yet the history that renewed memory can give us will not be easy or straightforward. On the one hand, as we observed at the outset, there is a real component of individual responsibility for some of the career failures of people on the tenure-track; on the other, most of the thousands of PhDs who never found academic jobs washed out of the profession through no fault of their own. We used them to staff our entry-level courses or sustain our graduate programs and then cast them aside. For that history, we have some reason to feel regret, even to regret who we have been. To address the emerging crisis of the near future in ignorance or denial of the past is thus to ground ourselves in moral bankruptcy.

The alternative—to take our history into ourselves and seek a more ethical academic workplace—does not appeal to everyone. Some consider an appeal to morality unrealistic. Academics, they argue, will simply pursue their own self-interest. But short-term personal gain for tenured faculty can seem a fairly empty value when pitted against the agony of the unemployed and the exploitation of the underemployed. Moreover, some faculty at least have cultural and psychological investments in educational institutions that are at considerable long-term risk. So there are grounds for principled argument in academia, and there are constituencies who can be reached by such arguments.

Unfortunately, achieving a fundamentally ethical workplace in academia is now impossible. If the job market remains disastrous, what would a completely ethical graduate program be like? We make an effort at answering the question in the book's last chapter. How would we employ apprentices without a future in a fully ethical manner? What are the responsibilities of highly paid faculty and administrators in an era of exploitation? We are left with degrees of compromise and relative fairness and unfairness.

Others argue that focusing on an individual industry's problems obscures the need for broader and more radical social change. But change that spreads by example from industry to industry can become more pervasive and fundamental. And people have the greatest potential to transform their own workplaces. Many of the issues that confront education, moreover, are similar to those in other industries—from the shift to part-time work to the collapse of entry-level salaries to the curtailment of workplace speech in a corporate and politically conservative environment. The campus workplace is also a good place to begin bridging the class divisions that help keep lower-grade workers impoverished across the world. Academics, if they are willing to critique their own identity formations—identity formations we begin to describe in the next chapter—can help show others how to address the inequities of the global economy. We cannot resist the inertial force of an exploitive history we hardly know. If we suppress knowledge of the brutal diaspora of the teachers of the last three decades, we will watch the next generation be scattered still more widely over even less fertile ground.

What this chapter documents, in an admittedly anecdotal fashion, is part of the price we have paid for the sink or swim, entrepreneurial academic culture of the last fifty years. For all the necessarily solitary features of academic life, it is now clear that individual ambition needs to be balanced with community responsibility and collective action. It is the message of this book. We are tempted to recommend, as we have before, Joe Hill's famous last words of 1915: "Don't Mourn. Organize." But this chapter is of course in part a work of mourning. So we will revise Hill's advice for a culture too long inclined to suppress its past and ignore its present: Mourn *and* organize.

CN

2. Anonymity, Celebrity, and Professional Identity

AS A GUIDE TO THE HIERARCHIES now structuring the academy—and as an index of our capacity to reflect on the disparities they create—consider several books published at the turn of the millennium. They include one of the most compelling and one of the more fatuous of recent books about higher education. What is notable are not just the differences in insight and relevance between these two books, but also the fact that they are differentiated as well by class, privilege, and generation. At the opposite ends of higher education's increasingly ruthless caste system, their authors also represent radically different subject positions. The two books in question are Michael Dubson's edited collection *Ghosts in the Classroom: Stories of Adjunct Faculty—and the Price We All Pay* (2001) and Sander Gilman's *The Fortunes of the Humanities: Thoughts for After the Year 2000* (2000).

The Fortunes of the Humanities gives us the purported wisdom of a solitary humanist, whereas *Ghosts in the Classroom* is a group project. Gilman's book is published by Stanford University Press, whereas Dubson's is essentially self-published out of his apartment. One can only guess that Gilman's frequently smug and self-satisfied book is warranted only by the presence of his name on the cover, since except for his interesting observations about German studies very little of the contents tell us anything we did not already know. Dubson's book, on the contrary, is almost anonymous. Indeed some of his contributors write under assumed names because they are so vulnerable. Those who use their own names come to us unheralded. Gilman is handsomely rewarded for his services to higher education, whereas the contributors to *Ghosts in the*

Classroom are underpaid, under or overemployed, and mostly uninsured, like most adjunct faculty. Gilman's job is secure; the jobs of these other authors are as insecure as employment in higher education can be.

In addition to his introduction, Dubson (2001) also contributes his own chapter to the book. It is offered under the pseudonym "M. Theodore Swift," not, as Dubson told me in an interview, because he needs to protect himself but because the pseudonym confirms his empty professional identity. If he is a cipher, a professionally empty signifier, he feels he should speak as one. That said, his essay, "I Am an Adjunct," is a riveting opening to the book:

> I am an adjunct . . . I bought the bag of lies we call the American Dream. I was intoxicated on the Nitrous Oxide idealism forced upon me in graduate school. I believed caring, working hard, doing a good job mattered and would add up to something concrete. Instead, I find myself on a wheel that turns but goes nowhere. I don't expect this situation to change. I know I have joined the huge group of teachers who become permanent adjuncts, who do a good job only to get one more chance to do it again . . . I have watched my self-esteem drop, drop, drop from doing work that is, theoretically, enhancing the self-esteem of my students. I have seen the tired eyes, the worn clothes, the ancient eyes of long-term adjuncts. I have looked into their eyes as they have failed to look back into mine . . . I have known thirty year old men living at home with their parents, forty year old women teaching college and going hungry, uninsured fifty year olds with serious illnesses. I have known adjunct teachers who hand out As and Bs like vitamins and help students cheat on their exams so they'll get good course evaluations. I've watched people fall into obsessive relationships with their idealism and their pedagogy because it is the one defense against despair . . . I am a dreamer. I am an idealist. I am a victim. I am a whore. I am a fool. I am an adjunct. (2001, 9–10)

Dubson's essay, a ruthlessly honest cultural manifesto and personal confession, is followed by twenty-four essays by other adjunct faculty. They are a mix of reportage, personal narrative, institutional interrogation, and reflection on the present and future of higher education. They mix cold analysis with both wit and rage, as some of the titles indicate: "Adjuncts Are Not People," "We Only Come Out at Night," "The Censorship of Part-Timers," "The Witch and the Wimp," "A Lover's Complaint," "Farewell to Teaching." This is the first book devoted fully to adjuncts telling their own stories in their own words. It makes for compelling reading, and it addresses the single most serious problem in higher education. Its audience is everyone concerned with American education. We cannot think of a more important book for all of us to read.

Gilman, to be sure, also acknowledges that "part-time, underpaid, and marginal members of the profession are doing more and more of the teaching" (2000, 60), but this is hardly either a stirring call to arms or a satisfactory account of the industry's most serious crisis. On the other hand, when he does address issues at length the results are not heartening. A banal chapter aimed at giving advice to young faculty—"How to Get Tenure"—is pitched so low it might better have been directed to their parents. As it stands, it reads as if it were written for an interplanetary visitor hoping to earn an earth-based PhD. Here are his recommendations: "1. Publish in refereed books and journals"—"2. Publish your work as part of a dialogue in the world of ideas"—"3. Scholarship must present a new or interesting manner of understanding a problem"—"4. Publish for a clearly defined audience"—"5. Write in an accessible manner."

Just who the audience is for his book is far from clear. The best chapters in the book, again, are those on German studies; they are a good model of writing for a general public. The range of references may not satisfy specialist faculty, but Gilman does a fine job of laying out the tensions in German departments for educated readers. Yet nowhere does he justify this emphasis in a book that declares itself a brief for higher education's entire future. Chapter seven, a sort of cultural studies program for the German American Bund, is offered to an audience already in the grave.

It would serve no purpose to berate a distinguished scholar for writing a forgettable book were it not that *The Fortunes of the Humanities* is entirely symptomatic of the problems of so many tenured faculty. On German studies Gilman can speak with authority because he is well informed. On every other topic he simply puts himself on stage as a subject supposed to know, a role he assumes whether he knows anything or not. Thus he smugly informs us "there is no worldwide conspiracy at the universities and against the humanities, for conspiracies are active, and the gradual erosion of the status of the humanities has been a passive undertaking" (2001, 5). Yet even in the United States conservative foundations and organizations have mounted an organized campaign against critical thinking in the humanities, but the "worldwide" picture is much worse. As we point out in chapter 6, the World Bank and the International Monetary Fund have applied an international policy aimed at reducing the humanities to instrumentalized, job-related functions. As we suggest in our introduction, if there isn't a conspiracy, there is certainly an ideology and a series of interlocking plans driving change. Gilman assumes his American experience teaches him all he needs to know, but America is not the world.

Similarly, Gilman worries that decreasing resources for higher education will increasingly deny people "the social mobility that education brings" (2000, 60). That is a valid fear, and if Gilman had troubled himself to read the relevant research he would have found that the poor had even less access to higher education at the end of the most recent democratic administration than they had at the beginning. Yet Gilman would also find that educational access for families at the lowest income quartile has never been other than marginal. Few of the poor have ever had the educational opportunities our founding myths have seemed to offer. The real problem is not the one Gilman identifies—potential decline—but the long-term and continuing failure to offer all citizens equal educational opportunities. Gilman's laziness about informing himself about matters outside his scholarly field undercuts every chapter in his book. Smug self-confidence reigns where wider reading should have taken over. The origin and the destination of his voice are one and the same: his own sense of self-esteem.

Gilman is hardly alone. Indeed, as we point out in greater detail later, he is much like many of the distinguished faculty on the Executive Council of the Modern Language Association. Accomplished scholars all, they have concentrated on their specializations until suddenly finding themselves responsible for making decisions about general issues in higher education. As recently as 2001, MLA Executive Council members were asking why on earth all these graduate students would want to unionize. Confronted with the execrable treatment of adjuncts, they murmured their sympathies but sniffed that it would be unseemly for the MLA to advocate for specific changes in their situations. Meanwhile they have no problem lobbying for increased attention to their scholarly specializations.

Higher education's difficulties, it seems, have thrust many faculty members into public roles for which they are ill equipped, though they are equipped with efficient mechanisms for deluding themselves. The broad problem of academics becoming public intellectuals gets a subtle and challenging interrogation in John Michael's *Anxious Intellects: Academic Professionals, Public Intellectuals, and Enlightenment Values* (2000). We count ourselves among those who have felt that the superficial, media-driven celebration of "public" academic intellectuals over the past decade has ignored the real problems inherent in the role they play. Others have raised serious questions about the problematic status of such so-called "public intellectuals," notably Bruce Robbins and Adolph Reed, but it is not until *Anxious Intellects* that we have had a fully successful and realistic account of the limits of what intellectuals can accomplish on the margins of American popular culture.

This is a canny, ruthlessly clear-headed book that sets aside all obvious political commitments to assess what a series of intellectuals have actually contributed to public life. Michael rejects all of the traditional models—the organic intellectual inhering in a particular community, the straightforward and hierarchical model of intellectual authority, and the class innocent invocation of a democratic public sphere—to claim instead that intellectuals occupy vexed spaces on the edge of opposing constituencies. Michael as a result gives us no easy basis for celebration of intellectuals' actual impact. The result is a superior book on the role of the intellectual in the contemporary world.

Yet in one crucial respect *Anxious Intellects* and *The Fortunes of the Humanities* are surprisingly congruent—in their relative blindness to the disease within higher education, the inability of most faculty to reflect on their institutional positioning and its compromised workplace ethics. Gilman, like most faculty, looks outward, complaining about curtailed public support. Michael, interestingly, for a book so relentless in urging self-reflection and reflexive political and institutional analysis, is rather quiet about the need to examine how institutional exploitation positions and undermines the authority of individual intellectuals. "The fact that intellectuals today must write and act, take positions and make polemics, in the absence of clear answers to basic questions about their own positioning, authority, and prerogatives," he writes, "is the very condition of intellectual work in the realm of popular politics today" (2000, 1–2). This is Michael's foundational argument and it soundly captures a key source of unease, ambivalence, alienation, and schizophrenia in university intellectuals. Yet we would argue that in one respect—their role as members of academic institutions—one can give clear analyses of the cost of elite prerogatives. Of course it is exactly that kind of reflection and moral and institutional responsibility that Dubson's book urges on us. The disjunctions among the books, all of them in different ways accounts of the current academic scene, suggest they derive from mutually separate universes.

So it was with the fall 2001 national Campus Equity Week, a series of local events staged simultaneously across the country to call attention to the need for solidarity, community, and dedicated activism around issues of campus workplace fairness. Organized primarily by contingent faculty, it succeeded in building their organizational strength, but left tenured faculty oblivious or indifferent. Most audiences—whether attending outdoor rallies or indoor scholarly panels—were composed primarily of part-timers or others already committed to the academic labor movement. Even among those tenured faculty willing, say, to sign a petition urging solidarity with contingent teachers seeking fair working conditions, the issues remain compartmentalized rather than foundational.

We are a long way from binding Michael's and Dubson's books together, from seeing them as one related set of issues and priorities. Yet as the gap widens between the salaries of administrators, academic stars, and the wealthiest disciplines on the one hand, and the salaries and benefits of contingent laborers and marginalized disciplines on the other hand, the structural relationship between the groups solidifies. For every person earning $50,000 to $100,000 or more for teaching a course there are hundreds earning about $1,000 or $2,000. The hourly pay for an assistant to the university president may be as much as $150; the hourly pay for a part-time teacher may be barely more than $2.50. With every budget cut the exploited group typically suffers still more while the protected class remains protected. Can we continue to pretend that one group is not living off the exploitation of the other? Is not the indifference of the lucky, the wealthy, the comfortable, the empowered, fast becoming an intolerable scandal, at least for an industry that seeks to be admired and supported for commitments of a higher order?

So what is the problem with tenured faculty? How have some of them become like institutional monsters, waiting at the center of the higher education labyrinth to devour unsuspecting graduate students and part-timers? What can we do at least to change the available subject positions for new faculty, assuming that many of their entrenched senior colleagues are lost to monstrosity? While we are not quite ready to proclaim that the only good tenured faculty member is a dead tenured faculty member, there have been recent moments, say, at Yale during the 1996 graduate employee grade strike, where but for Hazel Carby, Michael Denning, and David Montgomery, we would have been ready to celebrate a mass die-out of the dinosaur class.

Not long ago the organizing committee of the prestigious English Institute met to plan the following year's program. When these senior scholars looked to salt the event with promising younger faculty, the luminaries came to the agreement such people were nowhere to be found. No good work, they concluded, was being done by anyone under fifty. Our own experience is that we do not have to look farther than our own departments to find inspiring work by young scholars. But a certain species of academic superstar—all exempted from the depredations of an increasingly dehumanized academic workplace—believes he or she *is* the profession. No wonder they are comfortable with their belief that nothing can be done to transform the job system. Exploitation, after all, doesn't matter, since there's no one beneath their level worthy of fair and decent treatment.

Day Late, Dollar Short, a timely anthology edited by Peter C. Herman, does not solve these problems, but it does help us contextualize them.

The book begins the essential process of placing the intellectual agendas of the last three decades on the table with all the altered economic realities that are putting those agendas in crisis and reshaping their social meaning. And it also helps us see why most tenured faculty are ill equipped to understand the institutional worlds in which they now live.

The first general point to make, of course, is that most tenured faculty would not assent to my trope of monstrosity. In fact, they think rather well of themselves. As Crystal Bartolovich argues in her contribution to the Herman collection, "To Boldly Go Where No MLA Has Gone Before," an astute analysis of the MLA establishment's response to a resolution censuring Yale for its reprisals to grad employee labor organizers, academia "presents itself as a utopia of freedom and independence for its members, and yet seems capable of functioning only as a rigid hierarchy" (2000, 77). The academic system "manages to mystify its practices as benign" and encourages its members to "pride themselves on their ostensible enlightened distance from the rest of the universe." As Michael puts it, "intellectuals tend to hide their self-promoting agendas and aggrandizing self-interests behind claims to serve universalized truth, justice, or emancipation" (2000, 4).

A bit of history may help explain why faculty are unenlightened about their purported enlightenment. Consider an indicative fact, perhaps a decisive one. Over little more than two decades, beginning in the early 1970s, the total membership of the American Association of University Professors has declined by nearly two thirds, from 120,000 to 45,000. Part of the early decline represented a protest against the Association's decision to help faculty on individual campuses to unionize if they chose to do so. But most of the losses came from the combined result of faculty retirements and the failure of new faculty members to join in sufficient numbers.

Many faculty used to have loyalties to their institution and to the profession as a whole. Those loyalties tend now to be lodged in the individual academic discipline. But the older model was to a significant degree a collective one; it emphasized group identity and mission rather than individual gain. The rise of the entrepreneurial faculty member, however, helped craft disciplinary identities that are primarily self-interested, that see English or Philosophy or History less as ongoing traditions than as fields for self-advancement. As Michael Bérubé puts it in his epilogue to the Herman volume, "self-absorption, hauteur, and primadonnadom were raised to the level of professional principle" (1998, 223).

When an unreflective community investment in research meets this careerist model of disciplinarity, the result is a faculty member who sees self-advancement and careerism as transcendent virtues. Disciplines then reward and celebrate scholars—including scholars on the Left—without regard to their practices as teachers, colleagues, citizens, or indeed even as human beings. The individual scholar, who may consistently mistreat the people in his or her life, nonetheless thinks of himself or herself as heroic.

We all know the dispiriting betrayals by progressive faculty of their supposed values when self-interest or even mere inconvenience get in the way. We watched labor scholars at Yale become union busters, leftists at Columbia cross picket lines. As a recent PhD wrote to one of us about his experiences as a graduate student union activist:

> I joined the small TA union when I arrived at Santa Cruz in 1989 and walked picket lines and protests for eleven years, first as an underemployed graduate student, then as an underemployed part-time lecturer. The struggle at Santa Cruz was relatively unsung, overshadowed as we were by the proximity of Berkeley and the national prominence of Yale, but it was often bitter. The most bitter pill of all was the behavior, when push came to shove, of our faculty. We were shocked at how quickly the veneer of the teacher and mentor could be discarded to reveal the supervisor underneath. At solidarity meetings with faculty, we watched in disbelief as the faculty members who taught us to read Marx and labor history told us "now is not the time" and "this is not a real political struggle." On a rainy night in the middle of a bitter six-week strike, these "sympathetic" faculty members taught us—inadvertently—an unforgettable lesson in the power structures of the university.

In the end "now is not the time" means nothing more than "not on my watch, not while my privileges are at stake." "This is not a real political struggle" presumably reflects the mixture of denial and other-worldliness and guilt that permits faculty to claim the campus is not the real world. Meanwhile, graduate employees or part-timers without health care who become seriously ill feel that they are living in a world that is far too real. Of course some Left scholars understand exactly the relationship between past struggles, current ones, and their own benefits and place in a structure of power. But why do so many others not share awareness of their place in a heritage of Left activism? Here is our informant again:

> The left faculty members closest to me at UC Santa Cruz were very supportive of unionization. When the 1992 strike vote was taken, I told my faculty supervisor, Richard Terdiman (who later

served on my dissertation committee) that I would not be able to do any more work as his TA (in an upper-division literature course of 65 students). He told me, 'Jon, I'd be ashamed of you if you did otherwise.' But this was a very rare response. One faculty member teaching a lecture course in German cinema announced to his class (without consulting the TAs) that his two TAs would not strike, because of their commitment to the left politics of the class and of avant-garde German cinema. The two TAs stood up and walked out without a word (if the professor had inquired, he would have known that they were shop stewards in their departments)." (Letter to the author, February 16, 2001)

Like it or not, we have to conclude that a progressive politics invested primarily in one's ego and validated exclusively by career accomplishments can lead to a social blindness that contradicts most progressive traditions and commitments. Much in the professional reward system enhances this tendency. Over and over again we have seen remarkably destructive people receive the applause of their colleagues for their research accomplishments: a senior faculty member with a long history of harassing women, a history decisive enough to compel his absence from campus for a year, becomes the president of his disciplinary association and the occupant of a named chair; a faculty member who was repeatedly at risk of investigation for assault on graduate students receives a national disciplinary award for mentoring.

If these contradictions sometimes flow from the disjunction between local and national reputations, they also reflect a devotion to research accomplishments so slavish that it trumps almost any human indecency. In the psychodynamics of careers, professional honors symbolically pardon faculty members for personal offenses. It is time we stop doing so.

Indeed these disciplinary honors are ironic in another sense, not only because their recipients are sometimes not honorable, but also because they are largely indifferent to the discipline that is their field of endeavor. It is clear that many accomplished scholars actually have no interest in the future of their disciplines. The history of Sociology or Political Science effectively ends with the close of their own careers. A true disciplinary identity would make faculty quite concerned with the exploitation of contingent teachers because it undermines the discipline's capacity to renew and advance itself and to speak persuasively from within enlightenment values. For a Left faculty member especially, sensitivity to the history of labor injustice should combine with disciplinary loyalty to make reform imperative. But Left faculty who see the campus and the discipline primarily as potential claques, sources of applause and rewards, do not make those connections. Meanwhile, abstract advocacy for victims elsewhere in time or space places self-interested scoundrels on a professional pedestal.

The problem has been exacerbated by the changing economics of higher education. During the 1970s, talk of the entrepreneurial faculty member meant little more than someone devoted to a competition for federal research funds. To be sure there were some who focused on Pentagon or CIA funding and thus potentially built an implicit political commitment into their work and perhaps compromised the moral ground of a pure research agenda. But unmitigated self-interest still seemed at least to contradict the collective mission of higher education.

Then in the 1980s the pursuit of wealth once again became a national obsession unfettered by self-reflection or social commitment. Meanwhile, two things happened at universities. Federal research funding began to be replaced by often significantly more compromised corporate grants. And universities began themselves to adopt a ruthless business ideology, one eager to extract labor from campus workers at the lowest possible cost, one willing to sacrifice research independence and integrity for profit. These campus trends accelerated in the last decade. The entrepreneurial faculty member was now situated at the corporate university. Little had we realized the price we would pay for a careerism become wholly amoral.

These trends meanwhile intersected with a third development, less a trend than a permanent fact of life—the long-term collapse of the job market for new PhDs. And finally universities began to rely increasingly on part-time faculty, often paid less than the minimum wage when preparation and grading are added to classroom hours. The exclusively self-interested faculty member no longer had an honorable group enterprise underwriting careerism. He or she could now be counted literally as living off the exploitation of other workers in the same building or on the same campus. The monster had become a vampire.

The truth is that we have been breeding and training monsters in higher education for decades. How do you appeal to a monster? Perhaps you don't. If monsters cared about the *future* of higher education, they might reign in their self-interest. If they cared about the ethics of employment in their own departments they might already have done so. But we have told them that original publications absolve them of all subsequent sins. Do you even want to *try* sending a wake-up call to a vampire? We seem to remember that's a bad idea.

The truth is that many senior faculty cannot be reeducated. Nor can we tinker with a higher education system that has become increasingly more corrupt over a series of decades. But we also cannot afford to lose another generation of scholars to socially irresponsible subject positions. Higher education as we know it needs to be rebuilt from the ground up. As Bérubé argues in his contribution to the Herman volume, we need to recover and promote models of responsible academic citizenship. That is part of the implicit challenge of the Dubson collection as well. We need, in other words, to offer different identities and ideals to a new generation of scholars.

The entrepreneurial faculty member who looks out only for himself or herself is now positioned precisely to be coopted by corporatization. We need a new breed of citizen scholars who can identify not only with institution and discipline but also with community. If such citizen scholars are to emerge in higher education they are likely to come from the growing campus union movement, which encourages solidarity across job classifications about issues like the need for community-wide living wages, safe workplaces, and health care. We need not only to resist corporatization without representation; we need also to articulate an alternative vision of what a collaborative university might be like.

The University of Illinois recently issued a *Handbook for Good Ethical Practice.* It might well have asked what might constitute ethical employment practices at this or any other university, though it did not. It might as well have asked what an individual faculty member's ethical responsibility for his or her employer's practices might be. Under "Protecting University Assets" the booklet focuses on money and equipment and ignores the institution's human assets. Under "Being a University Employee" it urges us "to treat all members of the community with dignity and respect," but fails to ask what employment with dignity might entail. For some it requires taking out loans to meet living expenses not covered by inadequate salary and health care. The section on "Managing Conflict of Interest" does not help us consider what it means when self-interest and community interests collide, but that relationship is exactly what we must rethink if we are to retain and renew public respect for higher education. Toward the end, the booklet's section on "Good Business Practices" urges spreading responsibility for financial transactions across several employees; that is all well and good, but we need to ask whether the transactions themselves are inherently ethical. These are questions we need to take collective responsibility for posing. Of course this is also the booklet that announces "economic development" has been added to our traditional mission of teaching, research, and service.

It is obvious the administrators who wrote Illinois's ethical guide are not equipped to articulate an ethics for the corporate university. The "Charter of University Workers Rights" in circulation for several years instead at almost every point takes us where we need to go. It is first of all a list of good practices presently ignored, so far as we know, by virtually all colleges and universities in the country. But it is more than that. As experience in Boston has shown, promoting the charter as part of a city-wide living wage campaign across the employment spectrum is a way of building alliances and solidarity among the increasingly divided segments of the higher education workforce.

The prospect of such new identities within a collaborative university is what underlies some of the antagonism toward campus organizing today. Once we get beyond the comic performance of exploitive employers decrying the loss of collegiality if their part-time faculty should organize, or warning that the risk to mentoring relationships is dire if graduate employees seek fair wages and benefits through collective bargaining, and once we realize that many campus administrations spend more resisting unionization than they would likely have to concede in benefits were unions recognized, we are left to ponder why administrators are so remorseless in their opposition to collective action. It cannot just be a question of power, because there's little evidence power relations on campus are dramatically changed by existing graduate student unions, though a faculty union can make a significant difference in power relations if it is strong enough and promotes general principles of fairness.

What is fundamentally at stake, however, are the deep loyalties, goals, and identities of the participants in higher education. Pushed far enough, a focus on employee rights and related unionization drives instills very different loyalties in all members of the campus community. These, in turn, promote values of group responsibility and erode the unreflective subject positions of entrepreneurial department member and entrepreneurial disciplinary participant. The graduate student or faculty union activist has a different set of loyalties and priorities, a different sense of self and mission, from the graduate student or faculty member focused exclusively on personal achievement. The union activist will be resistant to cooptation by the corporate university, by a system of education designed to produce docile workers rather than critical citizens. A union activist is at least a little less likely to sell out for fame and fortune. Campus administrators are increasingly wary of staff members unwilling to be bought and sold.

It's not the traditional values of collegiality that collective action challenges. Indeed it can renew them in a different form. Nor is shared governance thereby threatened; instead organizing breathes new life into the concept. Nor is research devoted to the common good undermined by group commitment and community values. What is threatened is institutional devotion to profit at all costs.

The faculty monster was satisfied to be well-fed and deeply feared. He could even take fear for love. And so we praised the monster despite any cruelties he committed. It is time to demand moral accountability of our colleagues and our institutions. As we argued in our introduction, universities cannot promote enlightenment values unless they exemplify them.

CN

3. The Postdoc Paradox

IT IS NOW A FULL DECADE since I helped persuade my department head to start a postdoc program for our new PhDs. In retrospect, it is more than fair to say that neither I nor my department head was precisely thinking ahead. We tried; it's just that neither of us got the future right. If we had it to do over again I would still press to hire our own unemployed PhDs as postdocs, just as I did in the early 1990s. Yet we ended up with a program whose consequences are both greater and different from those we anticipated.

The impulse was straightforward: many of our new PhDs were not getting tenure track jobs in the year before or after they were awarded the degree. We wanted to give them a chance to stay in the profession while they kept testing what we were by then habitually calling "the market." Staying in town and teaching a year or two post PhD would give them a chance to teach more advanced courses and add more publications to their vitas. I had earlier predicted that some of our more unconventional cultural studies students would need a book to break into the profession long-term and secure a career. Yet they couldn't finish the book without the time to do so.

The postdoc program was grounded in a logic of responsibility. We had no contract with our graduate students guaranteeing them professorships here or elsewhere. Indeed like other schools we had added warning labels to our admissions package. Yet a number of us on the faculty felt a very deep sense of commitment to our students, and we were willing to transform it rhetorically into a general departmental responsibility. At the very least we had used them to teach the composition courses the

41

faculty preferred to avoid, and paid them less than the cost of living to do so.

The standard graduate student teaching load at the University of Illinois after the first year is 2/2, the same as the faculty teaching load, precisely twice the load the MLA recommends for graduate students; at the time the postdoc program started, grad students received about $10,000 for that service, several thousand dollars a year less than it costs to live in Champaign-Urbana. Graduate student employee salaries have since grown to over $12,000, but that is still below the cost of living. They either find additional jobs during the summer or take out loans to cover the shortfall. Since the 2/2 load seriously delays progress toward the PhD and the salary is abusive, they were and are clearly being exploited. Meanwhile, as we argue at length in *Academic Keywords*, at least some in the profession were coming to realize that the limited number of tenure-track jobs available made the notion that PhD programs were apprenticeships hollow.

As bad as the human damage, from my perspective, was the intellectual waste. These new PhDs had often developed genuinely important research programs. I admired the work they were doing, felt it was needed, and wanted them to be able to revise their dissertations, publish them as books, and continue writing for decades. None of that would be possible unless they stayed in the profession.

More important, I felt we had a responsibility at least to maximize their chances for a career. We couldn't guarantee a lifetime place in the profession, but we owed *something* more than thoughtless, automatic dismissal to people who had taught well and cheaply for us for seven years. My colleagues are fond of repeating that this guarantee of seven years of support is the longest in the country and something of which we can be proud. Yet seven years in a comp paper grading sweat shop is not the most benign gift higher education has ever offered. I felt we should fulfill our responsibility to the students we had taught and mentored and exploited for more than half a decade before bringing in new students and starting the process over again.

In a December 2000 motion passed by the MLA's Delegate Assembly that Marc Bousquet and I coauthored, we called this continual cycle of admission and disposal a "logic of replacement." It was Marc's phrase, and he has elaborated on it at length in a ground-breaking essay "The Waste Product of Graduate Education." One of the more striking ironies in this system, he points out, is that we continually dismiss our most capable and experienced teachers and hire new and inexperienced ones in the person of new admissions to graduate school. It seems we have to get rid of these new PhDs, the waste products of the employment system, in order to make room for new recruits to our graduate seminars. If we were concerned about the quality of undergraduate teaching we'd want to keep these people on the job. Instead we run a kind of processing and slaughter operation.

In a voluntary replacement system this would be called "churning," the term used to describe the process some groups undergo who keep losing established members and replacing them with new ones, but never actually experience growth. In the higher education system departments keep roughly the same number of teachers overall but continually exchange qualified for inexperienced ones. We keep training teachers and then getting rid of them, opting for less qualified replacements, a system that hardly seems rational.

Of course it's not only the need for more beginning graduate students that explains this system. The logic of apprenticeship called for increased job security and salary once apprenticeship came to an end and the PhD was rewarded. As many graduate students learn instead, the PhD can mean the end of their careers, rather than the beginning of a better career phase. Or if not literally cast out, many graduates move on to adjunct or part-time teaching at half pay. Rutgers University pays many of its graduate student teaching assistants a sound $6,000 per course; upon completing their degrees they are eligible for part-time teaching at $2,400 per course. What's more they have no job security. Is anyone wrong in considering such a system insane?

The motion passed by the Delegate Assembly called on the MLA to explore means of defining appropriate "continuing employment" for our long-term graduate student employees. One usually very sympathetic member of the Delegate Assembly cheerfully dubbed it "tenure for graduate students." Nonetheless, after lengthy preparatory discussion on the listserve, the motion passed. I pointed out that we weren't proposing any specific solution. Rather we were asking that a discussion begin about how the higher education employment system operates and how we might make it more responsible, rational, and humane. One version of "continuing employment," I suggested, was a postdoctoral teaching appointment. Two months later the Executive Council turned the motion down.

Meanwhile, back in Champaign-Urbana we were drifting in an unplanned but almost inexorable way toward continuing employment of a sort. When I proposed the postdoc appointment program to my department we were already struggling with staff shortages. Our faculty had been downsized from ninety to fifty-five in the 1970s and early 1980s when our undergraduate enrollment fell. When undergrad enrollments climbed again to their pre-jobwar highs, the administration chose, unsurprisingly, not to return the faculty lines. What's more, the English department had dramatically reduced the size of its graduate program over two decades, from a high of 350 to a current level of 120, almost exactly a two-thirds cut. So we were constantly short of teachers for undergrad courses and were hiring graduate students from several other disciplines.

Yet we had highly qualified teachers exiting our PhD program all the time. Some went on to part-time teaching elsewhere, some left the profession. In the year 2001 they could, if they chose, drive three hours south to Logan Community College near Carbondale, Illinois, and earn $900 for teaching a semester-long composition course. What higher principles were we honoring by encouraging that option?

In any case, departmental self-interest argued for rehiring our own PhDs to staff our lower level courses. It was easy. No interview necessary. We knew their abilities. They might not be the people we would hire in a competitive national search, where we looked for the people most likely to shape the discipline's intellectual development, but then we weren't offering competitive tenure-track jobs. We were offering temporary postdocs to answer our insatiable need for cheap teachers and to give our graduates a way of clinging to the profession with their fingernails.

Still, my department head was uneasy. A multiyear program might make these postdocs too comfortable. They might settle in with drowsy satisfaction at earning $3,000 a course, a bit more than they did as graduate students, and stop applying for other jobs, or so he thought. I countered that we were paying $9,000 a course to new assistant professors and that the income disparity and lack of job security, combined with constant media blandishment to buy cars and color televisions, would keep our postdocs hungry for other options. But we ended up with a one-year postdoc program nonetheless.

Then the year came to an end. Nothing had changed. We could take our postdocs out into the corn fields and garrote them, or we could rehire them. Amusingly enough, we performed a reprise of the "What if they are as happy as pigs in mud on these jobs?" interchange, with me countering again that even pigs may want to break out of the barnyard. So the one-year postdoc became a two-year postdoc. Year three gave us an opportunity to polish our acting skills yet again. We had a three-year postdoc. Year four, I believe, saw a more nuanced and future-oriented exchange of views. The focus shifted from concern with the unreliable ambitions of our postdocs to a more realistic concern with the programmatic structure we were almost haplessly putting in place. If my memory serves me well, it was at year five that we stopped talking. I did not need to show up to plead the postdoc's case. Indeed it seemed the better course to avoid the topic entirely. I was certain by then that we would rehire everyone still here when the freshmen showed up to sow comma splices among the soy beans.

Yet not everyone was still here. One of my own PhDs published a splendid book in her first postdoc year and went from $3,000 a course to $12,000 a course in a tenure-track job. Another colleague's PhD issued his book with a university press in year four; he landed a permanent job as well. One of my PhDs held on for five years in postdoc penury, publishing articles and working on his book. The project was not ready for publication, but it had become a far more eloquent and persuasive enterprise. He ended up in a tenure-track job at a flagship state university.

Those were among the kinds of successes I had in mind when I proposed the program. For some they came at a price. We were rehiring our own new PhDs as postdocs for $3,000 a course and soon enough hiring other schools' PhDs as $10,000-a-course assistant professors. Some of our own postdocs were outdistancing some of our assistant professors in the publication race. Resentment could hardly help but fester. My own five-year postdoc often seemed past resentment and near rage. Others simmered with a constant sense of injustice. And yet several hung on and won the kinds of positions they had always wanted. A year into the new assistant professorship, I am pleased to say, and the anger was gone. They were all glad to have been offered a way of staying in academia.

Meanwhile a thousand other flowers we hadn't known we were planting began to bloom in unexpected ways. As Jeff Goldblum, playing a chaos theorist, warns in the film *Jurassic Park*, life will find a way. An hour away was a comprehensive university where several of our decommissioned teachers had found refuge over the years. Graduate students who had never finished were hired as part-timers. Unsuccessful job seeking PhDs were given full-time terminal five-year appointments. Now these folks heard that we were hiring our own lost, tired, and poor. Here at least you can go home again. For despite offering apparently indefinite postdocs we were still short of experienced teachers.

We could hardly call people without the PhD postdocs, so we called them instructors. PhDs returning after a five-year absence? Postdoc seemed a little off the mark there as well, so they became lecturers. And steady pressure was raising salaries. We are now paying $4,000 a course for postdocs and lecturers; Indiana pays over $5,000 per course for literature classes. We had hoped to raise it to between $5,000 and $6,000 a course by 2003 or 2004, but state budget cuts demolished that plan. We do, however, provide full health care and vestment in a retirement system of choice. It's by no means the worst deal in the academy. Indeed you can drive an hour and a half to a community college and teach ten courses per year on the tenure track for just over $30,000 a year. And those are the lucky 15 percent of the faculty there; the rest are part-timers pulling in half that income.

Yet those inequities were established decades ago. Here at Illinois what began but a few years ago as a temporary strategy—we called them "emergency" appointments to meet urgent instructional needs—has now evolved into a new bureaucratic apparatus and a semipermanent second class of proto-faculty. No one knows what future these appointments hold, if any. A few years ago we were standing tall and saying "Six years and you're out!" Now we're not so sure. Whose interests are we serving in terminating these postdoctoral lecturers after six years? Needless to say, *they* don't want honorable execution on behalf of king, country, or some inhumane ideal image of the professoriate. They want their second class appointments regularized, with multi-year contracts and performance reviews. That too we had planned until budget cuts arrived in 2003.

And yet. And yet. And yet. We have aging PhD candidates with twelve or thirteen years of teaching experience at our campus, plus five years elsewhere in the area. Some Illinois PhDs have more than a decade in our employ, some with another five elsewhere. Do these people have any other job prospects? We're talking about people in their forties, with a few heading toward age fifty. Can anyone call these folks *apprentices* with a straight face?

Not that they've given up on the job market, though as I make my way through practice interviews with one forty-something hopeful candidate I suddenly wonder if our 'prentices face age discrimination. Nor are we the only department experimenting with free form faculty identities. The Spanish and Psychology Departments have been reinventing the professoriate as well. The administration is anxious to turn these arrangements into something with predictable ends and means, but these identities are mutating faster than viruses. No one knows where it all will lead.

The campus, however, has become accustomed to meeting a substantial portion of our instructional responsibilities at discount rates. Despite every certainty "it would never happen here," we have joined the large number of American campuses with a two-tier faculty—one named, visible, above ground and another morphing through underground darkness unheralded. More than a class system, it is a kind of species difference, like the future races in H. G. Wells's *The Time Machine*, or the genetically fated privileged versus flawed (and merely normal) classes in the contemporary film *Gattica*.

Illinois, I should emphasize, has not given up thinking it needs some humanities faculty who do research and bring public recognition to the university. It has simply decided it does not need quite so many of them. Like the Marine Corps, they are looking for a few good men and women. The others, well, the others need to function but they will not have the leisure to excel.

Do we owe these toilers in comp cellars any long-term guarantees? It would have been easy enough for the university to answer "no" at an earlier point in this historical narrative. And now we have discovered the central campus administration had already stocked body bags for them in case flexibility called for their use. But at some point something like permanent responsibility does take form. The University of Kansas recently fired Fred Whitehead, a twenty-year contract faculty member, without cause and without due process. There wasn't any doubt that he was doing his job well and was a productive scholar. The University President, a one-time literature scholar professing humane values, chimed in to assert Kansas owed him nothing, not even the standard year's notice. He was fired to save money; then they fought his unemployment insurance rights when he turned down a clerk's job as an alternative. The national American Association of University Professors (AAUP) wrote letters of protest but could not get its head around his employment category with enough clarity to investigate his case.

Needless to say, neither at Kansas nor at Illinois nor at most other schools do long-term contract faculty have AAUP-style due process and job security guarantees guarantees. Whitehead was canned five years before he could have retired, an act of special cruelty. Do we face such possibilities at Illinois? Well, after a certain number of years the odds that a part-timer or an annually rehired lecturer can find another teaching job drop below plausible calculation. Surely at that point continuing employment for someone performing satisfactorily becomes at least a moral responsibility.

If the potential for career-long institutional commitments was one unintended consequence of tinkering with the job system, others derived from the interlocking, interdependent nature of the various segments of university labor. You cannot make adjustments in one segment, it seems, without having impact on all the others. We reduced the number of graduate students with the best of intentions. Yet we managed at the same time thereby to open the possibility for part-time and contract faculty appointments.

On the one hand, we would not have been able to offer postdocs had we not first downsized the graduate program; that freed funding and created a need for more teachers. We thus *eventually*, after more than a decade, accepted a higher degree of career responsibility for the lower number of students we admitted. Yet the combination of downsizing and instituting a postdoc program also opened the door to a series of alternate and less secure faculty positions. I would not say that we *created* a two-class teaching faculty as a result; it was already implicit in the failed apprenticeship of graduate students. But the faculty class system lost all its disguises when we began classifying new PhDs according to an essentially arbitrary system.

The effects on the system would increase dramatically if a national postdoc program were put in place. That would have the effect of universally suppressing salaries for new doctoral recipients. It would also encourage schools without doctoral programs to institute postdoctoral programs, a particularly dangerous possibility, since that would give them a new way of decreasing the number of assistant professorships they offered. Under the guise of helping new PhDs, they would really just be looking for cheap labor. There should be clear and widespread professional disapproval of any school that does not produce doctorates employing postdocs. What Illinois did at least grew out of our sense of responsibility to our own PhDs, though we eventually hired a number of postdocs from other schools. The cheap labor system has to be fed, and in the end we fed it in any way we could.

The decision to branch out to a kind of informal, regional postdoc hiring system, notably, was reached by department administrators. It was neither discussed with department faculty nor announced to them in advance. As it happened, the decision to hire postdocs from other schools was the one really fatal decision in this whole sequence of events. Until then, we were operating out of a sense of community and sense of personal and professional responsibility, however flawed, to our own PhDs. After that, we were merely looking for exploitable bodies, an ideology that has now largely taken over the program. One fall we suddenly received a memo in our mail boxes listing several new postdocs hired from elsewhere. Each of them was awarded a paragraph describing their research areas and teaching interests. Even that system shortly disintegrated. After three years the department stopped producing the list of new temporary appointees, whether out of laziness or out of a plan to make them thoroughly invisible and expendable is impossible to say. By then department leadership had changed. The head who initiated the program had moved on to another job, and information of any sort was becoming scarce under the new dispensation. Like many of our permanent faculty, I stopped meeting these new "colleagues." Most of the permanent faculty had no idea who they were or what they did. One would regularly see people in their thirties walking the halls and wonder who they were.

Then new pressures arrived. After long efforts, we succeeded in getting a new departmental MFA program in creative writing approved. There was no evidence the state, the country, or the planet needed one. To facilitate matters, the creative writers cheerfully lied and said creative writers do not seek academic jobs when some of us wondered whether the academic job market needed more applicants. The theory behind the plan was that these additional responsibilities would encourage a cluster of deeply irrational creative writing faculty to begin behaving like adults, a plan that has since been exquisitely disproven. I was assured, however, that the MFA would have no effect on the postdoc program.

The program, it seemed, could absorb fifteen MFA students guaranteed three years of employment without batting an exam booklet. That confidence lasted a year. In the fall of 2002 the newspapers began to warn of severe cuts in our state appropriations. I walked the halls suggesting we might cancel two of our tenure track job searches to protect our postdocs' jobs. I found not one sympathetic colleague, nor am I certain I should have. Everyone with whom I spoke said our first priority had to be rebuilding the size of the tenured faculty. By 2003 we had fifty tenure track or tenured faculty, down from a high of ninety in 1970. The same year we had fifty postdocs, up from a low of *none* in 1970. In the summer of 2003 state budget cuts became a reality. We fired a dozen postdocs.

Meanwhile, surrealism and legalism were colliding with scarcity. So long as there were postdocs aplenty, we operated without clear rules of eligibility or priority. Now the university became worried that people denied reappointment might have cause for action in a system without guidelines. So guidelines were jury-rigged. A long-term postdoc with a fine teaching record and a PhD from our own department left the program for a semester. When he reapplied he was told he had lost his place in the priority list and would never again have a job. That crushing news lasted two weeks, when a faculty member's reassignment to an administrative job opened a need only the exiled postdoc could fill. He was back among the living.

Meanwhile, the logic of replacement was now operating with especially focused vengeance. Some of the creative writing faculty decided they were highly suspicious of MFA applicants with high test scores. It suggested excessive devotion to the rational, rather than the creative, faculties, so they began admitting candidates with unusually low tested verbal skills. We were faced with the prospect of replacing skilled rhetoric teachers with instructors possessing less verbal dexterity than the undergraduates they were supposed to teach. Determined to make matters worse, a few creative writers began telling their new MFA students that only their own fiction mattered. As a consequence we now had several composition teachers skipping a month or more of classes to devote themselves to imaginative pursuits. Department administrators, priests of academe all, hued to a coverup mentality.

As always happens in the academy, local peculiarities exacerbate or particularize national trends. But certain generalities nonetheless obtain. Our program has now become fundamentally irrational, but even when it "worked" it suffered from multiple fundamental paradoxes. Since we have an employment *system* in higher education, the effects, once again, of intervention in one area were quickly felt in others. Consider, for example, the impact of postdocs on expectations for tenure. It will be no news to many that requirements for tenure are being racheted up at many institutions. Several of our Illinois postdocs effectively earned tenure under the rules prevailing throughout the 1970s and 1980s and 1990s *before* they won their first tenure-track job.

Publishing your first book before you arrive on campus for a first-year assistant professorship makes it easier for the new employer to require a second book before tenure. A national postdoc program would make this still relatively exceptional demand fairly common. Even people hired immediately after receiving the PhD would have that heavy burden placed on them. That now happens at only a few schools, among them Princeton and Stanford. Revising a dissertation over several years is quite different from starting and completing an entirely new project. Indeed, the time required for publishers to obtain readers' reports and the time needed to make revisions necessitate the completion of a book manuscript by the second or third year of an assistant professorship. Imagine how hard it is to start and complete a new book in that time frame and you can easily estimate the impact on undergraduate teaching: such requirements amount to a demand that you abandon your students if you want to keep your job.

The only real defense against such practices is to award tenure to new humanities assistant professors with books within two to three years of their arrival on campus. If the tenure clock is speeded up and the appointment letter guarantees the first book will fully count for tenure, some of the potential abuses of a postdoc system can be eliminated. But some schools will refuse to follow these recommendations.

Postdocs also vary widely in their generosity and in their level of commitment to career development. The Illinois postdoc offered a 3/3 load, unlike the 2/2 load given assistant professors. We also offer assistant professors—but not postdocs—a semester free of teaching at full salary prior to the year in which tenure is decided. The assistant professors, who are occasionally less accomplished than the postdocs, also teach graduate seminars, while the postdocs do not. Other schools do better, sometimes offering postdocs a lower teaching load, a modest travel allowance, or research account to assist their careers, rather than just extract their teaching.

One simple measure of a program's fairness, of course, is the salary it provides. The closer postdocs are to full parity with assistant professors, the closer they are to the same compensation per course, the fairer and less exploitive the program is. When we started our program we paid postdocs about one third what assistant professors received per course. If we had succeeded in implementing the salary increases planned for 2002–2004, our postdocs would have been paid at nearly half the per course rate for assistant professors. Of course that would only be somewhat fair because our entry level salaries are relatively high. Community colleges sometimes pay part-time faculty at a 50 percent per course rate, but their full-timer salaries may be so low that 50 percent puts people below a living wage.

This suggests postdoc programs may only be tolerable if a campus adopts universal fair employment and governance policies. The "Charter of University Workers' Rights" launched at a February 2001 conference at the University of Massachusetts at Boston lists practices that probably no institution in the country yet fully honors. It asks not only for a living wage and fair benefits but also for public access to all salaries and grievance procedures run by elected peer groups for all employees. Like the AAUP, the authors of the Charter also endorse collective bargaining rights for all employees, an option most postdocs do not now have.

The paradox of postdoc programs is that they have both positive and negative effects. Instituting them can amount to progressive activism on behalf of graduate students who would otherwise be cast out of the profession if they could not find jobs. Yet the consequences—both foreseen and unforeseen—invariably multiply. When Illinois began its program there was, so far as I know, no "Charter of University Workers' Rights" in circulation. Nor was there a climate conducive to discussing such matters. My two demands at the time were that the program be created and that salaries be fair. I lost on the second count, but others have helped push salaries up in the intervening years. Meanwhile the graduate student union movement, successful in gaining recognition after nearly a decade of organizing, may make it easier for postdocs, lecturers, and instructors to contemplate group action. The project of reform never comes to an end.

CN

4. Disciplining Debt

THERE IS AN INSTRUCTIVE MOMENT in Richard Powers' novel *Galatea 2.2* (1995) when a writer-in-residence evolves from "token humanist" at a new Center of Advanced Sciences on the campus of his alma mater to co-designer of a machine capable of passing an MA comprehensive examination in English and American literature. (Although neither the Center nor the institution is identified, *Galatea 2.2* is set at the $50 million Beckman Institute at the University of Illinois at Urbana-Champaign, a facility conceived by Arnold Beckman, inventor of the mass spectrophotometer and founder of Beckman Instruments, whose $40 million gift helped make the Institute possible). The moment comes early in the novel, when Powers' eponymous narrator contemplates the Center's architecture, a "postmodern rehash of Flemish Renaissance" complete with "1200 works of art, the world's largest magnetic resonance imager, and elevators appointed in brass, teak, and marble" (1995, 5, 75). Yet, the more Powers gets involved in building a neural network capable of writing passable literary analysis, the more he feels the need for a refuge, an "antidote" to the suffusion of "future" the high-tech, expensively furnished Center represented. The English Building with stairs "patched in three shades of gray linoleum" and awash with nostalgia became such a habitus. This creaky structure, once a home for cockroaches the size of monarch butterflies, dominates Powers' "architecture of memory" which, in turn, induces him to make numerous treks across campus to visit it. Unlike the Center of Advanced Sciences, redolent with a *future* of maze-like neural circuitry and sterile hardware, the century-old English Building formed a monument to the *past* and a still febrile "erotics of knowledge" (1995, 75). He had learned to love literature in that building–and met a woman to love in a class he once taught there. No quiltwork of faded linoleum could extinguish the fire of his memory or diminish the feeling he sought—and found—there and nowhere else.

In this juxtaposition of teakwood with a motley of old vinyl, this contrast of affluence on one side of campus and penury on the other, Powers accurately depicts the state of the fine arts and humanities at the "pluralistic" multiversity: their increasing, in some cases abject, poverty and their diminished exchange value in late capitalism's conception of a well-educated person or a college graduate (these days, not the same thing).[1] Here we aren't referring to the presumed obsolescence of some disciplines and their slow death spirals into extinction (the fate of Professor Uzzi-Tuzzi's department of Bothno-Ugaric Languages and Literatures, for example, in Italo Calvino's *If on a winter's night a traveler*), nor to the absence of exotic wood veneers or polished brass in faculty offices. We've learned to cherish dourly painted cinder block and understand that these days even having an office of our own is a luxury that too many college and university faculty don't enjoy.[2] Nor, finally, are we inveighing against the construction of such high-tech facilities as Powers describes. Rather, we want to talk about *graduate student* employees in this chapter, and the financial straits into which an increasing number of them in the humanities and fine arts in particular are heading. We want to describe a crisis that is spinning out of control, one destined to ruin the futures of many of the very students we see every day, we teach in our seminars, and whose research we direct. We want, finally, to initiate a serious conversation about this crisis and advance possibilities for change.

It is important at the outset to recognize that during the decade of the 1990s a sea change—or, more accurately, a dangerous tsunami—occurred in the manner in which many graduate students, regardless of academic discipline, financed their studies. This is precisely why arguments implying that such inequities have always existed, arguments that tend to rationalize present conditions as really nothing new, need to be scrutinized, however historically accurate and evocative they might otherwise be. One of these, to take a notable example, is Robert Scholes's (1998)

---

1. The term "pluralistic" university is aptly defined in Clark Kerr's *The Use of the University*, 47–67, which also provides a helpful review both of the complex functioning of the contemporary university and of critiques of its at times contradictory goals and activities.

2. If the number of part-time faculty teaching at present—estimated at 48 or 49 percent of all teachers—is added to the number of graduate student employees teaching, approximately 18 percent, the sum is somewhere around 66 or 67 percent non-tenure track faculty. Most of these teachers do not enjoy their own offices—indeed, many are lucky to share offices or cubicles with several other instructors—nor do many tenure-eligible and tenured faculty across the country.

postulation of an uncanny parallel between the economy of academic labor in 1701 at the Collegiate School, later Yale University, its reliance on a rector who lectured to students and a completely expendable subaltern who worked under him, and the hierarchies of today's academic departments:

> The tutor . . . did the dirty work, while the rector pontificated. This division of labor, as may have occurred to you, is still with us: pontification at the top and overworked, under-prepared instruction at the bottom. (1998, 3)

Scholes adduces other similarities as well: "There was a rapid turnover among the tutors, then as now. They also multiplied in number, then as now" (1998, 3). True enough, as, rather paradoxically, both attrition rates in graduate programs and the rate of production of PhD's in the humanities are both staggeringly high.

As recent data compiled by the *Survey of Earned Doctorates* (2002) and the Modern Language Association confirm, English and foreign language departments across the country produced considerably more doctoral students at the end of the 1990s than they did at the beginning: for English, 1,077 in 1998, 1,022 in 1999, and 1,070 in 2000 compared to 796 in 1990 or only 669 in 1987; for modern languages, 643 in 1998 compared to 512 in 1990 (a 20 percent rise)—or only 430 just the year before (Laurence and Welles 2003, 9). Indeed, the number of doctoral recipients in English steadily increased throughout the decade (save only for slight declines in 1994, 1996, and 1999). And an optimist, one supposes, could argue that, except for the financially disastrous year 2002, so too did the number of tenure-track positions advertised. An aging professoriate hobbling toward retirement created academic jobs—some were even good jobs on the tenure-track—so things began to look up, in a manner of speaking: from 100 "definite tenure track assistant professor positions" in English advertised in the October, 1982 *MLA Job Information List*, to 207 in 1992, to a whopping 532 in 2000, to a near-recession economy 401 in 2002. Yet, according to the *Survey of Earned Doctorates*, since some 977 doctorates in English were produced in 2001, there was hardly any substantial reason to celebrate. Over half of that class of 2001 would not find tenure-track employment in 2002, even when factoring in the relatively few positions that become available later in the academic year.

But there are other numbers to consider, numbers that didn't exist in 1701 or 1801 or even 1901, and one in particular forms the subject of this essay: the average debt carried by a rapidly increasing corps of graduate students in the humanities. Here are the stark figures at Indiana University: in the academic year 1991–1992, the average debt of graduate students who borrowed was $13,323; by 1999–2000, that figure had tripled to $40,306. That's the average for all graduate students. But for those pursuing a doctorate in Classics, Folklore, or Anthropology, among other disciplines in the fine arts, social sciences, and humanities, as we shall explain, the average debt is appreciably higher. In other words, our graduate students' intellectual passion for languages, literatures, and cultures often comes with a heavy price tag, one that will take much of a lifetime to pay. Or not pay, thus the spectre of incurring all that comes with bankruptcy: a ruined credit rating, minimal ability to buy houses and cars, and so on. For the same system of values or, if you prefer, cultural capital that underlies the sharp discrepancies in salaries between professors of law, medicine, and business and most faculty in the humanities—the same rationalization that demands an assistant professor of Accounting or Law in his first day on campus be paid more than a professor of Art History, Folkore, or French in her thirtieth year of teaching and distinguished research—is destroying the futures of many graduate students in the arts and humanities. The diminished status of the arts and humanities at the pluralistic "multiversity" is thus legible not only in its congeries of architectural styles, in the juxtaposition of polished teakwood on one side of campus and a patchwork of faded linoleum on the other. It is inscribed on the backs of graduate students, many of whom are employees of the university teaching large numbers of freshmen and sophomores. The problem is, this reality remains invisible to many faculty and parents alike—and, with the enhanced "opportunity" to defer repayment and capitalize interest, the eventual severity of the problem often remains invisible to the student-borrowers themselves. Or it simply becomes the most enduring of the delusions from which young academics and would-be academics suffer. Something akin to the most pernicious of STDs, debt incurred in pursuit of the PhD is the "gift" that keeps on giving long after the affair is over.

This chapter is intended to make this problem more visible to everyone concerned. For if the number of students enrolling in colleges and universities in the next ten years does in fact rise by the 14 percent some experts predict, this will also mean that the 45 percent of public school students and 52 percent of private school students receiving financial aid in 1999 will also increase.[3] And, unless some major policy changes

---

3. This growth has been predicted by a number of groups. For a convenient graphing both of enrollment expectations in the first decade of the twenty-first century and the rising costs of higher education in the 1990s, see "The College Boom."

are enacted at the departmental, campus and even federal levels—limits on borrowing, a more scrupulous use of graduate student employees, and perhaps the restructuring of departments depleted both of institutional support and broader cultural capital–this epidemic is certain to get worse in the new millennium.

Debt and Disciplines

As students of this rapidly spreading pandemic, we thought we knew something about graduate student debt. Throughout the 1990s, we wrote about the topic, presented papers at professional conferences, read all the reports we could get our hands on, and talked to graduate students across the country.[4] So did other people. In *What's College For?* (1998) Zachary Karabell, relying upon statistics gathered in 1997 by a variety of reputable sources, decried the rising debt of America's undergraduates and its adverse effects on higher education:

> In the 1990s alone, the average debt burden for a college student grew from $8,200 to $18,800. Given that these students, once they graduate, tend to earn between $20,000 and $30,000 a year, those debts are heavy. . . . With ten, twenty, thirty thousand dollars of debt, careers in business become essential, while careers as teachers, social workers, or others in the nonprofit sector become less viable. . . . (1998, 6, 10)

Writing just two years earlier than Karabell, thus relying upon data from the first half of the 1990s, and addressing the dilemmas of graduate students in particular, Louis Menand described the typical PhD recipient in English as being, among other things, $10,000 in debt (1996, 78). But over $40,000—on average—which, in many cases, thus means much, much more? How much more? $80,000? $100,000? Even $150,000, to earn a graduate degree that will, in the best cases, afford the recipient-debtor a salary similar to that Karabell mentions for undergraduate degree holders? If they're lucky enough to land such jobs, that is, to fulfill the dream for which they have mortgaged their futures.

That's what the following data will show, unless someone is prepared to argue that graduate students at Indiana are somehow unique in this regard–and nothing we have heard from, literally, hundreds of graduate students across the country, from Yale to the University of Florida, from Ann Arbor to Irvine, suggests that this is so. In other words, these conclusions seem to us inescapable:

---

4. See, for example, "Debt" in Nelson and Watt, *Academic Keywords*, 99–107; and Watt, "The Human Costs of Graduate Education; or, The Need to Get Practical," 32–33.

1. Graduate student borrowing is spinning out of control with few if any institutional policies in place to check it.
2. The accelerated rate of borrowing during the later 1990s make almost any earlier data on the subject obsolete, which means that by the time you read this, the story of student indebtedness will most likely be considerably worse.
3. Debt is clearly related to discipline. Graduate students in the humanities, some social science disciplines, and the fine arts are far more likely to be affected than those in the sciences.

This last point is not meant to suggest that doctoral students in the sciences aren't taking out loans—many do. Nor are they are pampered or coddled, for far too many doctoral students and post-docs spend eighty, ninety, 100 hours or more a week in Chemistry and Biology labs working for inadequate stipends. But, for the most part, such student workers are not falling fifty, 100, 150 thousand dollar in debt, as considerable numbers of doctoral students in the arts and humanities are.

Acutely aware of these realties, the Office of Student Financial Assistance and the Graduate School at Indiana University formed a committee both to study graduate student borrowing patterns and to frame policies appropriate to its findings. Convened in the fall of 1999 and meeting throughout the winter, this committee brought together faculty and administrators from across the university. At a December meeting the committee was presented with data on 14,284 students (whose anonymity was protected, of course) who had borrowed money during the year to attend Indiana, data which provided more specific details on 2,981 graduate and professional students (this number includes MBA Law, and Optometry students). For students seeking post-graduate degrees in one of forty-six departments in the College of Art and Sciences, our topic here, we're talking about nearly half of all graduate students; that is to say, almost half (48 percent) borrow money to attend or stay in graduate school. Unless it's in a discipline like Theater, Fine Arts/Art History, or History, where 86 percent, 82 percent, and 69 percent of the graduate students borrow. Indeed, in a dozen of these departments the rate of borrowers exceeds two-thirds of the entire graduate student population.

And the statistics about how much they borrow were equally startling. By the academic year 1999–2000, for example, the students in Arts and Sciences had borrowed over $45 **million**. Of course, theater historians, semioticians, and cultural anthropologists were hardly alone in this regard. Some thirty-nine of 252 students enrolled in the Optometry School were over $100,000 in debt, as were six out of 487 Law students; another twenty-nine students in Optometry had borrowed between

$80,000 and $99,999. What was more troubling, however, were the relatively large numbers of graduate students who had fallen $80, $90, $100,000 or more into debt—and the programs in which they were enrolled. Of the fifty-five graduate students whose debt exceeded $100,000, only one was from a department in the sciences. The other fifty-four all came from the fine arts, humanities, and social sciences.

The data available from these departments—Anthropology, Art History, Comparative Literature, English, Folklore, French and Italian, History, Spanish, and various disciplines within the Schools of Music and Education—tell a sobering story indeed about arts and humanities at the corporate university. Twenty-two Fine Arts students between $50,000 and $127,000 in debt, twenty-two anthropologists between $50,000 and $129,000; thirty-one in History, fourteen in Comparative Literature, twenty-seven in Folklore and twelve in French and Italian all owe over $50,000—many well over this mark. By comparison, only four graduate students in Chemistry fell this far in debt, one biologist, and four mathematicians out of a total graduate student body of 170, 149, and 105 students, respectively. By contrast, those twenty-two anthropologists represent some 20 percent of the 103 graduate students in that program; the twenty-seven Folklorists in debt over $50,000 represent a quarter of the total students seeking graduate degrees in that department. Substantial debt, then, is commonplace among graduate students on one side of campus, but relatively rare on the side where the sciences and high tech departments live.

So, quite obviously, is borrowing in general, which follows the same demographic trend, thus corroborating what we believe to the be an accurate inference about the state of the arts and humanities on campus. Only sixteen students (out of 104) from mathematics, twelve out of seventy-five from Physics, and sixty-seven out of 170 from Chemistry borrowed anything at all (and over a third of the Chemistry students owed less than $10,000.) By contrast, 116 of 169 students from History, seventy-one of 102 students from Folklore, seventy-one of 103 students from Anthropology, and thirty-one of thirty-six students in Theater borrowed money to complete their degree programs. And the state of borrowing in the largest department in the College, English? One hundred twenty-nine out of 216 graduate students borrowed money to complete (or not) their degrees, although only twenty-two of these borrowers had accumulated debt of over $50,000 (a fact largely attributable to the existence of a Freshman English and other writing requirements). And the lists of graduate student-borrowers in Music? Almost endless.

Perhaps the most instructive statistics provided to the committee were those compiled for some 111 graduate students whose requests for further loans for 1999–2000 were either denied or approved only after a review/consultation process was initiated. To make it to this list, a student's application would have had to raise one of two "red flags": either the student had completed over 150 percent of the hours required to graduate and still had not done so; or, the dollar amount of outstanding loans exceeded the mean level of debt for 1999–2000 which was, again, $40,306. Many students on the list, while not so severely in debt as others, had completed well over the ninety hours required in most doctoral programs: in the worst cases, this meant fifty, 100, 125 hours *beyond* the requisite ninety hours (in fact, one student in Psychology had actually completed 218 graded hours of graduate coursework!). One obvious inference is that these are obsessive course-takers who continue to enroll in classes and seminars as a way of avoiding examinations and dissertation-writing. Another is that these students pay semester by semester to nurture the delusion that they will complete their dissertations, years, even decades, after completing their studies on campus. Most will not. The university requires that they be enrolled to "count" as graduate students, and they have consistently paid tuition over the years to maintain the fantasy.

This shorter list of 111 students corroborated what the much broader data showed: a clear pattern of the disciplines in which the heaviest borrowing was occurring. Only a handful of students on this more abbreviated list of troublesome cases were completing their research in Microbiology or Mathematics. Psychology was represented by a number of students, but the vast majority were from Humanities, Education, and the Fine Arts, especially a number of disciplines within the nationally renowned IU School of Music. Of the twenty-one students on the list from Music, one in Music Composition had borrowed over $142,000; another in percussion had borrowed nearly $123,000; several more in Voice had borrowed between $36,000 and $105,000. The data for students in choral conducting, music theory, and musicology were similarly discouraging, leading a number of us to wonder how, say, a high school choral conductor or musicologist could ever begin to repay this sort of loan.

This smaller list included nine students from Folklore, eight from Art History, seven from History, five from Spanish, and three to four each from French and Italian, Anthropology, Comparative Literature, and various departments within East and Central Asian Languages and Literatures. Only three came from English, again confirming the importance of the Freshman English requirement and the teaching positions it provides graduate student employees. In fact, English by itself has nearly as many graduate students as Art History, Folklore, and Comparative Literature combined, yet comparatively few students in English had found it necessary to borrow such large sums of money. The debt carried by the eight Art Historians and nine Folklore graduate students by themselves was alarming. The former group had borrowed nearly $700,000, with individual debt amounts including $117,574, $114,378 $109,380, and so on. The nine doctoral students in Folklore fared no better, with individual loans including one in excess of $156,000 and others ranging from $55,000 to over $115,000. Five students in Spanish were $137,000, $124,000, $119,000, $106,000, and $103,000 in debt. Another five graduate students in History had borrowed over $100,000 themselves, two of whom owed more than $120,000, and one over $150,000.

It is important to recognize both how this happened—how students could fall so far into debt—and what the reality of the loan repayment process will be once it has begun. The latter matter is both simpler to explain and starker in implication, and here we shall use interest rates contemporary with this borrowing and calculations provided by the Indiana University Office of Student Financial Assistance. Because most loans are structured over ten years, or 120 monthly payments, a student who borrowed $100,000 at, say, an 8.5 percent interest (with a one year grace period) will pay $1,226.53 per month. Structured over 120 payments, that student in History who has borrowed $150,000 would pay $1,839.79 per month or over $220,000 during the lifetime of the loan.

Of course, many student borrowers these days are compelled to structure payment plans in ways similar to those of mortgage-holders: over fifteen, twenty, even twenty-five years. At 8.5 percent, for example, a student borrowing $100,000 who structures the debt over twenty years will pay $852.07 per month or nearly $205,000 over the life of the loan. That graduate student in History and the other in Folklore who owe, at present, over $150,000, if they choose to repay their loans over the same 20-year period, will pay $1,278.10 per month or over $306,000 over the life of the loan. Can a Joyce scholar or theater historian ever expect to earn enough money to assume such a payment schedule? Even if these students, especially the fifty-five who owe over $100,000, graduated tomorrow and were successful in landing a tenure-track position at a distinguished college or university, none of these would ever earn enough money as assistant professors to repay these loans. To be sure, some might inherit money or win a state lottery, but others might do what so many graduate students we know have done: fall in love with another graduate student-debtor and thus begin a committed, long-term relationship with two repayment plans to contemplate.

To draw this point more finely, many loan officers in the earlier 1990s based the income expectation to student loan repayment ratio at eight percent; that is, a student's total annual repayment burden should not exceed eight percent of her post-graduation income. So, if a student borrowing $40,000 at even a rate as low as five percent structured payments over ten years, she would be required to pay $424.00 per month or $5088/year. Following the eight percent rule, she would need income of about $64,000/year to make these payments comfortably: i.e., without hindering her ability to pay for such necessities as housing, transportation, and so on. Because even the most successful young graduate students in the humanities in the year 2004—those who complete their degrees and find the elusive full time, tenure-track work or its equivalent within a year of graduation—can expect to make significantly less than $64,000 as a beginning assistant professor, their next ten years economically speaking may prove exceptionally difficult. And, of course, according to statistics compiled by the Modern Language Association, only about 34 percent of English PhD's and 40 percent of those trained in modern languages (the present boom in Spanish making it something of an exception) will find that tenure-track job.[5] Graduate students in Folklore and Art History face similar, if not far worse, job prospects. How will they ever begin to repay this debt, especially those who will soon join the growing legion of part-time employees earning $1,000, $1500, or $2000/per course?

And here, we are still considering the example of a student borrowing $40,000, a few thousand dollars less than she might expect to make as an assistant professor of Comparative Literature or English in the year 2004. The starting salaries on both coasts might be a little more, but so, too, are the costs of living; in 2003, for example, some fortunate few job-seekers in English landed jobs offering salaries in the lower fiftiess, complete with a modest research fund, moving expenses, and other perks. But others we know were offered starting tenure-track positions in the mid and high $30s, with the majority of successful applicants landing positions that began with salaries in the forties. Compare these starting salaries with the debt accrued by those students who have borrowed fifty, sixty, even 100,000 dollars at a higher interest rate, and you will quickly see what might happen. If these data at Indiana regarding student debt are similar to those at other research universities—and, again, graduate students across the country, from Florida to Yale, Tennessee to California, have convinced us that they are—the future of the doctorate in the arts

---

5. These figures were given in the MLA's 1997 report of the Committee on Professional Employment. As we have suggested above, although more jobs have been advertised recently, the increase in production of doctorates provides little reason for optimism.

and humanities will include, tragically, thousands of impoverished and bankrupt scholar-teachers.

How this happened might be explained as the inevitable consequence of a variety of factors located not only on campus, but in the economy more generally. One fact should be stressed at the outset, a fact many of our colleagues simply do not want to recognize or are incapable of doing so: Graduate student employees are, in the best of cases, minimum wage earners. Period. This means, according to the annual "Out of Reach" report of the National Low Income Housing Coalition, that in 2002 "Nowhere in the country could a minimum-wage employee afford to pay rent on a two-bedroom home." Further, in nearly three-quarters of the country even two full-time minimum wage jobs could not pay for such housing. Data published by *The Chronicle of Higher Education* in 2001, among other sources, confirm that most graduate teaching assistants in the humanities are indeed minimum-wage earners—if that. That is to say, stipend figures, like those describing graduation rates and years to degree, are at times not so transparent as they appear. At Indiana, for example, a new AI (Associate Instructor) in English earns a tuition waiver and about $12,000. But buried in the contract are some $1,000 in mandatory fees not covered by the stipend or contract. Then, there's the disparity at many institutions between stipends earned by graduate student-employees in humanities departments and their counterparts in the sciences. The range in English is $17,500 at Princeton to $8,400 at SUNY-Buffalo (State University of New York), with several schools—the Universities of Kansas, Minnesota, and Oregon, to name but three— reporting stipends of under $10,000 (i.e., under the present minimum wage). By contrast, numerous stipends in Biology exceeded $20,000, with the lowest numbers coming in at over $15,000 (Smallwood 2001, A25). Stated in another way, the lowest stipends in some scientific disciplines rival the highest earned by graduate student employees in the humanities, the majority of which place these workers' salaries well below the minimum wage.

Other factors are at work as well, many of which we have already suggested but bear repeating: the failure of fellowship and assistantship stipends to keep pace with inflation in those departments able to offer such instruments; an increase in the amount students are able to borrow from various loan programs; limited and/or inadequate policies in place to check this borrowing; the effect of deferred interest capitalized quarterly on these larger sums of money for longer periods of time; and the greater need for graduate students to "pre-professionalize"—to publish and present papers at scholarly conferences, thus spending more time in school and greater sums of money for the travel and related expenses such activities require. We want to concentrate here only on those factors related to loan programs, interest, and broader institutional policies, returning to specific recommendations at the departmental level elsewhere in this volume.

For example, in 1994 a student could borrow "only" $30,000 from the Perkins or National Defense loan programs; in 2000, that number stands at $40,000. Many students also qualify for a loan of up to $138,500 from the Federal Family Education program, the interest on only $65,500 of which is subsidized. This means, that if a student "maxes out" loans from just these two programs—never mind loans derived from private sources—s/he is looking at paying interest on over $100,000, interest which is calculated quarterly and almost always deferred until after graduation (and a one-year grace period). If a student borrows this much money in, say, four years of undergraduate school and six or seven more years of graduate school—a fairly common scenario among students who borrow—this means that interest has been capitalized between fifteen and twenty times before any repayment begins. And, at present, there's very little anyone can do about it, save for our commitment to make graduate programs more efficient—more years in doctoral programs mean more debt and more capitalized interest—and the occasional opportunities faculty and counselors have to discuss such topics with graduate students.

But such opportunities are rare. How often do graduate students walk into the offices of faculty in their department, those of their research directors or Directors of Graduate Study in particular, and initiate a conversation about debt? In our experience, almost never. The situation improves once this topic is introduced by faculty as part of larger professional conversations on graduate study and professional expectations. Stated in another way, once we began to discuss debt several years ago, graduate students began to volunteer more information about the problem, and we have met numerous students who have narrated to us their long, rather frightening loan histories. As recently as the mid-1990s, it was rather rare to find graduate students in English or History whose debt approached $100,000—now they're everywhere. Now, graduate students are beginning to carry the debt burden of medical students without any possibility of earning the income doctors in most specialties will (which is not to say that younger physicians have it easy by comparison or aren't experiencing similar kinds of difficulties—many are). People are beginning to talk about the problem; committees are working, but the problem is critical and demands a much wider, more urgent response.

How We Can Help

Solutions, it seems to us, might originate in a variety of initiatives. Some of them might require disciplinary conversations that will be both heretofore unprecedented and painful, though one hopes not so fatal as the suggestion of abolition of the department of Bothno-Ugaric Languages and Literatures in *If on a winter's night a traveler*. As Mark F. Smith reported in *Academe*, Washington has become aware of the problem, and as a result the budget of the Graduate Assistance in Areas of National Need (GAANN) program was increased some 36 percent for fiscal year 2000. Although this budgetary increase still brought the program's funds well below what they were in 1995—and some 60 percent less than the budget appropriation in 1992 (Smith 1999, 77)—it still represents an encouraging turn at the national level. But such news is all-too-rare and, as we write this in the wake of the continuing war in Iraq, the spectres of continued conflict in the middle East, tensions with North Korea, and an economy bled of its 1990s dot.com profits hardly augur well for solutions to the problems outlined here. And this is why professional organizations and institutions must provide leadership.

At the institutional level, Offices of Student Financial Assistance should follow Susan Pugh's lead at Indiana, initiating conversation and faculty awareness of this growing crisis. It is fair to say, we think, that nearly every faculty member we know who has reviewed the data reported here has been stunned; the vast majority confessed to having little or no idea that student borrowing had increased so dramatically during the decade of the 1990s and continuing into the present decade. And why would they be expected to know this?

Faculty and administrators might be encouraged to do a little homework on this topic, reviewing such data as we have presented here and reading studies like Robert Manning's *Credit Cards on Campus: Costs and Consequences of Student Debt*, published in 2000 by the Consumer Federation of America. Among the many illuminating points Manning, a sociologist at Georgetown University, makes is that all the data we and most studies present are inaccurate unless we also include the rising amount of credit card debt undergraduate and graduate students alike incur (2000, 9). These amounts are not included in student loan statistics, and in many cases they are formidable. Manning reminds us that "more than 4 out of 5 undergraduate students have credit cards (84.6%) at both [public and private] schools." More than one-fifth of all students use their credit cards to take cash advances (2000, 11), and as Manning emphasizes, even these data "substantially underestimate the 'true' problem of student credit card indebtedness at the national level" (2000, 12).

In other words, as startling as the data discussed here and in Manning's study are, they do not approach the reality (the Real?) of the matter, the spectre we can never fully know.

Readers familiar with Lacanian psychoanalysis or with Slavoj Žižek's application of this theory in such texts as *Welcome to the Desert of the Real* (2002) or his essay "The Spectre of Ideology" from *Mapping Ideology* (1994) might be able to predict where this is going: namely, for humanists to use the very theoretical sophistication they typically deploy in their scholarship in addressing these problems. For when a theoretician like Žižek, after Lacan, asserts that the "reality is never directly 'itself', it presents itself only via its incomplete-failed symbolization," or that "'reality, like truth, is by definition never 'whole'" (Žižek 1994, 21), those sympathetic to a psychoanalytical reading of such events as 9/11 or the sinking of the *Titanic* (two of his favorite topics) might well nod in agreement. Yet how many would nod similarly when a sociologist like Manning informs us that the reality of student debt accumulation is always already worse than the data suggest? How many of us are willing to turn our knowledge and reading ability away from our favorite literary and cultural texts and direct them instead to an institutional critique? What might a psychoanalytic reading of graduate student culture—with its debt, demands, and identification with faculty mentors—look like?

And to return to yet another faculty and departmental responsibility: without violating a student's right to privacy, to what extent should faculty be made aware of the general predicaments in which a particular student finds herself? What could they do? What should they do? Should the Office of Student Financial Aid develop a series of red flags and notify Directors of Graduate Studies when a student has raised one or more of them? What should or could such an administrator do? Should a department be made aware of the borrowing patterns of a group of students and be asked to formulate methods of improving the situation, either by increasing or varying its financial instruments, reviewing admission procedures and the size of incoming classes, or making significant revisions to the program itself? What would these methods be, short of dropping students who have no chance of graduating in the first place from degree programs? This would seem to be far too little and way too late.

At the departmental level, change must occur in making doctoral programs, especially those in the humanities, more efficient. There is a reason why only six of 487 Law students at Indiana were as far in debt as those students in doctoral programs in the humanities, and it is obvious: the program usually takes three years to complete, not seven, eight, or more years. As we discuss elsewhere in this volume, a coherent national conversation on doctoral programs and the nature of the PhD degree is long overdue. Various disciplinary organizations like the Modern Language Association have recently initiated such a conversation, but it needs to be continued—and broadened to include many of the disciplines mentioned whose students are languishing in a financial quagmire from which they will never extricate themselves.

Meaningful change will only occur, we believe, when an institution and department place the problem of graduate student debt at the top of its list of priorities. And if any amelioration is to be achieved, it will most likely be the result of concerted efforts at the departmental, university, and national levels. Absent such efforts, scholarly research in the arts and humanities will suffer tremendously in the new millennium, further eroding their already precarious position in the order of things at the multiversity. Most significant, thousands of genuinely committed graduate students will evolve into embittered, seriously damaged citizens, forever marked by their years of penury. A cellar office or mismatched tile floor in the departmental building is one thing; financial ruination is quite another. The multiversity must put aside its obsessions with corporate contracts and athletic programs, with entertaining wealthy alumni and creating administrative benefit packages that resemble those given corporate CEO's, and devote a little of its attention—and its resources—to students.

SW

5.   The Brave New World
of Research Surveillance

"HEY, FRANK, YOU FORGOT to put the gonad shield on this guy." Frank was a medical technician at the National Institutes of Health (NIH) in Bethesda, Maryland. The time was the winter of 1964. The "guy" who'd just had an x-ray without proper shielding was me. I was a college freshman employed in a dual role that winter, as a normal control in a cystic fibrosis study and as a laboratory assistant. I was also a student at one of the most progressive institutions of higher education in the country, Antioch College, in Yellow Springs, Ohio, which had a work-study requirement. Antioch typically placed about two dozen students a year in NIH jobs.

My lab job was fairly straightforward. It began by my processing tissue samples from children who had died from cystic fibrosis. But these were the days when neither family nor employee sensitivities were elaborately protected. I would receive a beaker with, say, a little human heart inside it. The label was never "Subject C-33" but rather "Tim" or "Sally." Tim or Sally was typically a child I had known on the ward the week before. I pulverized the samples and put them through a centrifuge. No better preparation could be imagined for a lifetime as a literary critic.

But NIH as a whole taught me many lessons about institutions and about academic researchers. It was a thirteen-story research hospital, full not only of patients but also of MDs, PhDs, and federal bureaucrats. It was an airless world unto itself and in some fundamental ways a madhouse. One of the PhDs in my lab sometimes began his day by killing experimental mice so they could be analyzed. Dissatisfied with mass execution, he acquired a little guillotine that enabled him to behead his research subjects one-by-one. It was his collaborators, alas, who had charge of me.

The main consent form that I signed to participate in the experimental program was my weekly salary check, $35, minus taxes, plus room and board. In other words, I was an employee and employees are expected to do what they are told. Officially I was being paid only for the lab job, but the main reason I was brought there was to participate in the cystic fibrosis study. One of my regular duties was to have an intestinal biopsy. And it was at one of those biopsies that Frank, as I am calling him, forgot the lead apron. The biopsy was performed by inserting a long metal tube down my throat, through my stomach, and into my intestine. The X-ray machine was kept on to guide the tube along its way. When the sample site was reached, a wire inside the tube was pushed forward. This opened a little metal claw at the end. A yank on the wire then made the claw tear off a piece of intestine, which was then pulled up all the way through my gut while I retched on the table. Still retching, I was wheeled back to my room.

Things became still more interesting when they learned from my medical history form that I had no sense of smell; so far as I knew I had been born without one. There was no question of a cure, but if they could find out why they might have another publication. Not part of their cystic fibrosis study, just an unexpected target of opportunity. They asked me if I would agree to a brain x-ray preceded by removal of a small quantity of spinal fluid and injection of an equivalent quantity of air. Because of the very small chance of introducing impurities with the air and the possibilities of resultant paralysis, they asked me to sign a form absolving both them and the federal government of any liability. I refused. Then the pressure began. It was not, of course, until two years later, in 1966 (Anderson 1996, 265), that NIH—under orders from the U.S. Surgeon General—introduced a committee system to evaluate the ethics of human subject research. The hospital had a preliminary system to review the general plans for research with normal controls in 1964, but no full-scale ethical oversight. Suffice it to say that it would have been very nice to have had an Institutional Review Board (IRB) in place in 1964.

That would have to wait for later history. Despite the indictment of Nazi physicians at the Nuremberg Tribunals, Americans showed little concern about medical experimentation in their own country; indeed Nuremberg may have helped assure Americans that such outrages only occur in exceptional elsewheres. Government regulation in the United States is almost always scandal driven, so it took incidents like the 1972 revelation of the forty-year Tuskegee experiments to generate congressional pressure to turn the surgeon general's policy into a formal regulation. Even then, the standards were only applicable to federally funded projects. Not until 1981 did a national commission recommend that the review policy be extended to all human-participant research in the United States (Anderson 1996, 271). In 1991 some fifteen federal agencies adopted a uniform policy, widely known as the "Common Rule."

But, after all, in 1964 I was an Antioch student. The college would protect me. It was while I indulged in such reassuring reflections that the responsible Antioch work-study supervisor, who held faculty status, called me to urge my cooperation with the study. It was clear he had consulted with the head of the department. Antioch needed these jobs; if I wanted a positive evaluation I had better sit still for the syringe. It would have been nice to have an IRB at Antioch as well, but they did not exist. I had many other NIH adventures, but this particular story came to an end because NIH realized at last that I was under eighteen years of age. My mother would have to cosign the waiver. She was a registered nurse and told them to go to hell.

Among the things I learned at NIH was the attitude that biomedical scientists sometimes harbored toward their research subjects. Research is a heady mix of intellectual curiosity, self-interested careerism, and an ideology constructed of high-minded ideals: the pursuit of truth, the advancement of knowledge, the good of the many, notions that are not simply catch phrases but entire transcendentalizing discourses. Their usefulness in self-deception and rationalization is both notorious and easily forgotten. A system of independent research review and curtailment is clearly essential when real harm is at stake. I do not consider experience a decisive or necessary category for intellectual or cultural understanding, but my experience did make a difference. And thus I will say that it is not easy to forget being the object of a certain kind of investigative gaze, to look into the eyes of a researcher and realize you are expendable. Yet IRBs, which operate without their own system of checks and balances, often without secure mechanisms of appeal, are equally subject to individual and group self-deception, even more so now that they are moving to review social sciences and humanities research more widely than ever before. Their staffs and members can also be corrupted by the ideals of justice and advocacy that energize them.

The 1991 regulations established the principles research institutions receiving federal funds had to follow. As of the year 2000, there were roughly four thousand IRBs operating in the United States, primarily at universities, hospitals, and private research facilities (AAUP 2001, 56). The Common Rule describes research as "a systematic investigation, including research development, testing and evaluation, designed to develop or contribute to generalizable knowledge," a definition that embraces much systematic social science research while leaving most humanities projects outside its orbit. Increasingly, however, the mission to protect people who are the objects of study has led some IRBs to begin reviewing even oral histories focused on a single person. Studies involving little real risk to their subjects are designed to be exempted from full review, but the definitions of risk can be interpreted very differently by different boards.

Among the texts that have had strong influence on campus IRBs is the 1979 *Belmont Report* issued by the National Commission for the Protection of Human Subjects in Biomedical and Behavioral Research. It established three principles for ethical research: respect for persons, beneficence, and justice. The first of these is most consistently cited by IRB staffs and committees in characterizing their mission. As the 2003 IRB chair on my own campus put it, "The Belmont principles transcend academic disciplines." Of course "respect for persons" can hardly entail respect for every human action, but IRBs are ill equipped to negotiate the difference. Instead they are driven to give unquestioned allegiance to a concept that might be given more nuanced application to, say, Ku Klux Klan or Nazi Party members, many of whom might merit humanity qualified with disapproval. Moreover, we might feel it appropriate to challenge Nazis or Klan members aggressively in an interview. An historian might well wish to investigate the self-understanding of a Ku Klux Klan member and might choose to present a neutral account of the organization, but academic freedom means that needs to be the historian's decision, not that of an IRB. One consequence of an unreflective commitment to "respect for persons" is that IRBs have great difficulty accepting research destined to be critical of its "human subjects" and to cause them pain, even though interviewers may treat them with cordiality during the research phase.

At the April 2003 University of Illinois "Human Subject Policy Conference," the Director of the Division of Behavioral and Cognitive Sciences at the National Science Foundation, David Rubin, recognized that disciplines are different and thus suggested "we need flexible solutions that impose minimal regulatory burden," but he also stated that "the protection of human research participants should be uniform." An historian conducting an oral history interview might well be willing to grant the interviewee final power over the disposition of the interview after it is concluded—whether it is to be preserved, whether it can be quoted. A journalist extracting an admission of guilt from an interviewee is hardly likely to make the same offer. Such disclosures can certainly cause pain and may do harm to individuals, yet both the common good and the historical record may call for a degree of ruthlessness.

When "respect for persons" is inflected with a heightened sensitivity to the risks inherent in biomedical research, the concept may be adopted with particular fervor. Then an IRB can effectively become a virtual police force in the service of liberal humanism—enforcing a philosophy of liberal humanism and its "respect for persons" across campus. What has been aptly described as "mission creep" (Gunsalus 2002, B24), as IRBs review more and more sorts of research, means that physical risk is conceptually leveraged to restrain a much wider range of scholarly inquiry. In some cases one encounters a kangaroo court ironically enforcing "respect for persons."

Yet IRBs typically find it impossible to apply these standards to all disciplines. The most consistent exception, as the argument above would suggest, is for journalists, who frequently write exposés of scoundrels. IRB members often solemnly announce that essays written by journalists for newspapers do not count as research, even though the same essay written for a scholarly journal does. The "research" project requires IRB scrutiny, while the newspaper article does not. Asking IRB members to adhere to fundamental ethical values and then apply them inconsistently and differentially does real harm to those who fulfill this service, and it is a source of the inner corruption I mentioned above. For in truth IRBs exempt newspaper journalism in part because they do not dare take on the press, not only because of caution about the First Amendment but also because of justified fear of the press's power. They thus excuse university journalists from evaluation of harm done to human subjects for political, not principled, reasons. The strain has been apparent in my interviews of IRB staff and members around the country, some of whom aggressively recite the catechism—"if it's published in a scholarly venue it's research; if it's published in a newspaper it's not"—while others blurt out that "journalism is unethical" and some express anger that they are barred from reviewing projects designed for newspapers.

What's more, IRBs have still other less Platonic forces operating on them. University lawyers will be warning them that social science research protocols could be the subject of objections raised by interplanetary travellers reporting violations of intergalactic rules and regulations. Think about it. Michael Rennie's space ship sets down atop the University of Illinois's Assembly Hall, and he warns us of worldwide consequences if we don't obtain consent forms from every undergraduate who fills out a survey. And there just might be the odd IRB head who thinks the potential loss of his or her job through failure to protect the university from legal action or government sanction was equally consequential.

My science fiction hyperbole is meant to be heuristic. One of the duties of university legal counsel is to generate accounts of hypothetical risk and advise administrators and faculty members how to avoid it. Yet we have little basis on which to judge the probability of law suits based on social science or humanities interviews and surveys. So there is a tendency to manage all research proposals on the basis of a worst case scenario, even when actual risk may not be much greater than the likelihood of a real world version of events in *The Day The Earth Stood Still*. The admirable moral imperatives propelling an IRB forward become entangled with legal constructs that compromise fairness and sanity, not to say academic freedom. Moreover, the federal rules governing IRBs suggest at least implicitly that knowledge of disciplinary practices be part of the context of all decisions, requiring that boards must be composed of members with sufficiently "varying backgrounds to promote complete and adequate review of research activities commonly conducted by the institution." The growing literature on campus IRBs shows again and again that boards assembled to supervise biomedical research often haven't a clue about the culture of history or anthropology or literature departments. In 2002 the Illinois IRB included not one humanities faculty member; a year later an anthropologist was added.

This is not to say there are no ethical or legal risks in research. The financial and institutional implications of biomedical research can be considerable; indeed I believe they should be. In the relatively uncharted legal flows of social science research matters are less certain. Yet IRB surveillance wields several double-edged swords. It serves to protect the rights of individual research subjects and to safeguard the institution against suits and regulatory reprisals. It also entails more institutional responsibility and liability. Once an IRB has reviewed a project in detail and approved it, it makes itself a party to any further action. A signed consent form is at once a source of legal protection and a potential proof of responsibility. IRB surveillance thus simultaneously mitigates and enhances legal risk. That suggests the necessity for further surveillance, further intervention, further caution. At some point we enter the airless world of NIH in 1964. The single most strict rule of the hospital back then was that no one open a window. The penalty for opening a window was immediate dismissal. Many of the patients had rare and untreatable illnesses. Some were in long term pain. Others had their social lives curtailed for years by their conditions. Thus as soon as the word was out that a window was open patient after patient would rush to the room to leap to his or her death. The academic equivalent is less dramatic: you give up doing what you are doing because IRB oversight has made it too burdensome.

In recent months here at Illinois we have sometimes lacked sufficient oxygen. In the spring of 2002, David Wright, at the time an assistant professor of English and African American Studies, was subjected to a largely insane review of an essay accepted for publication in the distinguished literary journal *The Kenyon Review*. He presented a version of the paper at a brown bag lunch, after which the head of African American Studies reported him to the campus IRB without first discussing the matter with David himself. Two questions were paramount: (1) had Wright asked permission to write about this student paper presented to one of his classes; and (2) was Wright required to report to the police the details of a murder recounted in the paper, even though it was a class in creative nonfiction, where fact and fiction are indistinguishable (Morgan, Bloom *passim*) and even though the paper described the perpetrator as dead as well? As it happened, the class in question had been conducted at another school, where Wright had taught before coming to Illinois. The IRB staff deemed that irrelevant because Wright was publishing his essay as an Illinois faculty member. Irrelevant as well was the department head's motive in reporting Wright to the IRB, even though that made the IRB a party to a professional vendetta. The staff felt the reason for the referral was beside the point; they had to deal with the facts of the infraction.

I was brought into the case by my department head after he was contacted by the IRB staff. Although they had not yet discussed the case with the faculty member in question, their e-mail to my department head proposed a series of actions, among them a requirement that the faculty member withhold publication until he obtained the student's permission and that he report the whole matter to the Los Angeles police. The case never went to the full IRB, but was instead handled by the IRB's Executive Secretary and its Research Compliance Coordinator. All this was to be discussed in a meeting between the IRB staff, the English department head, and several parties with standing or expertise. As a Vice President of the national AAUP, I was assumed to have some knowledge of academic freedom issues, a subject on which I had also previously published.

The first thing I did was call the staff of the AAUP's Committee on Academic Freedom and Tenure in Washington. They were astonished. Few cases, they said, were as clear as this one. Although it was highly unusual—and possibly malicious—for a unit head to report one of his faculty to an IRB, rather than discuss it with him, once an IRB had a case there was no fixed schedule for when they had to inform the accused faculty member that an investigation was under way. Yet one thing was absolutely clear: they could not reach even preliminary conclusions without informing the faculty member and giving him a chance to respond. The IRB e-mail to my department head was a serious violation of due process.

At least as bad, they argued, was to schedule that meeting without informing Wright of the investigation and giving him an opportunity to join the group. They told me I simply could not attend and become party to the event. I replied that I would attend for two reasons: if the IRB was going to violate due process, I wanted to be a witness; more importantly, I felt that attending the meeting would give me sufficient basis to call David and tell him the whole story, which is exactly what I did. I had warned him briefly two days earlier, but delayed giving him full details until I knew the IRB's position in detail and had a chance to question them. The IRB, following familiar administrative intimidation tactics, was planning to call David in for an interview later with only the most cursory explanation, thereby putting an untenured faculty member on the spot and extracting his compliance. IRBs often, of course, deal with arrogant senior faculty who feel it is their inalienable right to conduct any research they choose. I had met some of those folks at NIH. IRB staff learn to trample over nonexistent faculty "rights" in such cases. Due process, however, is not one of those nonexistent rights.

Among the things of note in the meeting was how unwilling and unprepared the IRB staff was to deal with the epistemological ambiguity of creative nonfiction, though courses in it are increasingly common. That issue, however, was brushed aside. Equally irrelevant in their view was the observation that the paper was distributed to the class and discussed openly. Both I and my colleagues have always felt some freedom to analyze classroom discussion, a freedom we would not feel about an office conference or a paper submitted solely for our personal evaluation. People visit classes, students talk about them. Classroom discussions are not like communications to a priest. Like other faculty members writing about classroom interaction, Wright had disguised the identities of the students and had even located the college in question in another part of the country. If we decide to write about such things, moreover, advance approval of a "research plan" is impossible: we are responding to events that are not predictable. Incredibly, but a few years earlier, when the Illinois IRB was run by different staff, they considered classes to be public events; now they were suddenly confidential.

For me at least the decisive moment came when I asked the IRB staff what would happen if Wright followed the advice I planned to give him: tell the IRB to place its concern where the moon doth not shine. The Executive Secretary replied that he was prepared to ask the university lawyer to insist that *Kenyon Review* withdraw the essay. He promised as well to call the Los Angeles police and report the semi-fictional carjacking and murder if Wright failed to do so. Trying to block a publication by a faculty member about to come up for tenure was obviously a serious threat. Any prior restraint on publication raised issues of free speech and academic freedom. If we opened a window in the meeting room, academic freedom would be flung to its death. The College of Liberal Arts and Sciences urged the IRB to drop the whole thing, but to no avail. LAS's only decisive input would be indirect: when they recognized David Wright's tenure case months later as the best received in 2002 they sent a message not only to Wright himself but also to African American Studies and to the IRB.

Meanwhile I had asked the AAUP's local president Matthew Finken to intervene. He called the AAUP office in Washington, where he had once served as an attorney, and wrote a letter to the chancellor, delicately but nonetheless unambiguously citing the national office's willingness to open a formal investigation if the matter were not dropped or if Wright were penalized or intimidated. In the end the IRB was persuaded to let the matter go. Along the way, many of the university's senior administrators had offered their advice. The IRB's independence meant that it was procedurally answerable to no one; it had come to a series of conclusions without even giving Wright a hearing and he had no formal mechanism for appeal, though there is nothing in the federal regulations to prevent IRBs from establishing appeal procedures and separate appeal boards.

My own belief is that the board's very first response should have been that the whole matter was none of their business. IRB administrators at other campuses whom I have interviewed have suggested they would have done exactly that. In point of fact the board only took jurisdiction because they happened to find out about Wright's essay. It does not represent a category of work that the IRB routinely or comprehensively supervises. Most IRB vetted research now comes to the board's attention when faculty members apply for internal or external support. But Wright was merely doing what thousands of faculty members across the country regularly do—using anecdotal classroom evidence to ground a professional narrative. It's the sort of occasional pedagogical essay that wouldn't warrant a research grant.

There are pedagogical practices, however, that now regularly draw IRB attention here and elsewhere. Anthropologists doing research in foreign countries and teaching field work courses in the United States are increasingly coming under surveillance. Given the rather narrow horizons of many IRB staffs, it has taken no small effort to get them to understand, as anthropologists have widely reported, that a pre-literate indigenous population halfway across the world is ill prepared to read and sign a consent form. I regularly interview nervous former members of the Communist Party now in their seventies and eighties. If I or my students showed them a consent form they'd show us the door. As others

(Sieber 2002, 1–4) have pointed out, consent forms can create the anxiety they are designed to ameliorate.

Meanwhile, our own IRB now expects undergraduates fulfilling an assignment to do practice interviews with their families to get signed consent forms in advance. In the now familiar pattern of institutionalizing every imagined anxiety, covering every imagined risk, the IRB wants to be sure a student's relatives do not feel coerced into doing an interview. Rather, they must feel free to refuse without fearing they are jeopardizing the student's grade. And a record of their signed consent must be on file. As recently as 2003 our own IRB insisted that a student needed approval before interviewing his or her mother. But not to worry. Provided the course instructor has filed the twelve-page IRB form, and as long as the mother is mentally competent to make her decision (there's a place to confirm that), university approval for the family conversation should be forthcoming in a matter of weeks. Better safe than sorry. Back in 1964 I was daring enough to call home without a bureaucrat's OK.

In 2002 it was worse still for University of Illinois anthropologists. Undergraduate students assigned to write papers about body language at the university gym were asked to get consent forms from everyone they watched. Although all students are members of the facility, the IRB contended the Intramural Physical Education Building was a private club and could not be treated as a public space. Students interviewing their friends and roommates about their reactions to magazine ads were required to get signed forms. At first the IRB also demanded the full twelve-page application from each undergrad doing a unique project. Now they seem willing to take class-wide proposals as long as they are supplemented by individual consent forms.

The fact that anthropologists have been teaching fieldwork courses for decades without difficulty does not matter. They are accustomed to supervising student projects. No matter. Big Brother knows best. The extra time and effort involved in getting IRB approval for family conversations will most likely have a decisively chilling effect only on large courses. So we hope. But the controlling principle, unannounced, unreflected, ill-considered—and, by the way, insane—is this: every single research interview conducted by a faculty member or student should be vetted by a bureaucrat.

I have myself—in the course of doing twenty-three books and over 100 articles over thirty years—conducted over 3,000 one-on-one interviews. Of course there are difficult moral issues involved. I struggle with them all the time. One useful essay by another scholar (Oakes 2002, 452–8) charts damage done to research subjects in a spectrum running from "annoyance" to "death." Journalism is lodged at one end of this spectrum, medical research at the other. My own interviews often produce a good deal more distress than annoyance, but they are not fatal. I may ask difficult questions. I am seeking individual historical truths. Often enough I end up with information I do not publish until my interviewees have died. I have withheld publication in some cases to save people distress, and I have caused real distress by publishing in others. For better or worse I make my own decisions after consulting friends and colleagues. In the end, a journal or a publisher makes a final decision about publication, after employing its own procedures for peer review. I've been denounced but not sued. And I persevere. So it goes. I need advice all the time from people doing research in similar areas. I do not need bureaucrats or faculty members from distant fields telling me what to do, especially when they set themselves up as the ultimate arbiters of ethics and professional conduct. There are no such arbiters. There are only the ongoing struggles with complex competing responsibilities.

In the fateful David Wright meeting the IRB staff dismissed out of hand the suggestion that we could rely on *The Kenyon Review* and the academic peer reviewing system, which has worked for decades, to decide whether an essay merited publication. If that does not offer sufficient warning for the future, I would add this: in all my conversations with IRB staff and members across the counry I have never encountered anyone who believed a publisher's ethical standards equalled their own.

Like everyone—save Wright—to whom I talked for this chapter, the IRB members all requested anonymity. They are afraid of the federal regulators, just as faculty members are afraid of their IRB. At every level of the system the persons in power declare "We are your friends. We want to work with you." And in every instance the person hearing the messsage wholly or partly discounts it. It does not matter whether this anxiety is well founded, since it is a predictable product of the power differential inherent in the system.

What would it take, we might ask, to extend the David Wright and the anthropology cases to the whole campus? Remember that Wright's case was about prior restraint of publication, not about a research proposal. It would take an immense staff and would produce a monstrous, intrusive surveillance culture that would substantively imperil academic freedom. Whether we face such a prospect remains to be seen. The whole IRB enterprise may either grow or contract, but it is unlikely simply to continue on its present scale. Yet it is difficult to see how IRBs can guarantee faculty research has done no harm to individuals without prior vetting of publications. Nor can they minimize the risk of suits without seeing what scholars are actually saying about people in their work. IRBs presently review research proposals, but most people have no idea what they will put into print until the research and writing are done. The impulse to focus on research *plans* is another awkward transfer from the medical model, where it is easy to assume the important human interventions will occur during the research itself. But with humanities and qualitative social science projects the analysis and reporting of research results are at least as likely to produce significant interventions in people's lives. Meanwhile institutions are increasingly likely to commit themselves to campus-wide surveillance; it's the simplest way to assure federal regulatory agencies your IRB is doing its job. It is easy to imagine how lawyerly anxiety and a rigid liberal humanism would combine to warrant curtailing faculty freedom of expression. The steadily increasing scope of the campus IRB mission is often justified by warning of government willingness to close down all funded research on a campus that endangers human subjects. But it is a long way from a university bio-medical scientist killing a research subject to a student potentially annoying a parent with an interview request. As C. K. Gunsalus asked in her opening remarks at the April 2003 University of Illinois conference, "Is an ounce of prevention really worth a pound of cure?" And what if it is pretty doubtful that we are getting that ounce? It is time instead for IRBs to just say no. As others have urged (Knight, personal communication), we believe it is safer in the long run for IRBs to declare most pedagogy and most humanities and social science research none of their business. Should faculty and students meanwhile be educated much more thoroughly about their ethical responsibilities in doing research? Absolutely. Are there cases where departments should supervise and alter teaching practices? Certainly. But E.T. should not need permission to call home.

CN

6. The Humanities and the Perils of Globalization

I. Consolations for Capitalists

IF YOU VISIT THE WORLD BANK'S WEB SITE (www.worldbank.org/), one of the first things you will see is its motto pledging to work for an end to world poverty. Here and there, to be sure, the World Bank has even had some modest successes at health and safety projects, though it tends at times to take credit for developments, like increased literacy in China, that it did not initiate. Not every lower-level staffer on the World Bank payroll, moreover, is a pure slave to global capital, though those who serve positive functions—funding water sanitation projects or nutrition information programs—are there because the WB believes their efforts will eventually facilitate capital investment and profit. Despite its overarching motto, "Our Dream is a World Free of Poverty"—as Michel Chossudovsky, Saskia Sassen, and others have pointed out—the WB overall has had more success at entrenching conditions that breed poverty than at alleviating them. Its sister organization, the International Monetary Fund (IMF), has now become notorious for enforcing draconian "structural adjustment programs" that strip social welfare programs so developing countries can repay their international debt. So brutal have those programs been that the IMF itself is now promoting plans to forgive some third world debt. Yet at the same time the IMF has seen fit to criticize what it sees as "excessive" government expenditures on social welfare in Europe.

It is increasingly clear, moreover, that the World Bank and the IMF cannot be separated in their intentions and effects from the other transnational institutions that business interests have helped establish in an effort to supersede the authority of nations. The most notable of these is, of course, the World Trade Organization. At the April 2000 IMF/ WB protest rally in Washington, D.C., one speaker called the WB, the IMF, and the WTO "the unholy trinity of greed." Together these organizations promote not free trade but corporate managed trade; they help to concentrate power and wealth in the hands of multinational corporations. They tend at once to stabilize international financing and to institutionalize local economic stagnation.

The chief ways that the World Bank, the International Monetary Fund, and the World Trade Organization intersect and amplify each other's effects are not mysterious. All want to maximize opportunities for international investment by multinational corporations; all want to promote "free" trade. While the WB and the IMF have broad authority to transform political and social practice in the countries beholden to them for loans, they have rather less power over the major industrial powers who finance their operations. The IMF thus has no power to regulate worldwide trade on a product-by-product basis. The WTO, on the other hand, has the effective power through fines to overrule laws in all its member nations. A WTO member country that is indebted to the IMF is uniquely vulnerable to external control. In such cases the WTO effectively enforces—at an intricate level—the WB/IMF principles for access to foreign markets and investment opportunities.

One could propose new operating principles that might reform these organizations, such as pointing the IMF toward extending microcredit rather than toward giant loans to corrupt governments, or stripping the WTO of its power to gut national environmental and safety regulations, but corporate domination of these organizations makes major reform unlikely. Taken together, the WB, IMF, and WTO comprise what Lori Wallach and Michele Sforza have called "an insidious shift in decision-making away from democratic, accountable fora—where citizens have a chance to fight for the public interest—to distant, secretive, and unaccountable international bodies, whose rules and operations are dominated by corporate interests" (1999, 14).

The changes at work are thus not only economic but also political and cultural. Indeed the ways these organizations penetrate national politics and culture would surprise many in the industrialized world. Wallach and Sforza describe the WTO as "the engine for a comprehensive redesign of international, national and local law, politics, cultures, and values" (1999, 70). All this, in the case of the WTO, grows out of its authority to overturn (or penalize nations for) any regulation that inhibits trade. Thus the WTO heard a challenge to U.S. laws restricting sales of tuna fish caught in nets that kill dolphins, while it also overruled restrictions against products contributing to air pollution. National policies banning products made with child labor or slave labor could easily be challenged in the future. At stake is the whole ethical consensus that undergirds public life in a given country.

The World Bank meanwhile has a much broader mandate than the WTO, which allows it to press for changes in a whole range of national institutions. Ronald A. T. Judy reports on the struggle in Tunisia over WB recommendations for the wholesale redirection and restructuring of higher education there. "What the commercial sector expects from the universities," he writes, "are properly trained business managers, accountants, computer specialists, information service specialists, and so forth" (1999, 27). The WB insisted that education be "more demand-driven and responsive to employers' needs." The aim of WB investment "is to organize the essential tools needed to maximize employment in the locally relevant portion of the global economy" (1999, 23). The WB intervention in Tunisian higher education has since been replicated in other countries. Moreover, as one Brazilian faculty member informed us in an interview, the WB adopts procedures that encourage privatization in higher education, making demands for financial guarantees that public higher education cannot meet. Much of the historical and cultural education that humanities programs in particular have offered, the WB sees as unnecessary to "human capital development." Thus Tunisia faced "a demolition of humanities education in favor of perceived instrumental market needs, pegged to Tunisia's integration into the global economy" (1999, 15).

These trends will not force themselves on American higher education by way of IMF edicts. The wolves will often arrive here in sheep's clothing. One of their emerging disguises is "lifelong learning." When we first heard the term "lifelong learning" it sounded rather pleasant. As the current motto for continuing education, it adds an upbeat, friendly connotation to what seems an increasingly pragmatic movement. Americans, the phrase suggests, will be encouraged to continue reading and thinking all their lives. Surely that will be a healthy change for a democracy. For those of us in higher education it might mean a second chance to reach students we had failed to inspire during their four undergraduate years. Perhaps people will want to take another philosophy course at age fifty. We might even require more faculty members to meet this new need.

Think again. Lifelong learning refers to a lifelong treadmill of job training and retraining. As higher education takes on this distopian mission it will become steadily and more intricately tied to global capitalism and the workforce needs of corporate employers. Think of lifelong learning as the password to the education treadmill, not as a practicum in the life of the mind. This brave new world was hailed with braggadocio in the inaugural issues of Jeffrey Kittay's magazine *University Business*, a publication devoted to the pleasures of selling out. But a more balanced— and surprisingly sober—account of these economic and social developments can be had in *Postbaccalaureate Futures*, edited by Kay Kohl and Jules LaPidus and published in 2000. By no means a critique of corporatized higher education, it is written rather by contributors who believe closer relationships between campus and industry are inevitable. They are concerned with facilitating these trends and maximizing their economic benefits. In the process they help us understand what makes higher education a potentially attractive investment. As Howard Marc Block puts it in an early chapter, "who wouldn't want to compete in a market where the 'competition' is hardly competitive?" Because higher education is a fragmented industry, new investors have a real chance of stealing market share. What's more, the market is exceptionally predictable: "the University of Virginia has a clearer vision than Taco Bell of how many customers it will have in six months" (Kohl & LaPidus 2000, 34).

The twenty contributors to *Postbaccalaureate Futures*—who include upper-level university administrators, government officials, leaders of educational organizations, and entrepreneurs—all believe that the needs of lifelong learners cannot help but reshape higher education as a whole. Stephen Mitchell, James Van Erden, and Kenneth Voytek put it bluntly. For individual workers, they write, "continuous learning is necessary just to stay in place" (Kohl & LaPidus 2000, 51). For the "proactive lifelong learners" (a phrase from a chapter by the editors) who act on this knowledge, a traditional degree program and discipline, one focused more on knowledge than job skills, is one of the major "barriers to operational excellence" (2000, 67): "rigid course sequences, academic calendars, degree requirements, and other requirements are institutional impediments to participation in KSCs [Knowledge Supply Chains]" (2000, 68). They offer a chilling alternative: "The ultimate solution to this bureaucratic roadblock may be a degree or certification awarded through a third-party broker" (2000, 67). Jules LaPidus calls them "'credit banks' where educational credentials accumulated over time and from a variety of sources can be stored and perhaps cashed in' when a sufficient number have been accumulated" (2000, 7). That would be one result of what Kay Kohl here calls "the erosion of traditional universities' credentialling monopoly" (2000, 22).

Along the way, other changes will accumulate. Kohl predicts the increasing "modularization of curricula" as institutions seek coursework more adaptable to changing job requirements. What is heralded here as "the diminishing half-life of skill and knowledge" (2000, 61) will compel us to "reduce learning transfer time" (2000, 25) and to "focus the curriculum only on skill gaps" (2000, 40). For "one-third of all jobs are in flux each year, meaning that they have recently been created or soon will be eliminated from the economy" (2000, 13) and "by 2020, most individuals in the workforce will need to prepare themselves for as many as seven or eight careers" (2000, 23).

For universities to meet these needs they will have to cede significant control over degrees and curricula to industry. One chapter goes further: "Shared staff or college staff located at company facilities are still better" (Kohl & LaPidus 2000, 64). Moreover, "constant analysis helps to reduce total system costs and cycle times, improve quality, and increase product or service functionality" (2000, 55), so faculty can expect relentless surveillance and evaluation of the effectiveness of the services they are performing for corporations. This Orwellian vision makes post-tenure review sound comforting.

Do we have a choice in implementing or resisting these changes? Toward the end of the book, Myles Brand, the former president of Indiana University, whose recent employment history we recall in our introduction, reminds us of an earlier prediction that "traditional campuses will disappear in favor of wholly technologically delivered higher education" (Kohl & LaPidus 2000, 194). Alan Bassindale and John Daniel offer some astonishing statistics from other countries: Turkey's Anadolu University has 578,000 students enrolled in distance learning degree programs focused on job training. The Indira Gandhi National Open University, an exclusively distance teaching "mega-university," comes in a close second, with 431,000 students enrolled in undergraduate and postgraduate programs (Kohl & LaPidus 2000, 123–4). Not surprisingly, Kohl warns us that American institutions as well "need to be perceived as responsive to the education needs of postbaccalaureate learners in the labor force if they are to retain public support" (2000, 27).

The shift toward contingent labor in American higher education will make help make such changes possible. It will also make it easier for administrators, rather than faculty, to control the lifelong learning curriculum. And in the process the critical function of the humanities will be marginalized and defunded. We will be on our way to the instrumentalized international model of education. With this background in mind, we would like to put forward a kind of counter-manifesto on the role of the humanities in general and literary studies in particular in the emerging global economy. We will conclude with a coda that specifies by way of example part of what we will lose as World Bank culture gradually replaces the humanities with instrumental versions of literacy.

II. The Counter-Manifesto

1. *Debt Restructuring:* The cultural form of contemporary debt restructuring is first of all a conceptual reversal. If capital was once thought to be at least in symbolic debt to literary culture, that time has past. Capital owes us nothing, and we survive on the margins of its sufferance. Literature is in debt to commerce; the debt cannot be repaid. It can only grow. And lack of interest accumulates.

2. *The New World Order.* As the old ties that bound literature to nation are undone and high culture's traditional capacity to underwrite empire becomes irrelevant, a desperate struggle ensues to find new ways of attracting investments in literary institutions. These investments are already under way, but their nature and function have undergone a sea change. Nations traditionally invested in literature and the humanities in part because of their symbolic capital; literature could be used at once to mystify and naturalize power relations. But our cultural accounts have crashed overnight. Global commerce does not need our symbolic capital.

3. *Labor value.* If literature in particular and the humanities in general no longer glow with a valued aura, the only remaining basis for investment is direct profit. Some books can be sold—among them the trials and tribulations of former First Ladies and children's book series with millions of devoted fans—though increasingly not books written by scholars. The literary institutions of academia in any case are not needed to market the relatively few highly profitable novels sold each year. Profit can, however, be extracted from the labor of those who teach in humanities departments. The symbolic capital of what we taught once offered us some protection from capitalism's more rapacious impulses. No more. Now the operative instinct is to extract the maximum labor and the maximum profit from delusional devotees of literariness and other high cultural products.

4. *Globalization.* Looking for new-fashioned symbolic capital, the acolytes of literariness have recently been cheered by the thought that multiculturalism could be the humanizing ideology of multinational corporations. Throwing down all old trade barriers, international humanities education declares "We are the world." Literature and its allied fields could mystify diversification, celebrate new markets in the guise of an expanded human family. But enough obfuscation already surrounds the expanding reach of

global capital. Bell Telephone, as comedian Elaine May used to say in one of her old routines, does not need your dime. Nobody is buying the little we can offer to recast the World Bank's offices as a Potemkin Village.

5. *Consolation.* Among their minor capacities, humanities fields have long included subsidiary rights to several useful human emotions. Deployed skillfully, their discourses could offer diverting consolations at once to exploiting and exploited populations. Literature, for example, was a safety valve for insurgent impulses. And even capitalists needed some consolations to compensate for rapacious services rendered to nation and race. But globalization decertifies guilt. Greed has evolved beyond the need to justify itself. Once more, humanities disciplines find themselves out of the exchange loop. The World Bank does not need their services.

6. *Conformity.* Increasingly, humanities tellers at the World Bank will have less and less room to maneuver. Neither the World Bank nor the International Monetary Fund seems to need multiple models of operation. One size is adaptable to fit all. Investments in symbolic capital generate at least a cautious tolerance for inconvenient behavior; the cost accounting is complex and variable. But cold calculations of profit leave little room for behavior that subverts the bottom line. What is the profit in rebellious forms of academic freedom? World Bank literature is altogether Orwellian in its implications. Unprofitable managers and sectors will not be tortured or interrogated; they will simply not be renewed. The only surveillance needed is the balance sheet. World Bank literature has no content, no meaning, no history; it is an empty commodity to be served by a docile labor force. And that labor force is more docile when it is distracted, overworked, and underpaid.

7. *Base Superstructure.* The relationship between the culture and economy of World Bank literature is increasingly unmediated. The elaborate metaphors we have devised to account for the relative if contingent autonomy of culture are no longer necessary. Literature and its institutions either sell or they do not; they either advance the interests of world capitalism or they do not. We are either part of literature's contingent work force or we are out in the cold.

8. *Resistance.* Resistance is more necessary than ever. And multiple spaces for its realization remain. Just don't expect it to pay. The displacements, contradictions, multiplicities, and conflicts of the postmodern world made symbolic resistance not only feasible but lucrative. Don't count on this arrangement surviving. The World Bank expects docility. The servants of World Bank literature will be expected to domesticate literature's unruly histories.

9. *Transition.* We are in a period of transition between the dichotomies of the cold war and the universal reign of world capital. In this period, homicidal ethnicities and fratricidal nationalisms are multiplying. But the forces of capital are determined to crush these tendencies. World Bank literature will not fully come into its own until the bland transit of commerce prevails everywhere. Literary investments in local rogue markets have no long-term future. But the need for alternative spaces—like the 1999 protests in Seattle, which made rejection of unchecked, exploitive capitalism apparent to everyone—could not be greater, for the conflict between World Bank culture and ethnic nationalism devolves into alternatives of reason and madness. These are not satisfactory choices.

10. *Denial.* Through nearly half a century of relative prosperity, those academics with tenure-track jobs have mostly thought the conditions of literary production and reception were something like a god-given order. For three decades the overproduction of PhDs has left thousands of young scholar-teachers without a decent wage, time for reflection, job security, or real academic freedom. Still, most tenured academics felt that the institutions of literature were unalterable facts of nature. Yet all the while a contingent economy of literary production and consumption was running its course and a new economic foundation with little place for the humanities was taking shape. The emerging economy of the humanities worldwide will no longer privilege scholarly achievement, no longer provide time for research or writing, and no longer even offer any high-status venues for publication. Those poets whose work can be recycled into the profitable text market will still be able to publish their books; the rest will publish on the web or out of their own basements. The scholarly book will have still fewer means of distribution. The World Bank has called in our loans.

III. Coda for World Bank Literature

[It] means completely abandoning the tradition of social justice through education and proposing a new experience of time, one that naively enhances the perspective of the 'modern' as a radical rupture from any past—it is effectively without a past of significance—and hence only directed at a boundless future that it determines or shapes. This experience of time is at the core of the economic concept of endless market growth and the financial notion of the boundless circulation of money (Judy 1999, 29).

One of us has spent a good part of the end of the last millennium in a curious if busy limbo between celebration and mourning. He has been at work, as the previous sentence cannot have signalled, editing and constructing a web site devoted to modern American poetry (http://www.english.uiuc.edu/maps). The site, which is described in detail in chapter 11, is designed to excerpt scholarly commentary about hundreds of twentieth-century American poems; it now has thousands of pages on line, with still more to come. The project has given one of us cause to read compilations of criticism assembled by a number of other scholars and to review scores of books on the subject published over the last half century: I wandered the library stacks at Illinois and carried home armloads of books, dusted off some neglected volumes in my own collection, and called friends to get the names of titles I might have missed. It was quite different from the sort of reading you do in preparation for writing. For one thing it meant reviewing criticism about more than a hundred poets. Unlike working on a scholarly essay, the aim was not to select those readings directly applicable to the conversation you might want to have with other critics, but rather to anticipate all the conversations other students and scholars might find beneficial. All the compilers of sites would read more widely than usual and read as an omnivore.

The sense of celebration came from pleasure at discovering how well many of these books have weathered the intellectual vicissitudes of a rapidly changing discipline. Construed as a long-term, ongoing conversation, the scholarship about modern poetry holds up surprisingly well. The differences that erupt as new methods, vocabularies, and interests arrive on the scene make less for obsolescence than for debate and challenge. Older readings sometimes reveal unstated assumptions underlying newer ones. But just as common are absolute reversals of meaning. The result is a drama about the contingent limits and possibilities of human knowledge, about the instability of textuality, about the historical construction of poetic meaning and readerly identity, about the social and political uses of literary understanding. That conversation may not survive globalization.

In some half-life of historical memory the discipline is fleetingly aware that academic culture did not have to evolve in such a way as to make this rich published conversation possible. The vast expansion of the postwar American university produced the scholars, students, publishers, research funds, and libraries necessary to this enterprise. The ratcheting up of tenure requirements helped instill in scholars the need to do the work of written interpretation represented in these books. The reward systems for publication and the symbolic valued attached to it helped shape faculty members' identities around their scholarly work. And a secure national and international market for book sales to libraries meant that presses would seek out, evaluate, and publish books on the subject. Finally, of course, the canon revision and expansion that have so radically reshaped American studies were driven substantially by a series of social, political, and intellectual movements both inside and outside the university. But no matter where you look in this multifaceted story, money, we so easily forget, is central to the account.

And that leads me to my cause for mourning. This conversation is coming to an end. Beginning in the 1960s and running through the 1980s a whole series of university presses were publishing books on modern poetry. Why not? They could sell 2,000 hardbound copies to libraries in the 1970s. By the end of the century, that number had dropped to barely 200, a 90 percent decline. My friend who received a letter from Cornell University Press saying they no longer do books about a single writer does not feel this inspires confidence. Nor do my colleagues who received letters from Minnesota and Texas saying those presses have stopped publishing literary criticism entirely. Some presses, of course, have been largely unaffected; Oxford and Cambridge have large international markets that enable them to sell a thousand copies of a given title, far less than was possible twenty-five years ago, but enough to turn a profit. As the British empire withdrew from its colonies, it left behind these publishing outposts as remnants of the cultural work England once did. But most presses have been very seriously affected indeed. In *Academic Keywords* (Nelson & Watt 1999) we reported that presses like Cornell and Stanford are issuing contracts limiting some book publications to 300 copies, but that news is already out of date. There are presses now doing runs of only 125 copies. At some point it is a pretty small tree that must fall in the groves of academe in order to publish a book. Even if someone is there in the forest they may not hear the soft rustle of a sapling hitting the ground. No World Bank planner will imagine there is need for infrastructure to support scholarly publication in the humanities.

It is striking how many presses have largely or entirely dropped out of the game during the period of increasing globalization. A dialogue about our heritage that was immensely valuable has become much more difficult to conduct. Nor is the Internet likely to produce the same sort of carefully rewritten prose. It is a wonderful medium for accessing the archive, a remarkable way to get material out quickly, and as we point out in chapter 11, an astonishingly effective way to repackage segments of scholarly writing for broad public access. But that credits the Internet as a tremendously effective *supplement* to traditional forms of scholarly publication, not as their replacement. Will any of us spend five or more years writing and rewriting an essay destined for the Internet in the same way we have done for our published books and essays?

At the same time, ironically, the canon revision that has occupied us for twenty years has left us a task of detailed research about scores of writers who have never had a book devoted to them. Look through the *Heath Anthology of American Literature* and see how many of the authors included there have at best a few articles published on them. How many of those articles are overviews with few close engagements with individual texts? If we were to predict the state of American studies over the next decade or two on the basis of recent research, we would include intensive single-author research for women, minority, and progressive writers among our priorities and expectations. There are necessary things one can learn in no other way. Detailed work about little-known or forgotten writers is also rather labor intensive. Over ten years one of us has conducted over 3,000 interviews about just one modern American poet. We won't be doing this for another ten poets.

Thus our regret at the passing of time and support for intellectual work does not represent nostalgia for a golden age. The texts that received detailed interpretations for much of this century were often written by conservative white males. Our regret is that the rise of World Bank culture means we may not be able to do this interpretive work for the newly recovered work of the Left. Without that work much progressive literature will remain largely empty of meaning, its potential for cultural and political work severely curtailed.

For we are not sure how many part-timers without adequate time and research budgets will be conducting 3,000 interviews about a poet, let alone how many faculty will even be interested in doing so where globalization has eliminated courses in literature. The economic and institutional infrastructure no longer exists to support the sort of work many humanities faculty have come to regard as a fact of nature. The collapse of the publishing market, the dramatic shift in the financing and nature of academic labor, and the Tunisian-style shift toward an instrumental curriculum will constrain what it is possible for literature and culture to mean to future generations. What literature means now is a product of economic and social forces. The next decade will be no less a function of those principles.

Indeed the cultural and political forces operating on the profession will dovetail with the economic constraints on higher education. We do not believe that global capitalism has quite the need for research in literary culture that nation states, however quixotically, have seen fit to support in the second half of the century. The function of the humanities in the global market is less likely to include a fundable symbolic component. We will be of value to the degree that we are profitable.

Being profitable means teaching courses as cheaply as possible, marketing them as widely as possible, and serving the needs of larger investment sectors. Being profitable is not likely to mean writing and publishing literary criticism. Being profitable means maximizing productivity, which means faculty should be cooperative and should focus on activities that generate corporate income. Being profitable means acquiring teaching labor at the lowest possible cost and minimizing its capacity for dissent. The time when literary studies and the humanities in general had a more symbolic form of cultural capital is coming to an end.

Nor are we likely to be able retain cultural capital simply by internationalizing literary studies and putting national literatures in dynamic dialogue either with traditions they have influenced or texts written in resistance to the dominant powers, much as those comparative enterprises are both worthy and desirable. It is not clear that a world economy needs a historical world culture in quite the same way that a nation state needed a national culture.

Detached in part from national imperialism, the blind will to profit does not require the same sort of rationalization, obfuscation, and mystification as it did in the past. Nations, of course, are often fundamentally exclusionary and racist; they can sometimes use literary idealization to disguise, justify, or compensate for these impulses. Coming from a consortium of multinational corporations, the motto "We bring prosperity to everyone" may not require the same level of service from literariness as did "We bring you Christianity," "We bring you civilization," or "We bring you American freedom."

There is nothing new in the humanities being entangled with or enabled and constrained by broader economic and social forces. What is new is a potential decoupling of the destiny of the nation state from academic disciplines. What is also *not* new, but rather reawakened after a long sleep, is an awareness that academia may suffer from these changes. Of course academics in many countries have themselves had a strong hand in their own collective undoing. They have shown capitalism how best and most thoroughly to exploit humanities professors. They have shown the way to a university without freedom and without the time to make a critical contribution to the culture. They have created a thoroughly managed and intimidated academic workforce and dangled it before corporations as an investment opportunity.

What is so disturbing in this is not only the sheer waste of the potential of so many young intellectuals, but also the risk to the continuing development of the intellectual traditions humanistic disciplines have sought to foster. For without the intensive research of several decades the expanded canon would not exist; recovered authors would have remained unread; their works would have remained forgotten and out-of-print. We would not now be living in an enriched and increasingly interdisciplinary literary culture. But the work of formulating and disseminating the meanings and implications of an expanded canon has barely begun. We have simultaneously encouraged this research and promoted economic practices that may bring it to an end. What is very clear is that we cannot proceed without talking very seriously about the global interdependence of our intellectual and economic futures. For we cannot continue to expand the canon with a cannon aimed at our heads.

CN

Part Two

Toward Alternative Futures

7. Organizational Affiliation and Change

IN THE FALL OF 2001 A MULTI-YEAR effort by Michael Bennett of Long Island University began to bear fruit. The Modern Language Association's Executive Council had before it for the first time two very different proposals. The more dramatic was a resolution to censure the Executive Council for failing to act on an earlier motion, which Bennett had written and which the Delegate Assembly had passed, to begin penalizing departments that were teaching too many of their courses with contingent labor, namely part-time faculty typically paid slave wages and denied basic job security and benefits. The second proposal came from an ad hoc committee, of which Bennett was a member, offering some practical suggestions for beginning to deal with the overreliance on contingent labor in many English and foreign language departments.

As typically happens in the MLA, a well-intentioned proposal arrives from the Delegate Assembly having been overwhelmingly approved but in a form not yet ready for Executive Council action. It could hardly be otherwise. A DA motion is usually written by one or two people and reviewed by a few others. The contituencies with a stake in the matter, in this case especially, most of the large literature and language departments in the country, have no opportunity for input before the proposal is passed. The document is then considered by an Executive Council with no guaranteed expertise in the matter and little patience for hard work. Like the well-known fable about a group of blind men gathered around an elephant and characterizing it by way of the foot or tail or trunk within their reach, the members of the EC self-importantly relate their opinions or their fragmentary personal experiences one after another.

After two or three rounds of this, it is clear no consensus exists and none can be reached.

Thus had Bennett's earlier motion been handled. A group of organizations then met to discuss the problem of staffing ratios, but they did little more than make it clear how knotty the issue was. I had cosponsored the original Bennett motion and was thus in what I regarded as the quite wonderful paradox at once of having proposed action and now being censured for failing to take it. I was more than ready to censure myself, for I felt the EC had failed its moral and professional responsibility to address the issue seriously and take some actions, whether those in the DA motion or others. The ad hoc committee gave us our needed alternative. Their proposals were not going to solve the problem, but they would move us in the direction of publicizing which departments had admirably high percentages of full-time faculty teaching their courses and which had dismally high dependence on part-timers. The range is considerable.

Meanwhile, in the course of considering the censure proposal, which would have come up for a Delegate Assembly vote in December 2001, the Executive Council for the only time in my four year experience actually worked collaboratively on a text and adopted it. Some of the most brilliant members of the profession threw themselves into this task with a kind of fervor I had never before seen in this group. The text in question: a letter proudly asserting that their failure to do anything meaningful about staffing ratios over two years of negotiations was a fine example of the human spirit at its best.

No one acquainted with Michel Foucault's work will be surprised to learn that organizational affiliation is always a double-edged sword: it creates opportunities for action at the same time as it installs powerful constraints defining what actions seem possible; it constructs and reinforces certain identities while casting out other identities as implausible or obscene. Like all forms of social regulation, as Foucault helped us see in other contexts, affiliation often promotes organizational and institutional ends less by punishing offenses than by rewarding compliance. Not that punishments, including monstrous ones, are ever absent from a properly affiliated imagination; they haunt both actual and hypothetical trespass. But affiliation also enriches subjectivity and positions identities in such a way as to win willing assent without seeming to extract compliance violently. Affiliation limits what it is possible to imagine, identifies outcomes we can fear, and naturalizes the status quo within institutions.

So it is with academia and with all the forms of affiliation promoted in this most paradoxical set of vocations, so many of them combining extreme self-consciousness and an unexamined life. As we point out in chapter 2, in academia one often subjects everything but the very social constitution of one's own identities to intense scrutiny. There is a gap, then, between the assent theoretical observations about affiliation might win and the willingness of many academics to interrogate the nature and consequences of their own affiliations. Affiliations may be constitutive and constraining, academics might argue, but they are often blind to their own constraining ideologies. For they have been, perhaps irrationally, persuaded they are themselves affiliated exclusively with freedom.

So long as the academic system worked efficiently, affiliation might proceed harmlessly on a dual tracks of equally focused inquiry and ignorance. From time to time, of course, multiple affiliations were brought together—or collided—in such a way as to produce desperately needed change. We saw that during the 1960s and 1970s when anti-war activism propelled academics into institutional critique and radically different forms of affiliation. We saw it again when simultaneous affiliation with feminism and the academy forced universities to begin confronting their multiple discriminatory practices. And multiple affiliations produced activist confrontations between black students and the institutions in which they were enrolled. Other marginalized groups have since followed their lead.

These multiple and conflicting affiliations have been both theoretical and organizational, though they have not necessarily operated on the same plane for every individual. Yet it is often only the friction between multiple affiliations that opens a space for reflective critique. Even in academia—the very institution supposedly most devoted to unfettered reasoned analysis—the horizon circumscribed by one set of seamless and mutually reinforcing affiliations can severely limit our insight. One belongs to a department, one belongs to a campus, one belongs to a discipline, and perhaps to its national organization. It is but one step further to the nation state. This is a hierarchy of interchangeable affiliations that obliterates difference and contradiction within a setting that is, ironically, rife with them.

Yet affiliation on the other hand can position one to effect much needed change. To abandon affiliation because of its inherent limitations and constraints is perhaps to be even less empowered. Necessary change seems most likely to occur, however, when multiple affiliations are in tension with one another. Out of those tensions—erupting across subject positions in dialogue and in conflict with one another—can evolve alliances that link affiliated subjects in new ways. And the social space occupied by multiple persons taken up in different affiliations in turn promotes moments of recognition and self-critique ordinarily suppressed by affiliations that merely reinforce one another.

It is time and past time for such patterns to assume prominence throughout higher education. We have been through three decades of a disastrous job market for new PhDs in which "apprenticeship" has been steadily emptied of its authenticity as a subject position. Affiliation has for many "apprentices" been a mode of enslavement.

This chapter, then, is about networking and acting for change in academia. It is about people occupying places in key organizations and using those affiliations to make a difference in higher education. It's about a movement of intellectual activists that has no structure and no overall organizational name. We have combined a general political analysis of affiliation with academic organizations with an on-the-ground account of actual efforts for change because we are convinced an abstract account alone will not suffice; people need to see how a commitment to activist affiliation plays out in daily life. I narrate this story in the first person, foregrounding my own role because it offers an instructive example, an example at the very least of how senior faculty members can make a difference if they choose. But I emphasize at the outset that everyone I interact with here is putting just as much time in these issues as I am. And this group includes graduate students, part-time faculty, and administrative staff, all of whom are successfully combining local and national activism in their multiple academic affiliations. The full story would comprise a three-dimensional map detailing all their activities in the context of their multiple and occasionally overlapping intersections. The "organization" here is the ongoing strategic conversation across multiple affiliations about what we are going to do. Our main aims are to reform the Modern Language Association and other disciplinary and transdisciplinary organizations, refocusing their efforts on the problems of academic labor, and/or to improve working conditions for graduate employees and part-time or adjunct faculty, and gradually increase the number of full-time, tenure-track faculty positions throughout the country. Underlying such reforms must be increased democracy for all the segments of the academic workforce.

Because I think this nearly accidental alliance has had some success, let me say by way of a preface that we have seen a series of alternative national organizational models fail. I have in mind in particular a series of progressive organizations in academia that frittered away their time creating structures and affiliations unconnected to action. When Teachers for a Democratic Culture was founded, I thought to myself "This isn't going to work; there are no actions for this group to take. It isn't going to radicalize anyone." I had the same series of premonitions when Scholars, Artists, and Writers for Social Justice (SAWSJ) arrived on the scene. Organizing and building membership either turns people into radicals

AAUP, as it happens, were often willing to support academic freedom for graduate students. But some otherwise distinguished AAUP members clung to the apprenticeship model and felt full academic freedom was necessary only for faculty. As I tried to point out, graduate employees are now often *in charge* of large lecture courses, talking to 500 or 1,000 students about race in American history, or about American imperialism. If these graduate employees do not need the protection of academic freedom, it is difficult to decide who does. Meanwhile, the rhetoric of apprenticeship was simultaneously undermining commitment to fair wages and even to the document's work load provision. Here multiple affiliations helped once again. The MLA in 1998 had affirmed one course per semester, or roughly twenty hours of work for compensation, as the appropriate maximum work load for graduate students pursuing a degree. AAUP members with MLA affiliations used the workload recommendation in the final report from MLA's Committee on Professional Employment to shore up the AAUP's position. The Statement on Graduate Students, meanwhile, allows some limits on academic freedom for graduate students learning about the discipline but secures their academic freedom as teachers, a reasonable compromise given the dual nature of graduate education. The document was printed in the AAUP journal *Academe*, approved by the National Council in June 2000, and published in the AAUP's *Policy Documents and Reports* (popularly known as the "Redbook") at the beginning of 2001. The MLA's Delegate Assembly endorsed it in December 2000, and it was printed in the summer 2001 issue of the *MLA Newsletter*.

Although the AAUP cannot enforce such recommendations, publishing them in the "Redbook" beside definitions of tenure and academic freedom gives them significant weight. Getting organizations like the MLA to endorse the entire Statement on Graduate Students will help local groups agitate for good practices on their own campuses. It will also give individual campuses a set of goals and principles to discuss.

To help that agitation along, I had drafted a resolution for the AAUP's national council in 1998, recognizing that all campus employees have the right to engage in collective bargaining if they choose. The National Council passed the resolution unanimously in November. In the fall of 1999 national disciplinary organizations began to endorse it. The American Studies Association passed a similar resolution on behalf of graduate student unionization in October 1999. Greg Bezkorvainey, a PhD candidate at the City University of New York, and I put our own resolution on collective bargaining rights before the MLA's Delegate Assembly in December 1999, which passed it overwhelmingly. The key to the resolution's language is that it does not urge collective bargaining but rather confirms the democratic right of each constituency *to choose for itself* whether to negotiate its working conditions together.

The following year MLA members ratified the collective bargaining resolution by mail ballot. In 2001 we decided to try to get the MLA's Executive Council to put this right into practice, in the form of a letter urging the New York University administration to begin bargaining with their graduate students in good faith. NYU graduate employees had voted to unionize and the National Labor Relations Board (NLRB) in an historic decision confirmed the vote. While I cannot comment on the discussion in Council, I can recount some of my conversations before the meeting. A number of the EC members had no concept of a "right" in this context, feeling that we should seek more information from the NYU administration about why it wanted to reject the results of a democratic election. Some council members could not understand that no administration arguments were likely to warrant their overturning a right ratified by the membership. Nor could they understand that arguments for and against graduate employee unionization tend to be quite formulaic. Thus it was foolish to expect any given university administration to advance a new and persuasive position. One association officer, having apparently been asleep for a decade, asked for an explanation of why so many graduate students want to unionize! In the end, an exhausting and sometimes brittle debate produced a letter, and shortly thereafter the NYU administration agreed to the NLRB ruling. That was during my third year on the council, but this story takes me back to my first year of service.

After completing my 1999 talk at Rutgers I headed off to two days of meetings of the MLA Executive Council, having been elected after nomination by a Graduate Student Caucus (GSC) petition drive. Despite 30 years of MLA membership, it would be my first visit to their offices. Two days around a seminar table in a windowless room had the potential to move MLA's first real action agenda forward. For the first time the organization would be acting, not just talking. It was beginning to seem possible that the result would be more than a structure to help affiliated people add lines to their vitas, and instead devote itself to securing higher education's future.

Two vitally important motions were up for a vote. The one that was potentially most controversial—to do a survey of part-time faculty salaries—had been jointly sponsored by the GSC and the Delegate Assembly Organizing Committee. This joint resolution came out of negotiations over a longer resolution first submitted by the GSC and its faculty allies. The need for this kind of data was laid out by two graduate students, Mark Kelley of CUNY (City University of New York) and Bill Pannapacker of Harvard, in a *Chronicle of Higher Education* article.

Gregory Bezkorvainey and I then decided to implement it with a motion, which we coauthored, then gathered a dozen faculty cosponsors from around the country. Approved overwhelmingly by the MLA's Delegate Assembly on December 29th, 1998, it called for the MLA to conduct the first ever nationwide survey of part-timer salaries, benefits, and working conditions. As the GSC understood the motion, 5,200 English and foreign language departments would be queried about their practices and then identified by name when the department-by-department results were published. Such data was not available for any discipline.

I had received a call a few days earlier from one of my graduate student co-conspirators warning me that the MLA was floating a suggestion to cut back on the size of the survey by contacting only a representative sample of departments, rather than the entire 5,200. This impulse partly represented a confusion over the statistical difference between reliability and replicability. Phyllis Franklin, then Executive Director of the MLA, believed a small sample, chosen on the basis of sound principles and buttressed by follow-up phone calls, would be more reliable, which was likely not to be the case. We could get reliable national data from a broad survey, but we could not guarantee replicability. I too wanted follow-up phone calls, but wanted them focused primarily on metropolitan areas where there were large quantities of part-timers.

I called New York to see if I could head off this initiative. Unfortunately, the call revealed other impulses to weaken the plan, namely a misunderstanding about the motion's aims. All the devils, it seemed, were in the details. The MLA staff was inclined to publish the data by region and institutional type, not by name.

The combined effect of these two changes—and the GSC certainly saw them as changes—would be to leave us pretty much where we already were. We already knew that some schools paid part-timers as little as $800 a course, whereas others paid as much as $4,000 or more. As of 2004, these figures have increased by about 25 percent. We knew the range, which repeats itself in most regions, and we knew the pay rates at a few specific schools. Steve Watt and I include some of this information in our *Academic Keywords: A Devil's Dictionary for Higher Education.* As Rich Moser of the AAUP had confirmed for me repeatedly, what part-timers needed in order to organize for change was detailed data in each region with all departments listed *by name* alongside their salary and benefits data. Part-timers have repeatedly said that it is impossible for them to gather this information. Central administrations claimed not to have it, and departments had little incentive to cooperate with part-timer requests for information. After the Delegate Assembly vote at the end of December, however, they were looking for the MLA to solve their problem. Phyllis' two changes would save face for individual departments—a strong motivation for long-term Association of Departments of English head David Laurence—but give part-timers little leverage to improve their compensation. To achieve that, part-timers needed to be able to cite exact salaries and benefits and make specific comparisons.

In New York I started calling friends around the country knowledgeable about survey methods for arguments to buttress my case. I needed to know, for example, whether we would significantly decrease the response rate by planning to publish the data institution-by-institution. Among the people I called at home were Ernst Benjamin and Iris Molotsky, then both of the national AAUP. Ernie had been doing faculty salary surveys for years and had drafted the important multi-organizational statement of principles on part-time hiring practices issued a year earlier. He would later help write the questionnaire for the part-timer survey. Iris was in the midst of gathering sample statements on graduate student rights. Both were seasoned veterans of organizational politics. In any case, by midnight, $100 of hotel phone calls later, I had the information I needed, which included the judgment that we would not lose a major portion of data by doing the survey the way we wanted.

Friday morning, at MLA headquarters at 10 Astor Place, the debate over the data gathering motion was extensive and sometimes pointed, but the proposal passed. It was helped in part by a companion proposal—to survey individual graduate programs in the field, then gather together and publish all the data about their individual admission requirements, placement rates, and pay scales, work loads, and benefits for graduate student employees. The schools would all be named, which would put this comparative data in one place for the first time. The disparity in degree completion rates and wage scales alone is astonishing. Neither students applying to doctoral programs in English or foreign languages nor those already enrolled in them have a broad grasp of the differences in departments across the country. Faculty advisors are equally ill informed. On the other hand, Philosophy was already embarked on a similar national survey of graduate programs and Math issued one regularly. There seemed little excuse for MLA cowardice when Math and Philosophy were already committed.

As with the part-timer survey, knowledge here is power. Moreover, it was clear to everyone that this information would be useless unless it was linked precisely to individual departments. Thus the MLA with either proposal would have to cross the bridge of identifying department practices by name for the first time. In the past the organization has preferred to describe good practices without specifying who does and does not adhere to them. That lets the Association of Departments of English, an

MLA division, serve as a friend of every affiliated department, ethical departments and rogue departments alike. But advocacy for exploited labor and advocacy for department overseers has come increasingly into conflict.

In any case, both proposals passed the Executive Council in February. Assuming the staff felt committed to the projects—it has wide latitude in deciding which projects are affordable—the data gathering projects for both part-time faculty and graduate student employees would be under way the summer and fall of 1999. As it happened, the staff in May presented a tentative budget for 1999–2000 to the Executive Council that included the survey. And in the end, despite earlier efforts to weaken the project, the MLA ended up carrying out the survey with impressive intelligence and dedication. Moreover, Phyllis used her long-term contacts to help build a coalition of disciplinary organizations who would each do smaller versions of the survey. Such, it seems, are the paradoxes of organizational affiliation, though it is hard to find anyone in the MLA hierarchy inclined to remember the GSC's role in this effort.

On Saturday evening Kirsten Chistensen and I, the two GSC candidates elected to the EC, went to dinner with Mark Kelley and Greg Bezkorovainy, then President and Vice-President of GSC. We updated them on the status of our proposals and heard their detailed plans for the coming year. We would all like to see more GSC representatives on MLA's Executive Council and more of the association's time, effort, and budget devoted to addressing the crisis of academic labor. We believe both things will eventually happen, though no doubt it will merely seem like business as usual to most tenured faculty, since the annual convention and MLA's major publications will continue on their way. Kelley had already dramatically increased the GSC's national and international visibility over the past year. On his own campus he helped draft a thoughtful response to the MLA's report on the job crisis, while nationally he and former president Marc Bousquet helped put two GSC representatives on the MLA's Executive Council. I would certainly not be there without their efforts. Bezkorovainy was our point person in extensive negotiations with the MLA over GSC's 1998 and 1999 Delegate Assembly motions and would become GSC President in January 2000. He would prove our best drafter of legislation and a wonderful negotiator, calmly and relentlessly promoting logic and reason in negotiations with the MLA.

The next morning I was on my way to the University of Nebraska at Kearney. One of my PhDs, Kate Benzel, is now a full professor there; she had invited me to give my corporate university talk, teach two classes (on Edwin Rolfe and Adrienne Rich), and meet with campus groups. I urged leaders of the faculty union to make increasing graduate student and part-timer wages an issue when they bargained for their next contract. Graduate students in English at Kearney were teaching two courses each semester and receiving $1,125 per course, for a total annual wage of $4,500. Until recently, they had no health benefits, but Kate, who had learned her lessons well, had waged a successful seven-year campaign to get them health coverage. I met with the grad students and urged them to organize and become a more effective force in campus negotiations. I also told them that Rutgers pays graduate student teachers about $6,000 per course. I would soon quote the $1,125 per course rate to a *New York Times* reporter who would use it in a story shortly thereafter. Back in Nebraska the Dean fired off a series of e-mails to faculty complaining about the misinformation printed in the *Times* article. "Things are a lot better than that at Nebraska. Salaries are now up to $1,170 per course." The Director of Graduate Studies had his own counter-argument: "We offer graduate students travel money to conferences." I asked him whether they could afford to eat once they get there. Meanwhile I heard of still lower salaries in Mississippi.

Wednesday afternoon I was back home, but Friday morning I was on my way to New York to present a first version of this chapter, which I had drafted on the plane from Nebraska, to a March 5–6 New York University conference on "Intellectual Activism: Coalitional Politics and the Academy." The conference included a fine Saturday afternoon open discussion about the implications of the No Sweat campaign on campuses across the country, which has been built around protests against university contracts with athletic clothing companies that exploit workers in overseas factories. The practices themselves are carefully discussed in Andrew Ross's collection *No Sweat: Fashion, Free Trade, and the Rights of Garment Workers.* Many of the student activists, we discovered, had parents who were veterans of the anti-war movement of the 1960s and 1970s. Others were first generation college students from union families. And others still, among the growing number of Latino students, understood sweat shops all too well. A number of the student leaders of the movement, notably, are graduates of the AFL/CIO union summer program. Multiple affiliations were at work again. We saw real potential to interest these students in labor exploitation on their own campuses. I suggested a poster reading "No Sweat There/No Sweat Here" above side-by-side photographs of athletic shoes and piles of composition papers. A campus living wage campaign is also a solid possibility. Such a campaign was already under way at Harvard, and a community campaign has been started in Champaign-Urbana. The Harvard campaign, of course, produced the extended sit-in in the president's office in the spring of 2001, along with a historic series of administration wage concessions.

On Sunday I headed to Syracuse, New York, first to attend a community meeting called to discuss a possible county-wide Living Wage campaign, a campaign embodying principles like those laid out in books such as Robert Pollin and Stephanie Luce's *The Living Wage: Building a Fair Economy*. It would encompass not only Syracuse University but also other large employers in the area. There was heated discussion about the potential impact on small businesses, along with details about wages in a variety of area firms. Though welcome to participate, I was really there to learn more about the issue and about how an academic institution would fit into a larger campaign about the workplace. One of the things I learned is that Syracuse University administrators—in keeping with the attitudes they revealed during the strike we discuss in chapter 9—have argued they should not have to pay a living wage in job categories where the prevailing local wage is less. Of course they *could* argue that gives them an opportunity to raise the local rate by putting pressure on other employers with their own salary structure. But the main reason for my visit was to meet repeatedly with graduate students interested in starting a unionizing campaign on campus and to give a general lecture on academic labor, meanwhile trying to recruit people to become active in MLA's Graduate Student Caucus.

Although my travel schedule is not always this heavy—this late twentieth-century version of the picaresque required taking fourteen planes over two weeks—this mixture of writing, lecturing, and activist organizing makes up a good deal of my life. I make no apologies for focusing my current efforts on the industry I know best—academia. For decades people have viewed activism on behalf of higher education as somehow illegitimate, déclassé. Exploited workers in other industries are noble figures, but university employees deserve no defense. The barons of the academy are free to grind their bones into dust. Real activism takes place outside the academy, in that place too many of us idiotically still refer to as the real world.

Of course this ideology has not served world revolution. It has rather left academic affiliation unchallenged and hidden and underwritten campus privilege. We saw that most dramatically when progressive Yale faculty with vertical and interchangeable affiliations made it clear they would only feel whole again when their striking graduate students were behind bars. At the NYU conference Stanley Aronowitz mentioned that a Yale scholar of the history of slavery turned his striking student in to the administration, but Aronowitz oddly declined to speak his name (David Brion Davis), despite its having repeatedly been cited in publications about the Yale strike. Yale postcolonialism theorist Sara Suleri turned in her student teaching assistant, then criss-crossed the country in a mink coat purchased with the profits from the Goodyear company's Asian rubber plantations; one suspects she regretted the coat was not lined with the hides of her teaching assistants. At the NYU conference, a recent Columbia University PhD rose to express his regret that three of his most well known progressive teachers—Franco Moretti, D. A. Miller, and Gayatri Spivak—had crossed Fall 1998 picket lines during the Local 2110 support staff strike. Again, unexamined affiliation rules their lives.

We are not demanding that any of these purportedly leftist academics become activists in the campus labor movement. For one thing academia is not the only site worthy of intervention. One of our colleagues does his activist work in Indonesia, taking on a good deal more risk than we do. But it is time to demand that academics on the left endorse efforts to transform their own industry. Their campus praxis must match the ideological investments of their scholarship. Affiliation must be reflexive and self-critical.

Nearly forty years ago, when I joined the fledgling anti-war movement, heading off with a dozen other college students to interrupt a speech by U.S. President Lyndon Johnson—we delayed the speech until we were wrestled to the ground by Secret Service agents—it seemed corporations could be cast out of the academy. We could put our bodies between Dow Chemical and the campus and retain the campus as another place, a place of difference, a place of idealized affiliation where the manufacturers of napalm were not welcome. Its compromised integrity would at least be critical and self-reflective. Now American campuses are in the process of courting Dow Chemical's business.

Thirty years of benighted, high-minded leftist contempt for their own workplace have helped leave academia vulnerable to all the ravages of corporatization. But it can be changed. Join us. Start small. Like all things, one action leads to another. Activist affiliation opens opportunities for yet more activism. Your colleagues, of course, may not approve. Michael Denning's colleagues at Yale thought he had lost his way when he stood with the Graduate Employees and Student Organization (GESO), for the duration. Two articulate graduate student activists whose ideas may better the lives of thousands of people, Mark Kelley and Bill Pannapacker, have been urged to curtail their activism by some of their faculty colleagues, fearful that the profession may cast them out in recompense for their more selfless version of affiliation. Except for Michael Bérubé (at Illinois until 2001) and a few assistant professors, many of my department colleagues view my national activism and my multiple affiliations as some sort of inexplicable obsession. What about my scholarship? What about real research (read lit. crit.), not the hundreds of interviews conducted in the course of writing *Manifesto of a Tenured Radical* and *Aca-*

demic Keywords? Of course I continue to do research in both modern poetry and the Spanish Civil War, just as Denning does in 1930s culture and Watt does in Irish literature, just as GSC activists continue to work on their dissertations, but the real world of the campus seems to require more.

Historically and in the present, writing has been and is a sufficient form of activism. But in today's academy activist writing is inevitably tested by workplace practice. If the two are in conflict, their inherent values in contradiction, then progressive scholarship and the core of a professorial affiliation become a sham. It is not simply that careerist affiliation is sometimes mistaken for intellectual devotion, or that the lines between the two have become increasingly blurred, though that is also true, but these impulses have been intertwined throughout history. What *is* new is the dynamic relationship with an audience dependent on imitatable models of careerist spirituality. We pledge love and devotion in exchange for discourses we can emulate to win jobs and tenure. Yet it is now time we stop honoring faux activists who refuse to condemn the exploitation of their lower-paid colleagues. There are now a series of movements and organizations with versions of affiliation that give all of us alternatives.

Yet work within such organizations, it must be emphasized, is neither easy nor guaranteed of good results. Nonprofit member-based organizations like the AAUP and the MLA purportedly exist to serve their members' interests. Yet the staffs tend largely to run the show. There is a tendency for a staff culture partly contemptuous of members to develop over time, and certainly members will often enough act foolishly and reinforce this bias. Affiliated members who seek to move such organizations in a particular direction are inherently at a disadvantage. The staff has a sense of organizational history and a detailed knowledge of the budget; members' new initiatives will often be declared financially impossible or legally dangerous. Short of embarking on full scale research projects it is difficult to prove the staff wrong.

Nonetheless, there are differences of both degree and kind in how such organizations function. Both the AAUP and the MLA have executive directors (the AAUP titles the office General Secretary) and an Executive Council or Committee of elected members. At the MLA, lawyers' advice is always delivered to the Council in a letter following negotiations with the Executive Director. MLA Council members never see or talk to a lawyer; there is no opportunity to dispute a lawyer's opinion and no way to prove what is often enough obviously the case, that the MLA's lawyers say what the Executive Director wants them to say. At the AAUP the lawyers meet with both the Executive Committee and the larger National Council. There is plenty of time for discussion and for differences of opinion to be aired. The result is more democratic decision-making, whereas at the MLA the lawyers have too often simply been weapons for the former Executive Director to use to impose her ideology on the organization as a whole. The AAUP lawyers are on the staff, but the MLA could still bring in its consultant lawyers for discussions.

That is not to say that the AAUP is by any means fully democratic or that it makes full use of its national officers. Most program initiatives still come from the staff, and some absolutely basic policy issues are debated and formulated with excessive secrecy. In order to assure maximum feedback on the "Graduate Student Bill of Rights," I circulated it to hundreds of people around the country. The aim was not only to produce the best text possible, but also to give the relevant constituency a role in the drafting of the document, to empower graduate students especially to feel it was at least partly *their* document, not just the AAUP's. As a result we received several dozen informative and thoughtful letters that were a real help in refining the statement. But some members of Committee A and some members of the national staff were incensed that I had released a draft, a document not fully vetted and approved.

Over the past several years a major debate has raged in the national office and among members of Committee A over whether the organization should, for example, pursue academic freedom cases involving graduate students and part-time faculty. I am among those who think it is imperative that we do so; moreover, we should publicize our interest so that people know they can refer appropriate cases to the Washington office. This issue obviously implicates the AAUP's mission and reason for existence in fundamental ways. Yet the discussion has remained largely internal to Committee A and the national staff. Even at Executive Committee and National Council sessions references to this debate—and its attendant power struggles—were uninformative and oblique until 2001. It is instead probably an issue the membership as a whole should discuss. Indeed they might feel more involved in and committed to the organization as a result.

The MLA's Executive Council is consistently far more passive than the AAUP's, which is actively involved in initiating proposals. Kirsten Christensen and I mostly found we were the only MLA Executive Council members with any agenda at all, with any program to put forward. The others regularly complained about how many GSC proposals were on the table but had no suggestions to offer of their own. The GSC representatives were not, to be sure, the only council members well informed about the state of the profession, but those best characterized as simultaneously professionally accomplished and politically clueless were always in the majority. We were in a long-running movie whose theme song might have been "Something is happening, but you don't know what it is. Do you, Mr. Chips?" The only time they all became energized was at the annual opportunity to appoint friends and colleagues to committees. In the Spring of 2001 the AAUP Executive Committee discussed strategies for dealing with the Supreme Court's "Yeshiva Decision" that overturned faculty bargaining rights at private universities. The MLA's Executive Council debated appointments to the Shakespeare Variorum Committee. In the Spring of 2002 the AAUP Executive Committee discussed the potential impact of September 11 on higher education. The MLA Executive Council debated appointments to the Shakespeare Variorum Committee.

Yet even ceremonial duties were often undermined by the Clueless Cadre, especially if they happened to intersect with a Kirsten or Cary suggestion. Toward the end of my tenure, when Phyllis Franklin was about to retire, several council members proposed a Distinguished Service to the Humanities Award in her honor. Thinking thereby to make the award more significant, they argued it should be given only once every three years. I countered that such awards were best offered annually. That way people were more likely to get in the habit of making nominations, plus the organization could respond to and recognize extraordinary service in real time, not when events had faded in memory. It was often easier to get publicity for annual awards as well; reporters could get in the habit of covering them. Since the suggestion came from me, it was immediately and vociferously attacked by several people. Eventually, a compromise—every other year—was adopted.

One indication of the psychology of some MLA Executive Council members is suggested by my favorite debate of my four-year term. An especially distinguished scholar had agreed to run and been elected but soon reported that Council e-mails were proving exceedingly invasive and disruptive. Mind you, we are typically talking about one or two e-mails a month, the lowest level of dialogue of any Executive Committee I know. Perhaps once a year there is a three day flurry of e-mails about a pressing issue. Other than that, you could easily forget you are on the council. Nonetheless, this scholar went on at length describing how painful it was to have a day of writing interrupted by a quite unexpected e-mail. We asked whether it was possible to take this wounded soul off the list completely, but then those rare council actions between meetings would be legally prohibited. We tried reason, gently recalling the small number of MLA e-mail missiles actually exploding in our boxes. Then we suggested just not reading the e-mails, but were told that the simple knowledge that they were there was pretty much unbearable. For a moment I wondered if this was just an experiment in performativity, a little example of feigned male privilege. But after half an hour it was clear the pain was real. In the end the staff agreed to vet all e-mails and send this council member only those he or she was legally required to receive. I suppose this person had run for the office out of the conviction that lending his/her name to the organization was a great kindness. No one at the AAUP seems to think that way.

These two organizations also have very different levels of consensus about their missions. Although the AAUP represents multiple constituencies with different views of higher education—from teaching-centered colleges organized for collective bargaining to decentered research-oriented universities—there is nonetheless a nearly universal commitment among its members to the organization's role in defining and defending the basic principles of academic life. No comparable consensus exists within the MLA. The MLA's elected Delegate Assembly for a decade has proven itself a progressive group committed to activist reform. The Executive Council and the Executive Director are mostly dead set against anything of the kind. So the delegate assembly pushes and the council resists. Yet now and again a Council majority can be assembled and action taken, the part-timer salary survey being the best example.

The politics of the MLA as a whole remain uncertain. Certainly progressive resolutions are routinely approved in membership votes, but with fewer than 20 percent of the members voting one is never certain how representative their views are. Of course such votes are the only indication of members' wishes, yet both the ED and the council feel free to dismiss such views as those of a radical fringe. At a meeting of English department chairs a few years ago, the current MLA president urged them to run for the Delegate Assembly because radicals were taking it over. Another recent MLA president stormed out of a meeting at the headquarters declaring that a graduate student would serve on the Council over her dead body. Well, it came to pass, as a result of a membership vote, but I have seen no funeral notice.

It is clear that an Executive Director who serves too long can become a tyrant and largely eliminate many meaningful forms of member affiliation. After I published an essay critical of the MLA in *Social Text* in 1995, Phyllis Franklin, the MLA's ED, called up one of the editors to express reservations about the essay and left the other editor with the impression she hoped they would not publish me again. It was a questionable maneuver for a supposedly neutral Executive Director, but from her perspective, presumably, any action was justified in defending the organization. Of course *Social Text* ignored the request, if that is what it was. I saw myself as trying to reform the organization, but she no doubt saw this as a leftwing counterpart of attacks from the right during the culture wars. More recently, council members privately expressed the opinion to me that the ED had taken a dislike to a quite effective member of the MLA staff and had discriminated against him in salary decisions. The consensus was that nothing could be done until she retired. Too much power can come to reside in an administrator who holds office too long, and both member affiliation and democratic process can be eviscerated as a result.

Some long-term staff also tend to resist historical change, becoming wedded to a view of the organization's mission that no longer matches reality. Both the AAUP and the MLA have begun to reach out to graduate students and part-time faculty against the wishes of some staff members. Yet both organizations have risked becoming irrelevant by ignoring major changes in the higher education workforce. Teaching and research are inceasingly being performed by graduate students, part-time or non-tenure-track faculty, or by academic professionals. The organizations need to protect these highly vulnerable members and to represent their interests.

The reform efforts of the MLA's Graduate Student Caucus have produced a series of initiatives designed to make the job market less rapacious and to improve employment conditions throughout the profession. The survey of part-time faculty salaries, widely participated in by all but a group of ivy-league schools brim full of contempt and privilege, produced dramatic results much more quickly than we anticipated. It was published in December 2000, and within four months department members from more than a score of institutions had called the MLA to report they had used the data to win substantial increases in part-timer salaries. Thus the GSC and its allies have by now increased the salaries of many hundreds of teachers across the country. Yet the MLA's long-term Executive Director, since retired, has been hostile toward most of these efforts. For the most part the council followed her lead. It was a wrenchingly difficult experience for the GSC's first representative to the council, Kirsten Christensen, a graduate student at the time of her election, to face the relentless hostility of well-paid faculty meeting after meeting.

Overall, at the MLA and other disciplinary organizations we are left with more hole than doughnut, with a cup barely moistened let alone half full. Our belief is that disciplinary organizations need to step in and fill part of the fairness gap, particularly since many workplace abuses are discipline specific. English-style exploitation bares relatively little similarity to Chemistry-style exploitation, except in the area of benefits to contingent labor. Disciplinary organizations moreover have the most complete knowledge of the practices of their member departments. Yet such organizations, still dozing through the long sleep of tenure, have had little success becoming policemen rather than court flatterers. They like to give awards, celebrate milestones, provide modest vita-enhancing opportunities to one and all. They see themselves as devoted to helping departments, not chastising them. That, once again, was why the senior MLA staff fought so hard to prevent the GSC-sponsored salary survey from listing salaries by department. They preferred summaries by geographical area and institutional type. Something harmless, slightly informative, but designed to ruffle no one's feathers, put no one in a bad light. The senior staff was not demonic; they simply were trained and retrained to tickle department heads under the chin, not embarrass them.

If it had not been for Kirsten and me, and then a couple of other well-informed EC members who stood with us, the salary survey would have been useless. As it is, it remains a neutral project of fact-gathering, but fact-gathering with teeth, since it empowered local people to improve their lives. It is, moreover, a first step in recognizing that, for much of the academic work force, the MLA's dowager cruise ship has devolved into a mere river barge. There is no dignity to lose in turning it in a new direction—toward taking responsibility for the workplace practices of the discipline.

This is what a large portion of the tenured faculty consider a program of "politicizing" the MLA. This despite the fact that none of us fancy the MLA endorsing political candidates. We're urging responsibility for the academic policies and employment practices of the departments in which our members work. In a broad definition of politics—concern with the structures that regulate social life—sure it's political. Just as disseminating deconstruction might have been political had it been overseen by folks other than the union busting aesthetes at Yale. But in the narrow sense of politics more widely understood by the general public—and subscribed to by most of the disingenuous conservatives who want the MLA to sponsor tea parties not union rallies—professional workplace oversight is not politics.

In time both the MLA and the AAUP will be transformed by demographic facts, as long-time tenured faculty and staff retire and as graduate students from the union movement continue to move into faculty positions across the country. The nature of affiliation with these organizations—the partial identities and opportunities for action they offer their members—will change dramatically as a result. But we cannot simply wait for these changes to occur. For higher education is steadily becoming a more exploitive workplace, and affiliation needs to be reconceived now if that trend is to be resisted.

CN

8.   Is It a University or
Is It a Country Club?

Four senior citizens and a faculty member received resounding
applause Tuesday [November 30, 1999] when they pledged to be
mauled by bulldozers if the proposed golf course goes through.
    —*Indiana Daily Student*, 1 December 1999

IT WAS QUITE A SCENE. As one century was coming to a close and another
beckoned near, and on the same day as units of the National Guard were
called to Seattle to quash demonstrations over the meeting of the World
Trade Organization, a lone policeman guarded the perimeter of a crowded
meeting room in the Memorial Union on the Indiana University campus in Bloomington. He wasn't decked out in riot gear or woodland-
camouflage BDU's, just his workaday blues. No gas masks or canisters
were in evidence here, just steam wafting out of a small styrofoam coffee
cup. And, even though, as it turned out, his services were never required,
the young officer helped complete the picture. So did the appearance of
the well-dressed administrator responsible for the university's public
relations who sat demurely in a corner taking notes and pondering the
implications of this extraordinary day.

The absence of police batons and tear gas, however, did little to
diminish the feeling that, for the five hours the students, faculty, and
members of the Bloomington community met with a sub-committee
from the University's Board of Trustees, this little corner of the world
had been transported back in time to the 1960s. The later 60s, to be
more precise. Back to a time of activism and campus unrest; of public
speeches, bullhorns and noisy crowds; of occasions for principled—and,
at times, unprincipled—civil disobedience; of moments where campus

117

and community alike were galvanized by such issues as Dow Chemical's recruitment of new scientists in student unions and university quadrangles doubling as parade grounds for ROTC drill teams. Placards expressing dissent or identifying local environmental or student groups were everywhere evident in the room, and petitions with the names of over 2,100 students decorated the walls. Undergraduates in tee-shirts and baggy jeans approached the microphone to address the four gentlemen in the front, impeccably attired in dark suits, playing their parts with stony implacability. Save for a pierced nasal septum here, a Sony Walkman and headphones there—new styles from today's subcultures and new technologies unavailable thirty years ago—this might have been 1969. Most of the crowd of nearly 200 were there to protest, resolved to sit or stand right where they were until afforded the opportunity to speak. Some grew irritable, exasperated by the gerrymandered rules of procedure which allowed a handful of the project's supporters to speak before protestors who had waited hours could be heard. I remembered a peaceful sit-in on campus in 1969 that started in much the same way.

But it was also different, however familiar the issues; different, however familiar the intensity of faces now ploughed by furrows sixty, seventy, even eighty years in the making. Undergraduates and retirees alike poured into this space not to protest a war halfway around the world, although the Bush White House has brought the peace marchers back to the streets, but to condemn the arrogance, elitism, and environmental irresponsibility of the increasingly corporatized university in the center of their town. This was the same university many of them had attended or once worked for; the one from which they were graduated fifty years ago or planned to graduate from in the spring; the one they encouraged their children to attend twenty-five years ago or hoped their grandchildren might attend one day. This was the university that, in fact, many of them loved and had built their lives and future aspirations around. This was the college town community to which newcomers in the crowd had moved and established homes: for some, the last move of their lives to enjoy their retirements; for others, the first move away from their parents to begin their lives as adults. This was the university that had totally, perhaps irrevocably, disheartened all of them, young and old alike.

As the throng assembled, the young Vice-President for Public Relations sitting inconspicuously in the corner jotted something on his notepad.

Note: This might slow things down a little.
Nahh–full speed ahead. We can get around this.
There's a lot of people here, though.
Question for next meeting: How do we quash these tree-huggers without appearing insensitive?

Joining this mélange of senior citizens and undergraduates, some of whom actually looked like hippies or, rather, a more chic *fin de millennium* version of hippies, were many of the over 300 IU faculty who had signed a letter opposing the project, their presence adding a smattering of salt and pepper and the texture of Harris tweed to the assemblage. (A week after the meeting, 300 signatures would grow to over 500, over one-third of the professoriate on campus.) A woman who must have been eighty years old initiated what would become a formidable procession of speakers from the audience, denouncing the *raison d'être* of the meeting as ridiculous. Surely, she mused, the university had more weighty intellectual matters to consider, and she admonished them with Fabian's aside from Shakespeare's *Twelfth Night*: "If this were played upon a stage now/I could condemn it as an improbable fiction" (3.4.119–20). Moments later, an agitated, less literary-minded opponent of the plan emerged from the back of the crowd, his snow-white beard sprawling over his considerable girth. He wasn't there to spread season's greetings. "I've taken a day off work," he bellowed from the corner. "I'm not budging till I'm heard."

It seemed certain he was going to add a snarling "God dammit!," but he didn't. His beard quivered from the self-restraint that small measure of civility required. Yet, save for an occasional hiss or boo later, the entire proceeding was polite, perhaps too polite. In the coming weeks, it would not remain so.

A middle-aged truck driver in a plaid lumberjack shirt, putter in hand, stepped up the heat, sternly warning the Trustees that trouble loomed if the Board elected to ignore the concerns of the community. An avid golfer, hence the brandished golf club, he nonetheless made his concern for the environment and his opposition to the university's plan apparent. A retired librarian vowed a more immediate economic reprisal: "If this plan even gets started," he said, "I will cease any monetary support of IU from $2 popcorn to season opera tickets." Near the end of the meeting others promised more significant acts of economic retaliation, like having their wills re-written to insure that the university would no longer be the recipient of their generosity. Maybe their money should go to support worthier causes, one of them suggested. Many in the crowd nodded in assent.

Faculty, concerned grandmothers, tattooed undergraduates, and environmentalists all stalked a microphone at the front of the room to speak their minds. A graduate student researching waterfowl tried to outline for the Board the likely consequences for several rare and endangered species if, as proposed, between 150 and 200 acres of their habitat are damaged by the development. The Trustees seemed to follow his argument, though it was impossible to infer understanding or sympathy from their mien. Taking a broader environmental perspective, a professor of biology rolled her wheelchair forward to emphasize the ecological importance of the forest and watershed endangered by this project. She outlined the fragility of the ecosystem, and reported that many of her colleagues took classes there to study and observe. Then, she challenged the Trustees to do the "brave" thing: to "have the guts to let Nature win this round."

The room erupted in applause that didn't seem to want to end. I felt honored to have been there, on that morning, to hear her speak and simply be in her presence. And in the presence of my friends, students, and colleagues who had made this issue such a *priority*—and who spoke with such passion and conviction, as I attempted to do some four hours later.

The occasion for this uncommon gathering, for this display of solidarity and community, was the announcement of an imminent trustee vote—to be cast exactly two days after the public meeting—on the latest brainchild of the university's administration and one of its harem of corporate paramours: a new golf course. That's how the project was characterized in headlines in local papers: just a golf course of championship quality, a badly needed one at that. A boon for duffers and pros alike.

But it was and is much more than that. It constituted prima facie evidence both of the university's disregard for its mission as an educational institution and its indifference to the public that supports it and its own faculty. It revealed insidious alliances within a large public university that, in the aftermath of the project's resolution, raised serious questions about the ethics of high-ranking administrators; about the relationship between business interests, alumni, the athletic program, and a few select academic units; and about a university project conceived largely without faculty input save for that of interested parties within the School of Business. Insofar as the project was contemplated within a pitching wedge shot of an internationally-recognized School of Public and Environmental Affairs and given the fact that none of the faculty of that School—or of any other academic department—were consulted about its ecological and other consequences, the project also speaks volumes about the governance of the university. In an editorial published the morning of the meeting, Michael Hamburger, Associate Professor of Geological Sciences and throughout a model of productive campus activism, asked the obvious question: "Why is it that this plan was undertaken with virtually no involvement of IU geologists, biologists, and environmental scientists with expertise in the areas of soil erosion, groundwater contamination, ecology, liminology, and wildlife biology?" (*The Herald-Times* [Bloomington, Indiana], November 30, 1999). Finally, this ill-conceived debacle provides an object lesson about the manipulation of language at the corporate university and the continuing need to interrogate every turn of phrase freshly minted in administrative offices. Perhaps this is the direction this narrative ought to go: toward an idea and the name that expresses it. I'd put it in the form of a question. Is the university an educational institution or is it a country club? More important, in the twenty-first century, can a public research university be the former without becoming the latter? Increasingly, not just in the Midwest but across the across the country, university administrators seem convinced that the answer is "no."

*****

Rumors abounded. Cyberspace in particular was made for such speculation, and conspiracy theorists in the Bloomington area grudgingly set aside their ongoing studies of the Kennedy assassination and Oliver Stone films to collect grist for their mills. Some ten months later, the firing of "legendary" basketball coach Bob Knight supplied many of the same folks with yet another obsession. But this story begins nearly a year before the General made his clamorous exodus from the Bloomington campus or, rather, its dénouement did. It still isn't entirely clear when the project really began.

Some believe the idea was promoted by a member of the Board of Trustees in the mid-1990s and presented to the then new, presumably amenable president of the university, although this genealogy can never really be confirmed. In a flurry of allegations and counter-attacks reported in local media, Clarence Doninger—then the Director of Athletics and later, it was revealed, Bob Knight's plucky nemesis—claimed to have first heard of the plan from unspecified administrators and "several people" who met to hear Mark Hesemann, head of the development group Indiana Club LLC. Hesemann, who received his MBA from the IU School of Business, now the Kelley School of Business, sits with Doninger on the senior advisory committee of the MBA Sports and Entertainment Academy within the Kelley School ("IU Officials Deny Group's Allegations," *The Herald Times*, February 26, 2000). Others know only that during the months preceding the public meeting with the Trustees on November 30, 1999, three businessmen formed a corporation—Indiana Club LLC—and joined forces with University Clubs of America. The murkiness of the pre-history of the "golf course" project starts right here. A Vice-President of the university stated publically that the university and Indiana LLC entered into negotiations in May of 1999, while documents in the Secretary of State's Office confirmed that the corporation was legally formed in late October, 1999. How could negotiations begin with a corporate entity that did not exist? And still more intriguing: the same documents listed the company's registered agent as a partner in the same firm in which Indiana University's Director of Athletics—again, Clarence Doninger—once practiced. Web chat rooms were abuzz with this apparent conflict of interest, although members of the Board of Trustees professed to know nothing about it when confronted at the meeting with the allegation of this particular–and significant—impropriety.

Whatever the precise timetable and however suspect the sub rosa negotiations, Indiana Club LLC secured an agreement with a company headed by professional golfer Jack Nicklaus to design a championship course on land owned by the university. After all, University Clubs of America, as one of its executives explained, had built similar facilities at Auburn University and at the Universities of Tennessee, South Carolina, Louisville, and Kentucky. Between 150 and 200 acres of the Lake Griffy Woods, land owned by the university just north of campus, would serve such a purpose beautifully, with the result that the environment might even be improved—or so he boasted. Indiana Club LLC would lease the property for a period of sixty-five years at a cost of approximately $1.2 million; these new partners of the university would invest between $12 and $18 million in the enterprise, although these figures were never discussed at the meeting. A decidedly less promising picture of the financial implications of the deal for the university—not for its corporate partners and certain well-connected administrators—would emerge later.

> *Glad he didn't mention the cost of this thing. Wouldn't want to give the impression that big money was behind all of this. Would be a little more difficult to spin these numbers the right way. SSShh!*

In addition to proceeds from the lease and the benefits of having such a course, the university would also derive additional revenues from greens fees and so on. The possibility that the university might just as easily incur any losses was never entertained; or, if it was, it was never mentioned in public. A privately-financed indoor tennis pavilion built some years earlier on campus had foundered, and the university eventually took it over. "Mightn't the same thing happen again?" a friend sitting next to me whispered. "Couldn't the same thing happen with this facility?"

And just what kind of "facility" are we talking about? One with not only a world-class golf course, but also with a swimming pool, tennis courts, clubhouse, 27-unit lodge and conference center, practice range, and so on. Individual memberships, which would be limited to 2,400, would range in cost from an initial fee of $10,000 plus $2,000/month clubhouse charges ("Founding Membership") to $6,000 plus $200/month for local residents. Faculty/Staff could be admitted to the club for $3,000 plus $150/month, with "Junior Varsity" memberships selling for $3,500 plus $150/month. Students would pay even less. Business memberships would sell at $20,000 plus $2,500/month (i.e., $50,000 the first year, $30,000/year after that). The club's fee structure, quite reasonable when compared to the much stiffer charges associated with more prestigious courses in Indianapolis, an Indiana Club executive assured the audience, would generate profit for the university, provide an enviable home for the men's and women's varsity golf teams, and still attract a "broad-based membership." The cost to the environment? None.

Such were the principal benefits supporters of the project, in the distinct minority in the room, outlined for the Trustees. Of course, there were other advantages too. The coach of the golf team complained that the present university golf course is both overplayed and under-designed. While it attracted far too many golfers, it failed to match the tournament-quality facilities of other Big Ten Schools. A Nicklaus course would solve the problem. The Director of Bloomington's Tourism and Visitors Bureau presented polling data which confirmed that a paltry six percent of visitors to Bloomington viewed it as a desirable "golf location." A new course at the university might improve those numbers, though later a faculty member in opposition to the project would use the notion of teaching at a "golf location" to great ironic effect. A subdivision and mall developer came to praise the university's willingness to do business and help oversee the project "every step of the way." Several businessmen and a realtor emphasized the course's potential benefits to the local economy. And the only student to speak in favor of the project, a member of the golf team, left nary an eye dry in the room after delivering his poignant oration. For it seems that, when his friends from other schools visited him, he was "really embarrassed" to show them the present university golf course. That just wouldn't do—can't have an undergraduate too embarrassed to show the golf course to his buddies.

Not surprisingly, another of the more enthusiastic proponents of the project was the Director of the Alumni Association, whose principal argument was echoed by an executive from University Clubs of America: the goal of the project is "to bring more alumni back to campus for social interaction" ("Critics Voice Concern Over Golf Course," *Indiana Daily Student*, December 1, 1999). This desideratum flew in the face of a recent survey of alumni cited by a bright undergraduate which showed that only one percent of the respondents had any interest in playing golf when returning to campus. No matter. This golf course was entirely consistent with the "goal" of the university to "provide a quality service." To whom, I wondered? "Provide a quality service" to whom? He never said, but it seemed clear he wasn't talking about students or the people of Indiana who help support the university. And he wasn't referring to the over 400,000 living alumni of the university. He wasn't even thinking about one percent of that number. He apparently had a much smaller number in mind: 2,400, to be precise—the maximum number of memberships to be offered by Indiana Club LLC.

Another rationale existed for the building of this country club, one evident in university construction projects and marketing schemes across the country. It is, finally, a rationale directly related to the undergraduate golfer's embarrassment when giving his out-of-town friends the Grand Tour of campus: namely, the premise that today's college or university must provide "state of the art" exercise and athletic facilities, shopping mall-style food courts, and other entertainments if it is to attract students, especially well-heeled undergraduates accustomed to such amenities who will pay most or all of their tuition. The University of Virginia, for example, recently invested $18.5 million in a fitness and aquatic center, complete with new Stairmasters, weight machines, and a swimming pool with a mega-screen projection system that allows students to watch movies while bobbing in inner tubes. As Mark Edmundson describes it in a withering critique of the consumerist ethos among the undergraduates he teaches at UVA, the campus "is looking more and more like a retirement spread for the young." Why? Because schools "want kids whose parents can pay the full freight, not the ones who need scholarships. . . . If the marketing surveys say that the kids require sports centers, then, trustees willing, they shall have them" (Edmunson, 1997, 43). Such an ethos contributes to at least two other unfortunate phenomena in Charlottesville, according to Edmundson: first, the "contemporary university's relationship with students" from the start takes on a "solicitous, nearly servile tone"; and, second, this solicitousness too often pervades the classroom, reducing a liberal education—Shakespeare, Joyce, and Chaucer—into a mere diversion or "lite entertainment" for many of today's students. Or, rather, that particular perversion of the liberal education is required if faculty are to receive passable scores on student evaluations, a topic too vexed to be considered here. But Edmundson's identification of a tone of servility is doubtless correct, and it appears to be getting more abject and disturbing. Only recently have I received e-mails from students in the first week of classes asking for a syllabus attached electronically for their review. The fact that they have missed the first week of class, which I always remind them, generally escapes them as they conduct comparative shopping exercises before "buying" a class.

Such transformations of both campus landscapes and student-faculty relationships aren't unique to major public universities like Indiana and Virginia. The trickle-down effect, however dubious when privileged in Ronald Reagan's economic theory, is everywhere in evidence on college campuses. In 1999, Occidental College in Los Angeles leveled an historic building and invested $14.5 million to create "The Servery," complete with an on-premises bakery, sushi bar, and an electronic sign "á la Disneyland [that] counts down the minutes until a customer's food is ready" ("Universities Going Upscale," *Indianapolis Star*, 5 December 1999). Convinced that it has lost students in the past due to outdated recreational facilities, Trinity College in Washington, D.C. hopes to raise $15 million to construct the first new building on its campus in nearly four decades: a sports and swimming complex. Community Colleges have followed this lead, as reported in *The Chronicle of Higher Education* (November 12, 1999). Collin County Community College in Plano, Texas, for example, has constructed new dormitory complexes complete with swimming pool, whirlpool units, satellite television hookups with 300 channels, and other amenities. Such facilities, the *Chronicle* reported, are especially critical factors in the recruitment of international students and athletes, one of whom gushed, "We've got it all right here—barbecue grills, the pool, everything. This is better than what they get at big-time schools."

In other words, universities seem convinced that they are engaged in a marketing war in they must package themselves as sites of what might be termed "first-class fun." If you work for a college or university and you doubt this assertion, take the following test: How many of the last five building projects on your campus were undertaken either to enhance the research capability of the faculty or to improve classroom space? The odds are, only a small percentage. At Indiana, for example, the building of a new University theater and Black Cultural Center and an expansion of the Kelley School of Business completed in 2002 provide some measure of reassurance that consumerism hasn't taken total control of IU's agenda. A custom-designed golf course, however, would also follow closely on the heels of the campus's new recreation and swimming complex (no mega-screen allowing film-viewing from the pool as at UVA, sorry), the construction of a new alumni association building across from the football stadium, a recently built office complex which is also home to IU Outfitters (purveyors of logo gifts and sportswear), the expansion of the University foundation (next to the golf course), the remodeling of dormitory rooms into more comfortable suites, and the emergence of food courts all over campus featuring well-known national chains (at the expense, in one case, of a restaurant in the union many faculty and staff supported). Today's students or "consumers," as IU president Myles Brand consistently termed them before leaving Indiana in 2003 to become head of the NCAA, demand such amenities.

Or do they? Without launching into an implausible defense of such delicacies as cafeteria "mystery meat" or green beans adrift in oily water—standard bill of fare in late 1960s' dormitory cafeterias—one wonders about this perceived marketing war. Does a public research institution really have to wage it? Do large numbers of prospective freshmen choose, say, Indiana University over the University of Iowa on the basis of their sushi bars or swimming pools? How many students select the University of Michigan over Northwestern or Wisconsin based on the design of the golf course, the number of tennis courts, or the presence of Starbucks coffee shops on campus (available at the student union of the University of Missouri-Columbia and in the center of the Ball State campus, for example, but a disconcerting distance of some ten steps across the street from the Bloomington campus). Do education, curricula, and the quality of faculty really count for so little?

> *The university of the twenty-first century: a country club and food court for students, first and foremost; a posh venue to entertain alumni second, with semi- professional sports to watch and lots of really cool places to play. Hmm.*

> *Weekend casino junkets after the big game? Hell, casinos on campus! Why not? Why should Harrah's and Caesar's get all that action?*

> *Note for next meeting: Tie in the Psych department's research on addiction and compulsive behaviors in advertising campaign.*

> *It's a win-win deal!*

All in all, more than a dozen people spoke in favor of proposed development. None had any formal relationship with the school save for the developer (part of the academic community by virtue of his business partnership with the university), the golf coach, his player, and a befuddled professor of business who saw nothing wrong with the plan. The greens for the course would be strategically separated from the trails he hiked on occasion and, living nearby, he and his family could jog on the course, if they wanted to, and maybe even fly kites in the spring. He was for the golf course, in short; it would be a fine facility.

"Golf course" and "facility," however, as I have suggested, hardly capture the scope of this project. When Mark Hesemann assured the Trustees that membership in the club would be "broad based" with students, staff, and faculty "welcome," he neglected to explain that his definition of "broad-based membership" extended no further than 2,400 plus the university golf teams. Hesseman's disingenuousness, Hamlet might say, showed him to be more "pigeon-livered" than "muddy mettled"; that is to say, he lacked Prospero's courage to claim the corporate university's version of the Caliban he wanted to create. What do you call a place with tennis courts, swimming pools, a championship golf course, and other amenities that is priced strategically above the means of most people? A country club, that's what you call it. That's what the public research university at which I had taught for sixteen years wanted to build on its campus. And it didn't want its faculty to foul things up or ask too many questions.

*****

The meeting on November 30 led to a variety of results, the most immediate of which was the Board of Trustees' decision not to rule on the proposal until various studies could be conducted, and it appointed a sub-committee to spearhead this effort. The full Board would reconvene in late January, 2000, to reconsider the proposal and results of the new studies. However, as J. Terry Clapacs, Indiana University Vice-President for Administration and new Atheletic Director, insisted, any new research into the ramifications of the project need not delay negotiations with the university's corporate partners. Full speed ahead.

Not surprisingly, local and campus papers—and those in Indianapolis as well—printed letters and editorials dissecting the matter, most of them critical of it. But not all. One of my favorite letters in support of the country club was sent to the *Indiana Daily Student* from an IU senior and golf enthusiast, who pleaded with the Trustees to consider facts, not "hot air" from ignorant English professors like me. The (il)logic of his position led him to the following tortured analogy: "English department faculty signing a petition to stop this 'injustice' when they can't tell the difference between rock and soil is about as coherent as a geologist who can't tell the difference between Shakespeare and John Grisham" (December 6, 1999, p. 7, col. 5). Come again? A PhD in one discipline permanently disqualifies one from having an informed opinion about anything else—or, rather, hobbles one so irreparably that s/he isn't capable of forming a defensible position on matters not specifically circumscribed by disciplinary boundaries? Most of us know enough about dirt to realize it isn't nearly hard or dense enough to beat any sense out of this argument—you'd need a boulder to do the job properly.

This letter was followed by one from a fifth-year graduate student in biochemistry who was quite understandably sickened by another of my observations: namely, that after a department like English loses nearly a dozen tenured or tenure-track faculty to outside offers in just a few years—and after other departments like economics and chemistry incur similar losses of key faculty—the Trustees had better things to worry about. Too many of the professors with whom this graduate student had worked had also taken positions elsewhere, and he couldn't understand why this problem didn't take precedence over the building of a country club. Neither could *The Indianapolis Star*, which in an editorial reminded the Trustees that their decision should be based on "academic appropriateness." The *Star's* editorialist paraphrased Professor Hamburger's question: "Is there a better use for . . . this 'extraordinary piece of land,' a living laboratory for the study of the natural environment" (December 2, 1999)? And this question prompts another: If the land weren't already quite clearly valuable for precisely this reason, why have IU faculty and researchers used it for so many years?

If the bulldozers leveled significant portions of the Griffy Woods to make way for groomed fairways and manicured greens—assuming they could get past those determined, hell bent for leather retirees—then IU would have succeeded in dissecting what is, at present, the largest block of contiguous forest in Monroe County, Indiana. The Protect Griffy Alliance (PGA—get the joke?), a grassroots organization formed in the crucible of this dispute, is perhaps most responsible for informing the public about this fragile ecosystem. Among the relevant environmental factors potentially affected by the building of this country club, the PGA contended, are the safety of 133 species of birds who make the woods their habitat (including the Cerulean Warbler, a species of "special management" concern); the potability of the water in the lake, which serves as Bloomington's emergency drinking water supply; the integrity of the ravines and slopes surrounding the lake and the potential for significant sedimentation damage; the precarious existence of plants and flowers indigenous to the area; and so on.

Keith Clay, professor of biology and a well-published plant ecologist, illuminated the more subtle environmental and educational issues involved. The area provides habitat for both highly diverse and rare species of orchids, ginseng, goldenseal, and other plants in part because of its structures of finger ridges and steep ravines, in part because of the terrain's mixture of sandstone and limestone. And while some of Clay's colleagues, ornithologists whose research has been disrupted in the past by university development, have sworn never again to be so dependent on university-owned land—"Are you kidding? The university is the last place in the world to conduct research," they advised—Clay and his graduate students have used the land in their research for the past decade or more. In 1999, five of his seven doctoral students were collecting data in the Griffy Woods, and over the past five years the dissertation research of at least fifteen graduate students has been conducted there. These are significant ecological and educational issues, not to be dismissed lightly.

But, of course, in the wake of the meeting, they *were* dismissed lightly and immediately, both by proponents of the plan and by a vocal member of the Board of Trustees (in this instance, one and the same thing). After assuring readers that neither he nor the Board would ever "do anything" to "impair in any way the environment we have out there," this trustee went on to explain that golf courses are located in "environmentally fragile areas all over the country." One of these already existed by nearby Lake Monroe, he observed, the main water supply for Bloomington. So, there was nothing much to worry about–that was the thesis. Golf course are always built around water and forests are often toppled. That's just the way it goes. He did take Professors Clay and Hamburger's point seriously, however, about the course affecting both the teaching and research of IU faculty. Speaking for the Board, he vowed to seek an "accommodation" with faculty on this point, while at the same time asserting that the project will finally serve the "best interests of all concerned." Professors Clay, Hamburger, and the over thirty members of the Biology department signing a petition against the country club were dubious that such an "accommodation" was possible.

Not surprisingly, the Trustee dismissed any criticism of the project, including mine, on ethical or more philosophical grounds. "I look at it no differently really than the private-public partnerships the university is engaged in and that other universities are engaging in all over the country," he maintained. Like the unfortunate reality that other golf courses are developed on environmentally sensitive sites, the fact that other universities—which ones appeared not to concern him—have constructed such clubs is sufficient in and of itself to refute all objections. Universities forge contracts with companies all the time; a handful of other schools regard the building of country clubs on campus as acceptable. This criticism, or "ethical and elitist concern" as he termed it, is thus totally misplaced. It need not be countenanced any further.

Let's ask the obvious questions anyway: Are many universities allowing the property entrusted to them, property utilized by faculty and students for teaching and research purposes, to be developed by private corporations for the reasons outlined here? Is the university in the business of devastating the environment, or does it function as a steward of the land it occupies and owns? Is the building of a country club, the price structure of which is designed to exclude almost all students, faculty, and staff, not to mention taxpayers of the state, consistent with the mission of a public university? Are these the ethical principles of a "great" institution? What distinguishes these principles from those of any corporation or business?

To take such questions in a broader direction, the direction of the multinational corporations and agrobusinesses that, increasingly, forge partnerships with universities, how different are the prime movers of this university project from the movers and shakers that comprise the World Trade Organization, whose meetings protestors in Seattle picketed and disrupted at the same time this local controversy erupted? Knight-Ridder Newspapers' commentator Michael Zielenziger launched an analysis of the Seattle meetings with a question that, redacted only slightly, seems equally apposite to the very idea of building a country club on land which many of us believe the university should be resolved to protect: "Is the World Trade Organization little more than a selfish cabal of economic haves plotting to gain riches by exploiting their poor and powerless brethren?" ("Equality Is Behind the Battle in Seattle," *Indianapolis Star*, December 5, 1999). Substitute university for WTO and the environment or—most precious of all—its own mission and institutional soul for "poor and powerless brethren"; the resulting question pretty much sums up the stakes of this issue.

I've always thought universities should be—and **were**—better. Maybe they aren't. But on that one day in November when students, faculty, and the community joined forces to protest this country club, this university **was** better.

As events unfolded in the eighteen months following this event, the university again proved itself to be better—much better. Yet, regrettably, along the way to this happy conclusion, it was also revealed that several administrators at the highest levels of the university had acted every bit as amorally, even corruptly, as the multinational cabals of "economic haves" meeting in Seattle to expand their influence and prerogatives.

*****

On January 17, 2000, four days before the Board of Trustees was scheduled to meet and decide the matter, Trustees president John Walda announced that Indiana University would cancel all further negotiations with Indiana Club LLC. The plan to build the country club was abandoned.

The Board didn't reach this conclusion quickly or easily. It needed a little push. After the November 30 meeting, the Bloomington and IU communities—now, speaking with one voice—sprang into action.

Throughout December and early January, a group of IU faculty lobbied the Board, asking for, among other things, formal studies of both the environmental and academic impacts of the proposed golf course. The faculty group also called for a complete examination of the economic viability of the project and held meetings assigning group members specific tasks. In addition to letter-writing campaigns, guest editorials, poster designing, and teach-ins, the Protect Griffy Alliance (PGA) mentioned above sponsored a widely publicized benefit concert at a downtown theater. On Sunday, January 16, 2000, musicians and singers performed to a wildy supportive and packed house of over 700. Writers read from their works; geologists and biologists outlined the ecological stakes of the battle; computer nerds manned terminals in the lobby so audience members could e-mail Trustees and the university president; bakers donated a wide variety of pastries and other delicacies. Parents and grandparents brought their children or grandchildren to hear the music and learn more about the ecosystem in which they existed. Public Access Television taped the program and replayed it for weeks. The next day, the country club was history.

There were reports, regrettably, that this highly effective activism, this instructive melding of what are locally known as representatives of the "town" and the "gown," at times included incidents that most theatregoers that night would not have endorsed: vandalism, the painting of slogans on sidewalks and walls, the smashing of windows, and, worst of all, the issuing of death threats to an administrator who was one of the project's most ardent champions. But these were isolated events. In explaining the Trustees' decision, John Walda underscored the Board's principal concern: "Facts are facts . . . and there were a large number of faculty members who thought that [the building of the country club] was not consistent with using a University asset like the land in question. I don't necessarily agree with that, but the fact is, that was a deep-seated concern" ("Golf Course Canceled," *Indiana Daily Student*, January 18, 2000). He went on to echo the sentiment expressed by so many faculty at that November meeting: the Board was troubled by "how the project would conflict with the mission of a public university."

Opponents of the golf course were jubilant, and the Board's announcement of its demise turned a candle-light vigil into an impromptu victory celebration. But a number of opponents of the plan were far from satisfied and wanted more than this simple victory. They wanted to know how it could have gone so far in the first place. And we want to use what they learned as a kind of primer from which broader lessons might be derived. They include the following.

1. Faculty, Student, and Community Activists Must Work To-gether. In a scathing article written just a few days after the Trustees' announcement, Steven Higgs in *The Bloomington Independent* lamented that even though the Board of Trustees "made the right decision, they really don't get it." Higgs was particularly bothered that "nowhere" in the Board's "six-paragraph statement do the words 'students' or 'Bloomington community' appear" ("IU Trustees Cave, Remain Clueless," January 20, 2000). Higgs was probably right when he claimed that "had IU faculty members been mum on the subject, the trustees would have brushed aside the same objections raised by students and the community." But there is little question that the combined voices and talents of faculty, students, and townspeople exerted a powerful effect on the outcome of this project. The labor strike at Syracuse University discussed in the next chapter provides the same lesson: faculty, however much they might enjoy the rarified air of the campus, exist in a larger community to which they are responsible. So does the university. That larger community, in this instance, forced the university to remember its public trust and live up to its ideals.

2. The Need to Follow Through: Investigate the "Sweetheart Deal." Immediately after the cancellation of the golf course project, the PGA initiated an investigation of the myriad dealings that led to the country club project. As Vito Corleone asked at a meeting of warring families in *The Godfather*, the PGA wondered how could things have gone so far. Throughout the early spring of 2000, it issued reports on what it learned—and, in many cases, the reports prompted both further controversy and questionable behavior.

On February 23, 2000, for example, the PGA called for a criminal investigation of the project, complaining that Clarence Doninger had failed to report a significant conflict of interest prior to beginning negotiations. Further, it alleged that Doninger would have received a free membership to the Club and been given thirteen others worth more than $100,000 to dispose of as he wished ("Golf Course Called 'Insider Deal,'" *Indiana Daily Student*, February 24, 2000). Other administrators were to receive free memberships as well. Doninger dismissed the allegations as "absurd" and fired back his own accusation: "Actually, [the PGA] have misrepresented the facts and may be legally liable for damages" ("IU Officials Deny Group's Allegations," *The Herald-Times*, February 26, 2000). This possibility didn't cause the PGA to back off, as it wrote a forty-three page report of what it had uncovered and made copies available at the public library for all to read.

The PGA was also skeptical about the financial deal IU struck and reviewed the numbers accordingly. Based on appraised real estate estimates, Indiana Club would pay IU an initial $480,000 plus an annual rent of $48,000 that would never be increased for fifty years. IU would also receive royalties from greens fees and cart rentals, earning as much as $68,000 per year. It could thus earn as much as $116,000 per year for a half century. Meanwhile, Indiana Club LLC projected to recoup its investment of over $13 million within a year or so, with subsequent years' income estimated at $4 million (Lisa Sorg, "Golf Course Still Raising Hackles," *The Bloomington Independent*, February 24, 2000). Four million versus a little over $100,000—somehow, this seemed like a much better deal for the developers than the University.

In addition, the PGA discovered that the bidding process to secure a developer for the project seemed very questionable. Lynn Coyne, Director of University Real Estate and Development, reported that in May 1999 some forty-seven firms were provided with information about the planned development and given thirty days to respond with a bid. Studying the resultant correspondence, the PGA learned that only seven firms had in fact responded to the mailing: six had sent one-paragraph letters, some of which asked for more time to consider the project. Indiana Club LLC, it seems, forwarded a 126-page proposal. The PGA also found it unusual that in January of 1999, some months before the bidding process was to begin, Indiana Club LLC had written a letter to an administrator saying that it was "proud to be designing a new golf course for Indiana University" ("Golf Course Called Insider Deal," 9).

Let's not be naive about this. These kinds of relationships between businesses owned by alumni and universities exist everywhere. No one is denying the importance of alumni development to the success of the American university in the twenty-first century. A country club built near the football stadium would doubtless have proved an effective venue for the cultivation of donors (though much of this money would inevitably have been channeled to the athletic association and units friendly to its goals). But ethical goals and educational priorities cannot be sacrificed in the process. And high-ranking administrators need to understand that their actions are being monitored, their business dealings scrutinized.

3. Investigate the Possible Cooptation of Academic Units in University Capitol Projects. Only a week before the decision to scuttle the project was announced, President Brand had been quoted as offering what Steven Higgs regarded as "the ultimate insult": "It's only a golf course. It's not the corporatization of the university." Maybe so. But President Brand's remark begs a question: what precisely might the term "corporatization of the university" mean?

Any definition of the phrase would be enhanced by an article published in the Fall/Winter 1999 issue of *Kelley*, a magazine, as its cover proclaims, directed to "Alumni and friends of the Kelley School of Business at Indiana University." This issue featured a story announcing the building of a Jack Nicklaus-designed course at IU and outlined several aspects of the plan's genesis. Four graduate students in the MBA Sports and Entertainment Academy, according to one of the Academy's co-directors, were retained as consultants to explore alumni opinion of the project. To that end, they "created and administered a survey to 3,500 IU alumni to determine their interest in a new golf course" and other amenities (Andra Jenkins, "IU Plans Bear of a Golf Course"). The quartet of students found that "60 percent of the respondents indicated a strong appeal for the proposed golf course"—not exactly a felicitous phrasing, but clear enough in its representation that a significant body of alumni supported the plan.

But did they? Funded in part by the IU Athletics Department, as the article's author clarifies, the survey hardly seemed scientific. Here's the giveaway: "More than 10% of those surveyed responded, including 28% of the 500 members of the Hoosier Hundred–IU's top contributors to its athletic program" (13). Thus, of the 3500 alumni surveyed—out of over 400,000 living graduates of the University—500 were known contributors to the athletic department. Not just any contributors either—the "whales," as Las Vegas casinos affectionately term affluent gamblers willing to open up their deep wallets when the occasion demands it. The big fish. Twenty-eight percent of this group, or 140 members of the Hoosier Hundred, took a minute off from their tailgate parties to fill out the survey. Of the approximately 350 respondents, then, 140 or 40 percent came from this group.

Clearly, this information raises serious questions. Was this a "real" survey or one rigged to achieve the result desired by those who sponsored it? More important, does the manipulation of a sham poll represent the quality of education these graduate students received in the gathering and interpretation of polling data? Mightn't it suggest that a course on the ethical use of survey results be added to the curriculum? Given these questions, the remarks of one of the four MBAs who designed this survey should give one pause: "[I] enjoyed working on a real project that enabled IU to make tough business decisions" (13). This was a "real" project? IU made some "tough business decisions" prior to the project's cancellations? The survey, at least as it was reported in the School of Business's own periodical, was little more than a ruse designed to provide the illusion of objectivity—or, let's call it what it is, false evidence—for a project that should never have been undertaken. One of the co-directors of the MBA Academy put it this way: "The IU golf course project clearly shows that Academy consulting provides real value to sports and entertainment firms" (13). There's that word "real" again—"real value" to business. What value might that be? In the name of graduate education, students were employed to produce data that allowed interested corporate parties and certain university officials to proceed with their plans.

Add that to your definition of the corporatization of the university. Business interests insinuate themselves not only into university capitol projects or faculty research agendas, but into the graduate classroom as well, perverting the aims of education in the process.

4. Lobby for Faculty Positions on Boards of Trustees. Two very instructive moments came as a product of the post-country club debates and investigations. One came directly from the Board of Trustees—or so it seemed initially.

On February 28, 2000, an editorial attributed to the Board of Trustees appeared in *The Herald Times* and *The Indiana Daily Student.* "Time to move past the golf course issue," the editorial's headline in the *IDS* advised. Responding to what it called "false and defamatory accusations against prominent Indiana University leaders" published in an earlier article in the *IDS*, the editorial deplored the misrepresentations of administrators' motives insofar as the "now-defunct golf course proposal" were concerned. It was determined to set the record straight:

> As Vice President for Public Affairs and Government Relations Christopher Simpson stressed in that article, there was no conflict of interest between Athletic Director Clarence Doninger and the proposed project. . . .

Later, the Board took the offensive in blasting local critics who persisted in criticizing the actions of IU administrators connected to the project:

> Scurrilous fliers targeting some IU administrators were posted around the campus and the community. The tactic was distasteful and wrong. There is simply no excuse for making loyal, long-time IU employees, who were simply doing their jobs, the target of these unfair public attacks. (*Indiana Daily Student*, February 28, 2000)

The editorial ended with the Trustees condemning a "strategy of misrepresentation and divisiveness" exhibited by the PGA and questioning the "motives of those who believe there is something to be gained by trying to inflame the community by throwing around false allegations about an issue that is moot." Signed: The IU Board of Trustees.

The only problem is, the Trustees didn't write the piece. In a small box in the *IDS* the next day, a "Clarification" was posted. In it, the *IDS* refused to withdraw any of the accusations it made based, as they were, on "public records and interviews with those involved with the issues." And Christopher Simpson was identified as the author of the Trustees' editorial "by suggestion and with the approval of the Board of Trustees" ("Clarification," *Indiana Daily Student*, February 29, 2000). Let's see if this rhetorical situation can be described without misrepresenting the motives of someone who was then, but is no longer, a "prominent Indiana University leader." (Simpson resigned his position and $160,000 plus salary in the summer of 2001 to start his own public relations firm, although he remained a consultant to the University for a reported $10,000/month for a year afterward.) Simpson wrote his defense of the motives of administrators, including his own, and recommended that we accept his account in an earlier article as truthful and accurate. He then declared such issues moot anyway and, at the same time, wearing the borrowed cloak of the Board, impugned the motives of anyone interested in investigating these issues further.

What was that he said about a strategy of "misrepresentation and divisiveness?"

At the same time that the identity of the Trustees' ghost writer was revealed, a real live Trustee—President John Walda—was contributing to a campus forum on the relationship between Trustees and faculty. Sponsored by the Bloomington chapter of the American Association of University Professors, AAUP General Secretary Mary Burgan and former Bloomington Faculty Council President Ted Miller joined Walda in a spirited discussion of the topic. Burgan urged that, among other things, faculty seek election to the Board of Trustees, which in fact one of my colleagues attempted during the elections of spring, 2001, losing although garnering a respectable display of support from the voters. There is little question of the wisdom of Burgan's recommendation. Until faculty voices can be heard at the highest levels of administrative power, boondoggles like the one described here can be virtually *faits accomplis* before rank and file faculty know anything about it.

By the way, the University's official position on the prospect of faculty serving on the Board of Trustees was a negative one; it opposed the idea in no uncertain terms.

5. Keep On Truckin' and Fighting the Good Fight. In the late 1960s, alternative cartoon icon Mr. Natural encouraged counter-culture types to fight the good fight with his motto "Keep On Truckin'." It's only fitting that this story end where it began: with principled opposition to an environmentally irresponsible plan with a dash of sixties' activism mixed in. Contrary to Mr. Simpson's admonition, Michael Hamburger and IU faculty from a variety of departments wouldn't let this story just disappear. They persisted with their goals of protecting the Lake Griffy watershed and of establishing a "natural lab" for future generations of geologists, biologists, and the community. They negotiated and planned; to be fair, so did the university administration. Eighteen months later, on May 11, 2001, the IU Board of Trustees announced that 446 acres of University land—including 185 acres of the Griffy Woods, forest and wetlands—would be set aside in perpetuity as a research and teaching preserve. No hackers would blast any divots from the ground, no chemicals used to create fairways would ever pollute the lake. By reaching this decision, Indiana University was able to achieve what, eighteen months previously, Biology professor Meredith West identified as a goal to which the University should aspire. The ideal became a reality:

> Instead of having the ace golf course in the Big Ten . . . we could say we went the other way. . . . We could say we decided to let nature win this round, that we decided to protect the environment and to use this for academic purposes. (Lively 2000, A36)

On May 11, University president Myles Brand declared the creation of the preserve a "wise decision for the long-run benefit of IU."

The following thought sped through an undisclosed synaptic network in the PR Office on campus:

> *Well said–way to get on the right side of this issue.*

Postscript: By 2003, many of the principal actors in this comedy—Athletics Director Doninger, Vice-President Simpson, and University President Brand—would no longer work for IU. That may be the last principle to derive from this story: the majority of faculty and certainly the community remain long after highly paid administrators retire or move on to their next "gig." Those of us in it for "the long haul"—those of us loyal to the university and the town or city in which it is located—need therefore to keep an eye on the longer-term consequences of plans hatched by parties who are too often only concerned about short-term solutions.

SW

9. Collective Action, Collective Bargaining, Collective Agency

I. Graduate Students Take Matters Into Their Own Hands

"IT'S SALLY. I'M IN." "IT'S TIM. I'M IN." The calls came in from advance members of GEO, the Graduate Employee's Organization at the University of Illinois at Urbana-Champaign. It was early one March morning in 2002. Sally and Tim, their names changed, were calling on their cell phones from men's and women's restrooms in the Swanlund Administration Building. It was just after 6 a.m. and the GEO was planning to take over the building. They had scouted the building over a period of weeks, never sending the same scout in twice. The doors to the building, it turned out, were unlocked about 6 a.m., but the security personnel did not arrive until an hour later, so there was a critical hour in which to place people in key positions.

Chief among those positions were the restrooms. A testament to thirty years of paranoid, post-Vietnam university architecture, Swanlund was designed with a central core that could be isolated from the rest of the building in the event of an attempted takeover. A sole stairwell offered only two doors per floor, each of which gave access to one wing of the building. The doors could be quickly locked electronically by the first floor receptionist. Then militants, homeless people, or a sudden impolitic body of undergraduates seeking grade changes, could be confined to the central core stairway. They would thus be denied access to all administration offices, along with restrooms, water fountains, and communications systems. But fire codes prohibited locking the doors on each floor from the inside. By placing people in the restrooms first, the GEO had assured itself control of the building.

The whole operation reflected a fundamental change in the GEO's analysis of its situation and in the tactics it was prepared to employ. After nearly a decade of organizing and no letup in administration resistance, facilitated by ambiguous state law, the graduate students realized something had to change. An unofficial campus election had demonstrated that a clear majority of teaching assistants wanted union representation. Salaries for a 2/2 teaching load remained below living costs. Health care coverage was a joke. And benefits critical to some, like child care, were nonexistent, despite three decades of reports urging the administration to act. Meanwhile, not one of the founding graduate student organizers was still on campus. Each year a new cadre of leaders had to be found and a new entering class of graduate students had to be educated.

Worse still, the leverage of a strike threat required sustaining a high degree of militancy among the membership. Renewing that level of activism semester after semester was particularly exhausting. It was a problem the anti-union administration enjoyed contemplating. So the GEO leadership finally asked itself a decisive question. What if the proper tactical challenge was not how to keep two thousand employees ready to strike but how to use sixty deeply committed activists ready to take personal risks and be arrested if necessary? The plan to occupy the administration building ensued. A small group of heroically obsessive planners let it be known in time that they had committed to memory comparable plans for other buildings. Meanwhile, the earlier vote had made it clear that the activists were seeking not to impose the will of a minority but rather to make majority choice a reality.

Swanlund's paranoid architecture had other features that helped the takeover. There were only two entrances to the building, one set of double doors each in the front and the back. So thirty students standing shoulder to shoulder at each entrance were enough to secure the site. The building housed the offices of the system president, the chancellor, and the provost, along with other high administrators, so it was the obvious symbolic target. By arriving so early, moreover, GEO could successfully prevent anyone from entering the building, rather than preventing anyone from leaving. Meanwhile, care would be taken to avoid any property damage, that being the offense that seemed most to offend fellow Americans. "Collateral damage" to civilians during air raids enrages few reporters and keeps few Americans awake at night, but turning over a potted plant, let alone soiling the stairwell in the absence of an accessible restroom, would clearly produce an irreversible backlash.

One hapless administrator did hurl himself at a diminutive long-term activist in a failed attempt to force his way into the building. Another found his eyes misting over when he talked about "these terrorists who frightened all the administrators' secretaries." But the secretaries all seemed to be enjoying themselves at a coffee shop across the street. Even the local police enjoyed the day. Union members themselves, they were confronted by smiling "terrorists" singing songs. The administration ordered that no food be allowed into the building, but the police decided that it would be thoroughly unAmerican to block a pizza delivery.

The day's events had been planned by a heroically obsessive cadre who devised a minute-by-minute plan for the takeover. While half a dozen advance scouts, like paratroopers parachuting behind enemy lines on the eve of the Normandy landings, took over the bathrooms, the sixty door blockers and spokespeople waited invisibly indoors at the university YMCA a few blocks away. Like all successful military operations, there was even a diversionary strategy. In the week before the event, signs went up all over campus announcing a major demonstration at the student union building for that day. Plans for the administration building meanwhile were kept secret. "Loose lips sink ships" sufficed as a wartime motto then and now. The Union Building rally was actually a feint, announced because the Board of Trustees were meeting there that day and thus guaranteed to draw campus security away from Swanlund. There was no Union Building rally, though even some who knew about the Swanlund takeover did not know the posters were a ruse.

As the day progressed, other actions in the plan fell into place. Celebratory banners were hung from Swanlund's upper floors, and union leaders poked bullhorns out the front door to make a series of announcements: "The new University of Illinois administration hereby declares that there will be free child care available to all employees beginning next semester." A large group of allies with placards and chants assembled on the sidewalk and people gave impromptu speeches. Television crews with cameras, expecting a big demonstration at the Union Building, were available to film the events and do interviews.

Everyone expected arrests to follow. Surely the campus's previous chancellor, ferociously and relentlessly anti-union, would have done just that. But a new chancellor had recently arrived from the University of Michigan. The previous chancellor had managed to make Chicken Little look somnolent on this and other matters; his last legacy to the campus came when a federal judge fined him for violating faculty and student First Amendment rights. The new chancellor had cannily taken no public positions on unionization, but it was unlikely the generally businesslike

Michigan experience with collective bargaining had infected her with hopelessly rabid proclivities. Meanwhile, the very public Swanlund take-over provided her with a necessity to act; nor could she bounce the prob-lem to the Board of Trustees, whose prior approval would ordinarily have been necessary for a policy decision. So the provost was delegated to make an offer, refined by front step negotiations at Swanlund after GEO refused to hold discussions with him in the building. "It's our build-ing now. You get your office back after the union is recognized." The offer was now clear: vacate and we will recommend the Illinois Labor Relations Board conduct an election in which teaching assistants can vote for or against union representation. The victory, months later, was overwhelming.

Not every element of Swanlund's multi-layered security system proved relevant that day. Bookending three decades of still more personal admin-istrative paranoia, the university president had concluded the building's core isolation mechanisms were not sufficient to guarantee his own se-curity. Precisely thirty years before, the university's chancellor, just prior to devoting himself to doing no good in California, hired a security firm to do a report on his first floor office, then appended to the south end of the English building. The report alarmed him. Turn-of-the century lock-ers installed back when the building housed the women's swimming pool were located in the basement just under his desk. Vietnam War protest-ors could stuff the lockers with dynamite, set delayed fuses, and make their escape before the chancellor was sent some distance farther than Sacramento. And the grounds before the building were decorated with piles of small, loose boulders, even easier to hurl through windows than Paris paving stones were two centuries earlier. The lockers were filled with cement, and the Buildings and Grounds department was com-manded to find some all-weather glue that could be poured over the rocks to bind them into a solid mass.

But glue would no longer do. The president now opted for a door with steel restraining bolts his secretary could operate from her desk. But what if GEO arrived with lasers and acetylene torches? Perhaps he was worried his inability to compose eloquent sentences would push an unstable faculty member over the edge. Perhaps he was asking himself what might have saved Davy Crockett at the Alamo. So one last redoubt was established. The door to his private bathroom was reinforced, and a bullet-proof vest was set beside the toilet. No wonder the man has no time to establish child care on campus. All this wonderful information, incidentally, was obtained by yet another GEO activist, who ingratiated herself with a university security officer one day and found him eager to brag about his accomplishments. But even the GEO activists did not need Davy Crockett's kevlar enhanced commode. What they will now need to get the university to bargain in good faith remains to be seen.

As with every union action, there are general lessons to learned from this one. That same year the California Faculty Association had pressed the system chancellor to negotiate in part by following him around with larger than life puppets that satirized him wherever he went. When he finally agreed to talk, he immediately asked whether the puppets would now disappear. A certain amount of street theater characterizes California union activism. At the fourth annual Conference on Contingent Academic Labor (COCAL), held in San Jose, California, in January 2001, we were greeted by the part-timer's living symbol—the Freeway Flyer in full regalia: black academic robes, black wings, and an oversized chicken's head—when we stepped off the plane. She leapt into the air and squawked, flapped her wings, and generally terrorized the clueless passengers crowding the airport lounge. Not that they knew who she was or why she was there. As we later learned, many parents confuse part-time faculty in higher education with *substitute teachers* in high school. So there is much work to be done in educating the public and achieving fair employment practices in higher education. Meanwhile, at the conference site itself even the entertainment came with an edge. At one point fifteen contingent faculty members were on stage to perform the academic version of "The Twelve Days of Christmas." They called it "The Twelve Days of Bargaining" and it constituted a list of the alternatives to fair wages and benefits that administrators might like to offer their part-time faculty. "On the first day of bargaining," they began, "the college offered me: one lottery ticket, instead of a salary raise." And so it went, on through two freeway maps, three self-help workshops, four feet of floss, five sweatshop pencils, six pats on the back, seven yawning trustees, eight spoons of Maalox, nine minutes of prep time, ten cups of coffee, eleven extra students, and twelve penny raises. Perform it in your own department or at your next disciplinary conference. Add your own words. It is time for street theater in higher education.

The GEO building occupation provided another, equally cheerful form of street theater, not unlike the effective community response to the ill-fated country club at Indiana. Nonviolent civil disobedience over campus employment issues often has a better chance of winning good publicity and good results if it is both exquisitely well planned and cheerful, rather than merely confrontational. Yet, unlike the strategies employed in Bloomington, disruption of daily life, making business as usual impossible, can be a critical feature of any successful collective action. The tactic of using a small, committed group of activists willing to take chances is one many other campus groups need to consider. But let us look at another labor confrontation in greater detail—this time at Syracuse University—then see what lessons it offers.

II. Faculty, Academic Freedom, and the Strike at Syracuse

"Speak freely, Syracusian, what thou wilt."
—*The Comedy of Errors* (5.1.286)

Egeon, Shakespeare's long-suffering merchant from Syracuse, is afforded this opportunity by the Duke of Ephesus in the final scene of *The Comedy of Errors*. This freedom to speak and ask questions without restraint, in fact, makes the play's comic dénouement possible; without the ability to inquire into and thus ascertain the truth of other characters' personal histories, Egeon might never have recovered his long-lost wife and son. Nor would the play's closing lines, spoken by one servant long separated from his twin brother, ever have been uttered: "We came into the world like brother and brother,/And now let's go hand in hand, not one before another" (5.1.425–26). Free speech at Syracuse University during the fall semester of 1998, however, was a little more difficult to obtain for faculty, students, and university employees and, when finally exercised, could hardly be construed as "free." But the price was well worth it, as we hope to show.

In this report from one of the more instructive labor fronts of higher education as the last millennium came to a close, we promise to resist further comparisons between Shakespeare's farce and the week-long strike of the Service Employees International Union Local 200A (SEIU) at Syracuse University during the first week of September, 1998. We will also refrain from making analogies between the casts of characters conventional to Elizabethan comedy and labor action, not only because such a comparison would inevitably grow annoying, but because the SEIU strike featured a *dramatis personae* quite different from that in Shakespeare's play. Victorian melodrama, with its rapacious factory owners or mortgage holders and their helpless victims, seems a slightly more relevant analogue. Yet while villains may surface in this drama—Syracuse Chancellor Kenneth Shaw, in office from 1991 to 2004, comes immediately to mind—the story yields no single hero, as most varieties of melodrama require. Rather, however implausible this may seem, the strike at Syracuse produced a collective hero more like those of agit-prop drama of the 1930s than melodrama: this includes the faculty, working in concert with striking workers and concerned students. Indeed, politically active Syracuse faculty—and many of their students—

provide an example of what can be accomplished in labor disputes on campus once academics become aware of one increasingly obvious fact of life at the corporate university: namely, that they are workers, pure and simple. These days, faculty may share much more in common with cafeteria workers than with higher administrators who, even if they "rose" through the ranks from an academic department to their present positions, have grown increasingly distant from the former colleagues they now manage. As a dean we know explained so frighteningly well, "I'm a businessman now." And so they are.

Rather than vilifying a single administrator, however, we would prefer to lay out the facts of the strike as they were reported, both in public documents and in interviews. For what happened at Syracuse has occurred across the country and will continue to do so unless action is taken to resist it. Moreover, we hope to support the thesis Ali Zaidi proposes in his excellent essay on the strike that "current labor unrest and the erosion of the humanities at universities spring from a common cause" (Zaidi 1999, 28). That common origin is in part revealed by the at times striking disjunction between such managerial strategies as outsourcing, on the one hand, and the administration's public relations' salvos, on the other, much heard during the strike at Syracuse and at other sites reported in this book. That is to say, it is one thing to extol the virtues of academic freedom and intellectual community, as Syracuse's administration did, and quite another to support them. More vulgarly, if administrators want to "talk the talk" of higher ideals and lofty intellectual missions, they need "to walk the walk" as well.

Take Chancellor Shaw himself, for example, in the early pages of his 1999 tome *The Successful President*, published by the American Council on Education and Oryx Press, where he offers this cogent analysis of the labor action: "As I write, we are recovering from a week long strike by our service workers' union, which was followed by a storm packing 75-mile-an-hour winds that downed trees and electrical wires all over the city. I've been credited with both." The only other allusion to the strike in the entire book is an oblique one at best: "Faculty are disappointed when you fail to be their head cheerleader" (1999, 22). In her "Foreword" to Shaw's book, then Secretary of Education Donna E. Shalala, now President of the University of Miami, advanced a somewhat more sanguine view of Shaw's managerial strategies at Syracuse: "He promoted the university's restructuring as positive change by using it as an opportunity to involve the community in decision-making . . . to renew the institution's values and mission. . . . The result was a greater sense of hope on campus" (vii). Perhaps. Shalala's allusion to Shaw's 1991 plans for restructuring the university—plans he infamously compared to the process of sausage-making as "Ugly in the process, but, if done well, healthy in the outcome" (qtd. in Zaidi 1999, 32)—included a salary freeze for staff, a personnel reduction of 15 percent, and a strong reason for nearly 20 percent of Syracuse's tenured faculty to opt for the university's "supported resignation plan" (Zaidi 1999, 32). Contrary to Shalala's rosy depiction of renewal and community, Shaw's arrival clearly did not inspire hope in all corners of the university, although the earlier renovation of the Chancellor's 20-room mansion could possibly have encouraged some. You be the judge in this case of the extent to which the university's actions helped foster a "greater sense of hope on campus," or to what extent faculty and staff were relieved to know, as Chancellor Shaw informed them, that his proposals for re-structuring the university mirrored similar plans at Chrysler and IBM. You decide about what "values" were reflected by whom during this prelude to an electrical storm.

The strike of SEIU Local 200A lasted a week, August 31 to September 5, a strategic time for at least two reasons: students were arriving on campus for the fall semester, and the university was hosting the first "big game" of the college football season as the nationally ranked Tennessee Volunteers visited the Carrier Dome to play the highly regarded Orangemen. National media were in town to cover the game; parents and alumni were on campus in unusually large numbers. The strike involved some 750 food service workers, physical plant employees, parking lot attendants, and library assistants, some of the university's lowest paid workers. How low? In a strategy employed on campuses all over the country, the salaries of various employees and managers at Syracuse were published so readers could draw their own conclusions. Table 1, excerpted from an online "Who Makes What at Syracuse University," tells an all-too-familiar story.

This is not the occasion to rail at the obscene salaries of many Division One basketball and football coaches, or to query the $320,000 raise Paul Pignatore, Syracuse's football coach, apparently received for 1997–1998. Head football coach at the University of Alabama Mike Price, fired in May, 2003 for his alleged solicitation of prostitutes while on a golf outing, reportedly lost a seven-year contract worth $10 million; in the same week, Larry Eustachy, forced out as head basketball coach at Iowa State after being videotaped partying into the wee hours with undergraduates, was the highest paid public employee of the state at a salary of $900,000 per year (not counting some of the perks big-time coaches often enjoy). One of the authors of this book learned a similar lesson about football's primacy some years ago when, as a new assistant professor of English at the University of Tennessee, he displayed the temerity one Saturday morning of driving to campus and parking in his assigned

Table 1

Position	Salary (1997–1998)
Senior Secretary (Grade 18)	$14,343 ($7.35/hr.)
Parking Lot Attendant	$15,000*
Custodian (Grade 3)	$18,700
Library Assistant (Grade 25)	$17,700 (after 1 yr.)
Regular Part-Time	
Writing Instructor	$11,930–$21,720**
Full-time Faculty	$57,732 (mean)***
VP (Student Affairs)	$124,161
VP (Public Relations)	$135,506
VP (Enrollment Management)	$151,698
VP (University Relations)	$167,867
VP (Business)	$180,871
Vice-Chancellor	$197,837
Chancellor	$242,284
Men's Basketball Coach	$265,126
Men's Football Coach	$656,463****

Notes:
* This salary is the average of workers who have been on the job for four years.
** Part-time Instructors in the Writing Program earn between $2,386 and $3,620/section. Most teach a 2/3 or 3/3 load.
*** This average is for 1996–1997.
**** This figure does not include deferred compensation or media contracts and represented a $320,679 increase over the 1996–1997 salary.

lot. A couple of hours and ten graded essays later, he returned to his car to find a parking ticket lodged behind the windshield wiper and a tow truck poised for action. Naively believing a mistake had been made, he rushed over to the campus police office and introduced himself as a faculty member with a permit to park in the lot. After a ripple of laughter subsided, and the ticket was ripped up, an officer delivered the news: "Hell, boy, this is a football weekend. Your parking permit ain't no good today."

More relevant in the present context—and of greater concern to the strikers–were the huge disparities between the top and bottom of the Syracuse salary schedule. Of greater interest to readers of this chapter are the growing ranks of highly paid administrators on campuses all over the country. And six years later in 2004, the situation has clearly worsened. In addition to the chancellor and vice-chancellor, the Syracuse list included nine vice-presidents with annual salaries between $124 and $180 thousand. Residing at the less comfortable end of the pay spectrum was a full-time "senior" secretary earning a little over $14,000/year; if that secretary also happened to be a single mother with children, she would fall significantly below federally-estimated poverty levels. A grade 20 secretary, which one can become only after years of service to the institution, could still earn less than $22,000/year. There is an obvious issue of gender inequity as well in some of these data, as Zaidi emphasizes: "SU ranked ninety-fifth out of 109 university libraries surveyed by the Association of Research Libraries in 1996–1997 for average salary of professional library staff; and, while women held 70 percent of these jobs they received on average 20 to 25 percent less pay than their male counterparts" (1999, 29). And then there is the obvious connection between corporate tactics at the highest administrative levels and the treatment of faculty teaching in the humanities. For example, *only* a "regular part-time" instructor in Syracuse's Writing Program who is at the top of the pay scale ($3,620/section) *and* is given a 3/3 teaching load could come close to earning $20,000 a year. Many such "senior" instructors have taught for Syracuse for ten years—or more—and make considerably less. Salary, of course, was not the only issue on the table during the strike. Employee benefits and the university's increased reliance upon temporary, non-union labor evolved as major points of disagreement in the negotiations, as Syracuse, like so many universities today, follows the leads of the United Parcel Service and companies like Thomson Electronics (makers of RCA televisions) in ruthlessly causalizing its workforce.

In the spring of 1998, in March, in fact, as one Syracuse professor told us, faculty began to discuss their role in what appeared to be an imminent dispute between the union and the university when the contract between the two expired on June 30. Preliminary discussions between the two sides began in May, and in late June the university made a "final" offer to the union, which it rejected and began work without a contract on July 1. On July 16 the university requested the assistance of a federal mediator, a decision with which SEIU concurred, and later that month the university made a second offer, which was also rejected without a full membership vote. On August 16, SEIU polled its membership and received overwhelming support for a strike, if necessary (by September 2, the vote of employees supporting a continuation of the strike rose to 96%). In an August 28 open letter to "Members of the Syracuse University community," Chancellor Shaw laid considerable blame on "paid agents" and "designated union officers" for failing to allow the union membership to "ratify or reject the proposed contract." For its part, the union countered by accusing the university of "not negotiating in good faith" and was particularly emphatic on the point of not signing any contract which failed to address the institution's replacement of full-time workers with "temporary employees working at minimum wage and without benefits" (*Herald-Tribune*, 29 August 1998). And even after a new contract was voted on and approved by an eight to one majority of union members, some could not quite forget or forgive the university's conduct. Ron Hart, a dissenting food service worker of twelve year's experience, compared negotiating with the university to talking to "a brick wall. We had to fight for every tooth and nail. I have nothing against them [the bargaining committee]. They fought hard" (*Herald-Tribune*, 7 September 1998). (What was that Donna Shalala said about Chancellor Shaw's instilling a "greater sense of hope on campus," about involving the community in decision-making?) After the new contract was signed on September 8, union representative Coert Bonthius described his adversary in a letter of appreciation to faculty, students, and other supporters as a "corporate giant" which "refused to acknowledge our issues and our lives. The arrogance of power!" ("Letter to Supporters").

Of particular interest to our thesis is the manner in which this power—and corporate arrogance inimical to the mission of higher education—was exercised *against faculty, students, and other supporters* of SEIU. Before the strike began, for example, before Carrier Dome hot dogs ("Dome Dogs") could be ordered for the showdown between Tennessee and the Orangemen, Syracuse administrators clearly perceived a need to constrain support for the union. So, on August 25, some ten days before the kickoff—and days before the caravan of students' U-Haul trailers arrived on campus—Gershon Vincow, Vice-Chancellor of Academic Affairs ($197,837 on the list), sent a memorandum to the Academic Deans Cabinet to apprise it of the "special attention" that might be required in "the situation of faculty members" who "choose not to cross the picket lines to teach and advise students." Such faculty "should expect a reduction in pay," the memo advised, and their fringe benefits might also be impacted depending "upon the circumstances" ("Memorandum to Academic Deans Cabinet," August 25, 1998). One of the most attractive of these benefits allows both employees and their dependents to take courses at the university free or at greatly reduced tuition rates. In the event of a strike, however, "family members using tuition benefits to take classes" were to be asked in class to report to the Financial Aids Office to have their fees recalculated. And, not surprisingly, non-union staff were admonished that they would lose their jobs immediately if they refused to cross the picket line. Chairs of departments were warned they would no longer hold their positions if they failed to report to higher administration the names of all staff and faculty who did not appear for work.

But this was just the beginning, as an anonymous August 28 memo disseminated by the Graduate Student Organization (GSO) outlined (the language of the memo indicated to many that its author may have been a well-intentioned lower administrator). Union members were not allowed to distribute information on school property, an abridgement of freedom of expression private schools like Syracuse are permitted to enforce. And neither were individual students. The memo reminded graduate students who "hold scholarships, fellowships, graduate assistantships, research assistantships, and teaching assistantships" that they do so as "university beneficiaries." In a sense, graduate students were cautioned to seek the counsel of their respective departmental or academic advisors if they intended to show their support for the strike ("GSO Memo," August 28, 1998). Apparently, in his desire to make good on one of its advertising promises that promoted Syracuse as the "number one student-centered university" administrators forgot that graduate students are not only essential workers, but students too. And this group of students was firmly warned that, as individuals, they could not distribute any information about the strike on campus and that they needed to be careful about any display of support for the union.

Chancellor Shaw and his fellow administrators don't make their high salaries for nothing, it seems, and they quickly realized that the Stalinesque squelching of academic freedom they desired might cause a public relations problem (more than the university's highly paid Vice-President for Public Relations could handle, at any rate). So, in web sites that were erased once the strike was settled, the university trumpeted its commitment to freedom of speech as it simultaneously worked to stifle it. In a September 4 memorandum to "Members of the University Community," Shaw again affirmed the university's pledge to honor "the principle of free speech," but explained that "freedom of expression . . . ceases at the point in which its exercise infringes on the rights of either participants or non-participants." Consequently, the abridgements of speech outlined in the earlier GSO memo were still more or less in force: union members and students were prohibited from distributing information on campus; students were enjoined from wearing hats or t-shirts supportive of the union or the ongoing strike; and faculty, threatened in more ways than those described above, were advised that they could not carry signs sympathetic to the union or its action.

How a student wearing a shirt or a geology professor carrying a sign could infringe on a "non-participant's" rights is difficult to determine, but what is quite clear, as Shaw acknowledges in his September 4 memo, is his motive for writing the memo in the first place: the possibility of anything or anyone disturbing football fans the next day as they filed into the Carrier Dome. Still, perhaps some dissent could be allowed, for, as the chancellor clarifies, the university certainly believes in freedom of speech. But how? Where? In a tactic one faculty member described as the establishment of "cages" of free speech, Shaw designated an area 100 feet from Gate N of the dome for "peaceful protest" (Gate E is the main entrance to the facility). How many football fans and alumni would pass by Gate N? (Another faculty member suggested to us that this area was closer to the garbage dumpsters than to the main entrance, but we have been unable to make a precise cartographic measurement.) What could the strikers do? What could faculty do? One answer was to contact all faculty members whose offices lined a well-travelled walkway and encourage them to post signs in their windows. Fans walking to the game could hardly ignore them.

Another more general strategy that worked all week was to hold classes at various locales off campus: the Westcott Cinema, Salt City Performing Arts Center, Good Earth Cafe, and numerous churches. And while a university spokesman announced that only a few professors refused to cross picket lines, the *Herald-Journal* (September 2, 1998) reported that between 75 and 100 faculty participated. What is particularly impressive is not just the number of faculty who, albeit threatened with the loss of salary and even dismissal, supported the union, but the diversity of their backgrounds. Professors from philosophy, anthropology, law, engineering, economics, English, and other disciplines were quoted in local newspapers in support of the strike. And, contrary to university assertion that, because students pay tuition to learn, a faculty member who refused to cross picket lines was acting in violation of a teacher's principal responsibility to educate students, Dale Tussing, an economics professor teaching a course on "U.S. Poverty and Discrimination," used the strike as an instructional tool to impress upon students the effects of corporations hiring a contingent, hence expendable, workforce. John Oldfield, an engineering professor, conducted classes in his home, vowing to make sure students "don't lose out." An anthropology professor conducted class in a park gazebo; a professor of law posted notes and assignments on a web site established for the course. The next day, readers of *The D.O.* (*The Daily Orange*), the campus newspaper, were greeted with the prominent headline "Faculty Leads Chapel Protest" and the subheading "Hundreds of Faculty, Students show their support for strikers." Quoted prominently was English and Women's Studies Professor Rosaria Champagne, who confided, "I'm here because if I let this mistreatment of people, people I work with, go on without some sort of a fight, I couldn't live with myself" (*The Daily Orange*, 3 September 1998). Three hundred students were also in attendance, a turnout that even horrible weather could not diminish.

Throughout the week, faculty, the director of the Law Library, and socially conscious alumni also addressed letters to administrators both supporting the strike and expressing their understanding of the larger mission of the university. An alumnus of the law school who described himself as an annual donor, reminded the chancellor that the "University should provide a model for the private sector rather than replicate the worst techniques from the labor battles of the past" and indicated that his continuing support of Syracuse hung in the balance. In a widely circulated letter, Rosaria Champagne urged Chancellor Shaw to "return to the bargaining table and thus model for our students a commitment to respectful dialogue." And while other faculty wrote to Chancellor Shaw registering their dismay at what Dale Tussing called "a polarized and confrontational situation" exacerbated by "brusque and rude approaches by university personnel." Mas'ud Zavarzadeh and Donald Morton, perhaps the campus's best-known leftists, launched a rhetorical attack on Vice Chancellor Gershon Vincow for his efforts to intimidate the faculty. "Attack" would seem the appropriate term as their August 31 memorandum begins with the following: "In your usual repressive managerial style, you have sent a threatening text to the faculty and staff of this university in which, once more, you resort to the usual boss tactics of pressure, intimidation and what can only be called suppression of contesting and oppositional views." After castigating the vice-chancellor for the depth of his "institutional ignorance" and decrying the "absence" of his "historical understanding of labor practices," Zavarzadeh and Morton reluctantly expressed their support for SEIU Local 200A, announcing their intentions not to cross any picket lines.

What is the source of their reluctance to support the strike? In an issue of *The Alternative Orange*, the house organ for radical thought at Syracuse, Zavarzadeh attacked trade unionism on the ground of Lenin's argument delineated in his 1902 pamphlet *What Is to Be Done?*. Trade unionism, echoes Zavarzadeh, is "one of the most reactionary forms of 'economism.' Its goal is not transforming the social division of labor but, on the contrary, strengthening it. . . . Trade unionism merely gives exploitation a 'human face' by such tactics as increasing the minimum wage, adding vacation days, and other ameliorative gestures" (Zavarzadeh 1997, 58). In sum, the goal of a "revolutionary transformative practice" is hardly furthered by unionism or by strikes; these gestures fail the litmus test of sufficient radicalism because, for Zavarzadeh, they accomplish "nothing but temporary and merely local 'reforms'" (1997, 58).

Well, maybe. If this isn't the place to dissect the Leviathan-sized salaries of college football coaches, it probably isn't the place for interpretive skirmishes over Lenin either. Suffice it to say that, contrary to

Zavarzadeh's criticism or perhaps acting in blissful ignorance of it, faculty at Syracuse realized how essential "putting a human face" on the labor dispute would be to galvanizing faculty support for the union. So, they held meetings in which faculty could hear from the very people who cleaned their offices, from the librarians who facilitated their research, and from the secretaries whose labors made everyone's professional lives work more efficiently. Without this personalization of the strike, without showing faculty how interrelated their daily labors really were with those of the university's clerical, maintenance, and library staffs, the real victory in Syracuse—solidarity—might never have been achieved.

On that eventful Saturday in September, millions of viewers watched Tennessee come back in the waning minutes of the game to beat the Orangemen, jump-starting its drive for a national championship. But a much rarer, more important victory was achieved that weekend in Syracuse: the banding together of faculty, students, and a union to improve the lots of an institution's most exploited and vulnerable workers. Certainly the union felt this way, as Coert Bonthius's letter of gratitude to its supporters explained:

> What is clear is that the strike became a rallying point for all of us. It was a unifying process. . . .
>
> That our, and I do mean OUR (as in all of us) strike was successful is an understatement. . . . The strike was a real life drama unfolding in front of all of us. It was the struggle of normal people struggling to be heard over the inertia of everyday life which is controlled by corporate interests. And we were heard!
>
> Without all of you by our sides there is no question that our success would have been less certain. . . . We must continue to work together and to build a real community.

The "real life drama" thus ended with an essentially comic impulse: the building of community. In so doing it resembled the final ideological thrust not of Shakespearean farce but of such agit-prop plays as Clifford Odets' 1935 *Waiting for Lefty* and Langston Hughes' 1938 *Don't You Want to Be Free?*: solidarity.

Equally important, the strike of SEIU Local 200A might also teach workers at the corporate university some essential lessons. Three in particular seem obvious: start planning early, put a "face" on labor issues, and don't immediately alienate students and their parents. That is, faculty elected not to add to the chaos of students moving into their dormitories or apartments by aggressively picketing until the term actually began, nor did they interfere with fans flocking to the Carrier Dome. At the same time, they had already worked to secure alternative venues for classes on the first day of the term. Most important, they stood up for employees less powerful than themselves; they organized teach-ins, wrote letters to administrators, and thoughtfully reassessed the issues underlying the strike in terms of their own identities as educators, citizens, and fellow workers at what Stanley Aronowitz (2000) has recently termed "Knowledge Factories."

We'll say it again: an improbable collective hero.

Like a lot of recent stories from the higher education front related in this book, the country club project at Indiana University, for example, discussed in chapter 8, this one wasn't quite over when the ink dried on the new contract. At least one other issue remained unsettled: which side would be successful in securing the higher moral ground after the dispute was settled? The question arose earlier as well when, in addition to its press releases condemning union recalcitrance and undemocratic practices during the negotiations, the administration attempted to garner the approbation of the public for its position. When, for example, faculty and students suggested that football fans supportive of the strike should not buy "dome dogs" during the big game, the university responded that because a percentage of the profits from the sale of hot dogs was contributed to local charities, such a strategy would succeed only in harming these charities. After investigating the matter, faculty learned that only 15 percent of the profits went to charity; the lion's share went to the university or athletic department. But the lesson was clear: in response to labor movements, many universities will do whatever they feel necessary either to demonize their opposition or make dire predictions of life at the university should their opponent win. Graduate student unions know this tactic all too well, as administrations typically argue that unionization would forever damage faculty-student relations, thereby undermining the mentorship graduate students need from their faculty advisors. This has seldom proved to be the case.

But Syracuse wasn't quite finished. Two weeks after the strike was settled, Chancellor Shaw decided he wanted to punish some faculty and, at the same time, further his ongoing project of improving public relations at their expense. Grasping disingenuously for the high moral ground once again, he apparently forgot the homily he had preached just a few days earlier: "Now is a time for healing. I understand that it will take time to recover from the strike. . . . Yet there is no need for lingering resentment and blame. This is time to look ahead and support each other and the university" ("Service Workers Approve Contract," *Herald-Journal*, September 7, 1998). Such sentiments don't last long in the boardroom. Invoking the history of civil disobedience and alluding to the examples of Ghandi and Martin Luther King, Shaw announced that those professors "who chose not to meet their classes" should "voluntarily inform their deans of the time missed, so that their paychecks can be adjusted accordingly." The greatest teachers of civil disobedience have always accepted the consequences of their action, Shaw argued, so the faculty should do the same. Uncertain about the quality of health coverage Ghandi received from the British, but acutely aware of the hours they spent in providing their students with a week-long alternative education, faculty supporters of SEIU met and decided to ignore Chancellor Shaw's recommendation for self-punishment.

All of which raises one final issue: in these times of financial restructuring conducted in the name of greater flexibility and of administrative remonstrance of faculty who haven't punished themselves sufficiently for their activism, one might reasonably ask what restraints administrators have imposed upon themselves. As Aronowitz reminds us concerning the dire financial exigency in the 1990s at his own school, "[D]uring the last budget crisis many CUNY presidents and the chancellor's office exempted professional administrators from the retrenchment plan, and planted the burden of the layoffs or thinly disguised force-outs on low level administrative and clerical staff" (2000, 66). Much the same could be said about the episode at Syracuse, for if there was much conversation about administrators tightening their own belts to help restore the university to financial health, it must have been drowned out by the sounds of hammers and electric saws used to renovate the Chancellor's house prior to Kenneth Shaw's arrival. If economic flexibility is to trump any other consideration—academic freedom, free speech, the cultivation of a community—then that flexibility needs to be achieved by a restructuring of all levels of the university, and this includes those who earn the highest salaries on campus. Such re-structuring, moreover, ought not further erode the intellectual mission of universities, which as Aronowitz complains, has already been reduced "to a mere ornament . . . a legitimating mechanism for a host of more prosaic functions" (2000, 62). For a brief moment in the fall of 1998, committed faculty, students, and workers reintroduced values that are too often lost in the corporate university's redefined objective of certifying a workforce that, at the same time, seem so often to be "intellectual corpses" (Aronowitz 2000, 63).

But, amid all of these discouraging issues, Coert Bonthius of Local 200A at Syracuse should perhaps have the last word for now: "The strike did not, as the Chancellor warned, fracture this campus. On the contrary, the strike unified this campus in support of building a true 'community.'" We should all take note.[1]

---

1. We wish to express our gratitude to two faculty members and one former faculty member at Syracuse for discussing the strike with us. We also wish to thank Ali Zaidi for his assistance with this chapter

III. The Lessons of Cincinnati

Both the Illinois and the Syracuse stories suggest the powerful effects collective action can have. It can unify not only a single campus constituency but also a whole range of groups—graduate students, workers, and faculty—who usually remain within their own spheres. But the "faculty" itself by now in large institutions is no longer a coherent group or even much of a shared ideology, let alone a common identity. Part of the decline in the sense of shared mission and identity among faculty reflects generational changes in values like those we described in chapter 2, but the decline is also an result of departmentalization. One of the long-term effects of disciplinarity and its decentralized administration has been the gradual erosion of the very concept of "the faculty."

So long as the university had a shared commitment to general education—to preparing students not only to hold jobs but also to be informed participants in a democracy—the relative insularity of departmental culture presented little danger to an institutional mission. In the corporatized environment, however, job training has taken precedence over other aims. The faculty at many large institutions meanwhile has had few if any occasions over decades to think of itself coherently and collectively.

Even less have many large faculties had occasion to *act* as a group. The relative autonomy of departments was not devised as a strategy to divide and conquer the faculty, but that is now one of its practical effects. Not only do faculty in engineering or agriculture have little culture in common with faculty in philosophy or art, they often have no sense of common purpose and no sense of solidarity with one another. They are thus often unprepared to act together effectively to challenge the allocation of resources or to intervene in the redefinition of the campus mission.

Discussions of diminishing faculty influence in higher education usually begin now by citing the slow but relentless shift from full-time to part-time instruction throughout the academy. And indeed that is the single worst problem we face at present and will continue to face over the next decade. But it is no longer an isolated or unitary phenomenon. Selectively vilified in the culture wars, put on notice by periodic legislative demands for accountability, the dwindling professoriate has become a target of opportunity for competing interests and constituencies, all of which seek to remove the faculty from the center of higher education.

In 1999 the Washington, D.C.-based American Association of State Colleges and Universities (AASCU) issued a report titled "Facing Change: Building the Faculty of the Future." It makes a number of good suggestions, including improvements in compensation for part-time faculty.

But it also consistently views the faculty largely as a resource to be "managed," as "human capital" to be "defined, directed, and deployed with originality and attention to institutional mission." The "institution" itself, the report implies, is identified with its administrative and bureaucratic apparatus. It's hard to imagine the faculty in this report as a source of insight or inspiration about a college's mission, or even possessing a broad view of that mission, let alone as a site of resistance to a mission undergoing change. Indeed, as the report heralds the corporate partnerships that will help higher education transform itself to meet the new demands of the market, it insists that each faculty member make an annual statement of "short-range goals compatible with the mission of the institution."

This is a far cry from the view, held deeply by many tenured faculty, that they *are* the institution. Faculty in the AASCU's view are to be rewarded for their accomplishments, but nothing collective and broadly institutional flows from individual achievement. The AASCU report in this regard echoes the fall 1998 statement of principles for college and university governance issued by the Association of Governing Boards of Colleges and Universities (AGB), a Washington, D.C.-based organization that represents most boards of regents or trustees at major universities.

Notable among the chilling innovations in both reports is a new definition of the place of the faculty, which is now characterized (along with parents, alumni, and legislators) as but one of several "stakeholders" in higher education. The kind of redefinition the AASCU and AGB are promoting cannot take place in a day, but it augers a slow erosion of faculty influence that may actually be more threatening than such direct assaults on tenure as that mounted in the 1990s by the University of Minnesota Board of Regents.

According to both documents, the faculty has interests to represent, but it is merely one of several such groups presenting their claims before the administration or the board of trustees. The AASCU report depicts the administration as setting policy, whereas the ABG gives the board the final role in setting the institution's mission. Of course boards have always been able to set large-scale policy, but most faculties are accustomed to having primary control over how policy is actually enacted or carried out. In practice, the university's mission is largely set by what faculty teach and how they teach it, by what programs faculty and administrators propose and implement, by budgets that faculty and administrators allocate, and by the research that faculty undertake. In a very real sense, Boards end up approving, after the fact, the ongoing and developing mission that lurches and trickles up from below. Both the AASCU and AGB would like to change this pattern, establishing firmer control and direction from above. As a first step, they have moved the faculty from the center to the periphery; it is no longer to have a uniquely significant role in shaping institutional destiny. The war against the faculty thus entails reducing not only the number of full-timers but also reducing the power they can wield.

Part-time faculty are not merely less likely to resist this sort of change; they are essentially unable to do so, their role in governance being already marginal or nonexistent. On many campuses the only way to maintain a majority of the faculty in full-time tenure-track positions will be to unionize and win an enforceable percentage of full-timers by legal contract. But the AGB seeks to undermine that strategy as well. In an extraordinary passage, the statement on governance mandates that people involved in unionization should be barred from playing any other role in college or university governance.

The AGB offers no justification for this recommendation. Why should committee memberships or department headships be denied to union activists, that is, *to some of the very people who have shown the most interest in and commitment to campus governance*? Why should union advocacy for salary equity or workplace reforms prohibit further participation in campus life? No explanation is offered. Apparently the AGB considers the case self-evident. Are blacklists to be kept of faculty, staff, and graduate student employee union advocates? We know the answer, for some campus administrations are already trying to carry out this plan.

Meanwhile efforts are under way to redefine the faculty in other ways that would substantially reduce its authority. Post-tenure review can suppress faculty dissent if it does not adhere to AAUP principles. The American Association for Higher Education (AAHE) is exploring alternatives to tenure for full-time faculty. A series of their working papers recommends substituting term contracts for tenure, thereby making faculty more easy to dismiss and less able to resist administrators and boards of trustees. The Pew Foundation has funded research on alternatives to tenure. The Mellon Foundation is interested in how distance learning may reduce the need for full-time classroom faculty. A series of such initiatives is beginning to coalesce into a de facto movement. This movement is united not by conspiracy but by corporate ideology—the ideology shared by many of the CEOs serving on boards of trustees—but the danger to higher education as we know it is no less.

The dangers are multiple; this movement threatens not only the dignity and status of the professoriate but also its intellectual independence. Recognizing that tenure and academic freedom have long been linked, the AAHE has sought to "decouple" them, meanwhile increasing the number and nature of the exceptions to academic freedom as we know it. J. Peter Byrne's 1997 AAHE working paper "Academic Freedom Without Tenure" proposes contractual guarantees of "academic freedom" for faculty "subject to their academic duty to clarify the distinction between advocacy and scholarship" and "subject to duties to respect colleagues and to protect the school from external misunderstandings." But the ultimate guarantor of free speech for faculty members has for half a century been the difficulty of firing them, something the AAHE's recommendations make a good deal easier. Job security enables and protects unpopular speech. Tenure secures the principle of academic freedom.

If tenured faculty are at the center of the institution, their guarantees of free speech can to a significant degree radiate out to protect the speech of untenured or part-time faculty, undergraduate and graduate students, and secretaries alike. When the center can no longer hold, the system of linked guarantees collapses and academic freedom begins to disappear. Then faculty can be dismissed for criticizing the institution's corporate mission or for politically or culturally controversial speech in the classroom or in the public sphere. Less dramatic erosions of the faculty role are already evident in institutions largely staffed by part-timers. The curriculum, notably, ceases to be the provenance of the faculty; it becomes the responsibility of administrators, people who often lack up-to-date disciplinary expertise. The AASCU report anticipates even less faculty control over the curriculum as courses are broken down into segments to be taught by part-timers.

An institution whose faculty is disempowered is certainly more "flexible," more ready to respond to short-term corporate hiring needs. Specialists can be hired or fired at will to run job training programs. As we showed in chapter 8, profitable corporate partnerships can be negotiated without concern for their social, political, or environmental impact. Students who want to pay for a degree with no component of art, history, literature, or philosophy can be sold one without faculty interference. Sham "apprenticeship" programs can be marketed to graduate students who will have no faculty advocates and no jobs when the apprenticeship is over.

If activities like these are major priorities, then the presence on campus of full-time faculty devoted to the institution may at best be an inconvenience, at worst an impediment to "progress." Better to hire people to perform narrowly defined tasks: teach this class segment, design this curriculum, grade these exams, supervise these lab technicians, evaluate these teachers, carry out this research contract, review these application files, write this syllabus, advise these students, design this online course, hire these part-timers. The war against the faculty entails identifying and separating all the roles faculty members perform, eliminating those that inconvenience administrators, and contracting for the others as piecework.

Faculty have recently tried to reinvigorate the notion of "shared governance" as a way of alerting people to these growing changes. For decades no one much talked about shared governance because it was taken to be the natural condition of the university. But the war against the faculty aims to make them merely governed, employees without a role in shaping the nature of their institutions. The values evoked by "shared governance" are already slipping away. Only organized resistance will preserve them.

These were among the lessons apparent in our third story, that of the University of Cincinnati and its faculty union. Unfortunately, there is also a harsh final lesson, one that gives fair warning to the Illinois and Syracuse activists as well: solidarity does not last forever; it needs to be reinvigorated and renewed.

In the fall of 1999 one of us had the opportunity to visit the University of Cincinnati, to help them celebrate twenty-five years of faculty unionization. At the Cincinnati commemoration faculty from a wide variety of departments recalled one another's contributions to a common struggle. They recounted and celebrated one another's words, strategies, analyses, and actions during a series of strikes and contract negotiations over more than two decades. During that time they forged relationships and commitments that transcended the ordinary departmental competition for resources. They learned to respect one another's abilities and capacities. And in moments of real challenge and crisis they forged a solidarity *as a faculty* that could continue to serve them in less desperate contexts. At the 1999 celebration, faculty from professional schools rose to recount the heroism of colleagues from humanities, while faculty from humanities departments recounted the actions taken and strategies devised by those from professional schools and the sciences. That shared history could be recalled not only to build solidarity for new collective actions, but also to help negotiate current conflicts and differences.

Unfortunately, by 1999 trouble was also brewing at Cincinnati. Several of the founders of the union were 1960s activists whose identities were forged in the homefront fires of the Vietnam War. Those young faculty hired in the 1980s and the 1990s—at Cincinnati and across the country—were more narrowly careerist and less likely to share union values. A number of them failed to join the union when they arrived in town. Eventually some of the founding activists began to retire; others lacked the stamina for ceaseless activism. And so the percentage of faculty belonging to the union began to erode. A crisis was already under way by 1999. Indeed the commemoration was partly a strategy devised to reverse the trend. But maintaining membership requires continual organizing. It means walking the halls semester by semester in continual recruitment drives. Meanwhile, the Cincinnati faculty were not required to pay dues unless they were members. Those unions that have agency fee agreements, requiring all faculty to pay dues whether or not they are members, usually have larger budgets and can hire full or part-time organizers to schedule faculty commitments to membership drives. And Cincinnati's bargaining unit also included the medical school, where union membership was never high.

Meanwhile, administrative culture had changed. The union was recognized by administrative consent in a time when administrators sometimes thought honoring the faculty's wishes for self-government was appropriate. Over time, most administrations become convinced they should resist any employee group's democratically chosen form of representation. In this climate minority unions are at risk of efforts to decertify them. On the other hand, even now a union with 80–90 percent of its bargaining unit signed up is likely to get a certain degree of cooperation from administrators. The union might, for example, automatically be asked to participate in faculty orientation sessions. A union with 80–90 percent membership will find it easy to sign new arrivals on campus; a union with less than 50 percent membership will find it far more difficult. Success and failure each become self-fulfilling conditions, generating more of the same.

The Cincinnati faculty union had negotiated a good contract after a successful strike years earlier. By 2001 it was too weak to pose a threat; it had no leverage and could do little more than take whatever the administration offered. From the outset the Cincinnati union had signed up with the AAUP, whose faculty-oriented model of unionization is radically different from the AFT (American Federation of Teachers) or the NEA (National Education Association). Both the AFT and the NEA are fully organized national unions that set policy for local chapters on individual campuses. The AFT has long had politically conservative national leadership and generally resisted strikes; the NEA has been dominated by an anti-intellectual leadership opposed to research. The AAUP, on the other hand, simply helps faculty on a given campus set up its own independent union. It will assist in organizing drives and give advice during contract negotiations. It will provide models of good contract language and provide a variety of other services, but it will not decide policy and impose it on a local. The AFT does the job *for* the faculty. The AAUP helps the faculty do the job *itself.*

The AAUP model thus emphasizes faculty independence and self-determination. It also expects faculty to join with local union staff to do the work necessary to assure the union's strength and survival. For many years the Cincinnati chapter did just that. Then it began to drift and decline. Looking for a miracle, it voted in 2003 to create a joint affiliation with the AAUP and the AFT, hoping that the energetic K–12 AFT leadership would supply its missing clout with the city and the state. But in the end only the hard work to build membership and renew faculty solidarity can save the day.

Increasingly, many campuses resemble Cincinnati; they are places where faculty are losing ground and losing power, losing the right to shape the mission of the university. We need to organize as communities to regain the authority to educate our students to be thoughtful, critical participants in a democracy, not just to be employees filling corporate needs. As some faculty and some administrators have grown apart, some of us have ceased to share a common view of higher education. Of course not all administrators are on one side of these issues; nor are all faculty. But we believe the gulf between those seeking docile students to service the economy and those seeking critical students with diverse cultural functions may be growing. Only an organized force can resist the hegemony of a corporate definition of our mission. We know no way other than collective bargaining to counter the corporate university.

Much more is at stake, then, than the faculty's loss of its privileges. If salary and benefits were the only issues, the public might be expect to shrug its shoulders at the prospect of yet one more professional group losing its privileges. Where faculty organizing overlaps with other professional groups—from flight controllers to medical interns—there is a need to have an organized alternative force to corporate power, one designed to give protection and quality assurance to those the professions serve, from airline passengers to hospital patients to students.

Unions of this sort cannot focus exclusively on their members' short-term financial gains. They need to do collective bargaining that takes up the needs of all campus workers and invites them to help define the larger aims we are here to serve. Neither of these functions typifies most faculty unions. So in reviewing the history of faculty unions we need also to ask how they need to grow and change.

For the structural interdependence of the multiple segments of academic labor increases daily. An influx of new students to many administrators is an opportunity to hire more part-timers to teach them. As the ratio of full-time to part-time faculty decreases, all faculty wield less authority over the curriculum, the budget, and every other aspect of campus life. As part-timers and graduate students take over more teaching responsibilities—and do so with less academic freedom—academic freedom diminishes for everyone in the university. As more part-timers with subminimum wages enter the campus workforce, it becomes increasingly easy to lower entering salaries for ladder faculty. New categories of non-tenurable full-timers with higher teaching loads, lower salaries, and diminished control over course content become difficult to resist. Who *is* to resist? The diminishing tenured faculty? The full-time faculty unions of the present and future can no longer hide from these trends.

What we need to do above all else is to recognize the nature of this struggle—a struggle not only over finances but over the nature of the campus workplace and the aims of education, a struggle finally over the meaning of citizenship in a democracy. For that struggle we need as faculty members to rethink our relation to ambition, achievement, competition, and careerism. A faculty culture devoted exclusively to individual achievement cannot survive the ruthless proletarianization of the professoriate. Yet we are not urging that we abandon either our personal careers or the systems that recognize genuine achievement. We are suggesting rather that we add identities to those in which we are already invested. We are suggesting that we make time in our lives and careers for more collective action, not that we abandon the study and the lab.

SW & CN

10. The Economics of Textbook Reform

I

IT WAS IN THE SPRING OF **1999** that I learned the British edition of my forthcoming *Anthology of Modern American Poetry* would have to be cancelled. My publisher, Oxford University Press, had come to the conclusion they could never sell enough copies of the book to recoup the huge investment they were facing in reprint permission fees. They had hoped to make a profit on the project, not immediately, to be sure, but after a year or two. Now it looked as if the amounts they were being charged to reprint the poems we were including would throw the book permanently in the red. No small irony there, given the number of left-wing poets I had selected; politically and philosophically in the red, the book was now financially in the red as well. Capitalism was to get the final word in blocking the dissemination, at least on the continent and around the world, of some of America's fierce but forgotten political poets.

The publishing industry is a perfect Marxist example of how base and superstructure are not only entangled and interdependent but also contingent and mutually determining. Yet many readers—Marxist and non-Marxist alike—assume a great deal more independence for the cultural realm than is warranted, especially where intellectual production is at stake. It is becoming increasingly clear that not only large expensive books like this one—an anthology with a total budget (including staff salaries) of over $200,000—but also modest scholarly books with direct production costs of only $5,000 are dependent on specific markets and thus clear financial conditions of possibility. I want to review the intellectual and financial history of this book to give a detailed example of what I mean.

The largest single cost by far for an anthology reprinting previously published poems, plays, or short stories is permission fees. Once I had established whether the poem was still in copyright, it was Oxford's job to track down the copyright holder and request the right to reprint the relevant poem or poems. Despite working very efficiently, it took my permissions editor six months to do the job. Sometimes it required several letters just to identify and track down the copyright holder. A significant number of publishers did not answer until multiple letters, faxes, and phone calls had been tried. In one case (Holt), Robert Frost's publisher, we received no reply despite five months of trying. So I asked Oxford to send an express mail letter saying we would reprint the poems (and give a fee of $50 per poem) unless we heard otherwise within forty-eight hours. That got a response.

This was merely one of a number of cases where we had to invent some unique way to handle an individual problem. Often Oxford and I had to play good cop/bad cop or the reverse. Only I, for example, could write a letter threatening to drop an author from the book unless a fee was lowered. It also fell to me to set recommended fee reduction levels for the smaller presses and individual agents, since Oxford had more experience with the larger houses. When tensions rose with a given correspondent, we would routinely switch roles and start again.

Some publishers, like Random House, will set a fee per line of poetry that runs through their whole list of poets. Other publishers, like New Directions, have different fee structures for different authors and poems. Thus a short, famous, frequently reprinted poem may cost more to reprint than a longer little-known poem. We paid more to reprint a six-page excerpt from William Carlos Williams's "Asphodel, That Greeny Flower" than we did to reprint the entire twenty pages of his *The Descent of Winter*. Farrar Straus charged more per line to reprint Randall Jarrell's universally anthologized "The Death of the Ball Turret Gunner" than for any other poem.

Despite the bad news about the consequences of high reprint fees for the British edition of *Anthology of American Poetry*, the American edition was not threatened because the estimated market was much larger. But there too we steadily had to increase the permissions budget. It had started in five figures and was now in six. Tough bargaining by both Oxford and me was necessary to hold to even this substantially increased sum. We wrote the usual letters requesting reductions, letters every publisher's permissions department expects to receive, and most large publishers sent back the anticipated 15–20 percent cuts in their requested fees.

In some cases, however, when the requested fees were especially high, we had to be more aggressive. One literary agent, notorious for charging high fees and for refusing to reduce them, happened to be representing two poets we wanted to include. I wrote back with a simple offer: "Cut the fees by 50% or we will drop one of your writers, who will then get nothing; we'll let you know which one we're cutting when the book goes to press; it's up to you." Of course I had to be willing to follow through with my threat, which indeed I was. As it happened, the agent agreed to cut the fees in half, and the poets both made it into the book.

Yet after six months of bargaining we were still over our increased budget. So I began to cut poems. The University of California Press was charging us $25 each for poems by Robert Creeley and Charles Olson. No need to cut there and nothing to gain in doing so. So I cut an Elizabeth Bishop poem (Farrar Straus) and a James Merrill poem (Knopf), saving a thousand dollars or more for each poem. Three Robert Frost poems (Holt) hit the cutting room floor at $500 each, as did two E. E. Cummings poems (Norton/Liveright). Ditto with a Louise Erdrich poem (Holt). Another $500 saved. On the other hand a prize-winning poet I very much admired, whom I shall not name, came in at $8.50 per poem; we obviously could use as many of his poems as space allowed.

Some publishers saw the Oxford anthology as a way to gain additional readers for their poets and thus as an indirect way of increasing sales of their books of poems. That is sound reasoning, especially in the current market, where the bookstore shelf life for volumes of individual poets' work can be very short. In many stores a volume of poetry that sells out in a few months is never reordered. Very few poets get to see a series of their books kept in stock and many widely read and much-loved poets have no long-term bookstore presence whatsoever. A few major anthologies, however, do get reordered and restocked. They are one of the most dependable ways—and sometimes the only way—for poets to get new readers.

A major component of increasing reprint fees is short-term greed. Commercial publishers owned by conglomerates often refuse to look beyond the impulse to maximize this quarter's profits. So they charge what the market will bear. In the case of the British edition of my anthology, greed overwhelmed the book and killed it. That is an increasing danger for anthologies, one that puts the presence of poetry in the culture at substantial risk.

University presses often behave differently. I cited the University of California Press as an exception to the pattern of extortionate fee demands, and I could as well have mentioned a dozen other university presses. We were charged fair prices by such university presses as California, Illinois,

Pittsburgh, and Wesleyan. At the moment, the high rates charged by many commercial publishers—often twenty-five to fifty times what university presses charge—are balanced by the lower rates from campus presses. If universities upped their rates to commercial levels, the game would be over. Anthologies would die out overnight.

Indeed, certain kinds of anthologies are dead (or moribund) already. In the wake of their massive textbook *Understanding Literature: An Introduction to Reading and Writing* (2004)—a text with a permissions budget of nearly $300,000—Walter Kalaidjian, Judith Roof, and Steve Watt are editing separate volumes on poetry, fiction, and drama. Teachers of drama, no matter how innovative or radical their tastes, still need books ranging from Sophocles to to the twentieth century. But such tables of contents aren't cheap. Arthur Miller's *Death of a Salesman* costs $15,000 to reprint, and plays by major contemporary playwrights—David Mamet, August Wilson, Harold Pinter—cost at least half that. So smaller specialized anthologies like Watt and Gary Richardson's *American Drama: Colonial to Contemporary* (1995) can neither stay in print nor be revised. Less commercial anthologies are becoming rarer still, since publishers do not want to take on the financial risk.

The only good news is that some writers and agents understand that exorbitant permission fees mean high book prices for students and respond to requests with uncommon generosity. Adrienne Kennedy comes to mind, as does Luis Valdez, true to the activist impulse that motivated his playwriting career in the first place. In organizing the Oxford anthology we also encountered notable and immensely welcome acts of generosity. Melvin Tolson's son gave us *Libretto for the Republic of Liberia* for free. In return we annotated the poem elaborately to make it fully available to readers for the first time. Yet our most memorable demand came from an individual poet, not a corporation. I had wanted to include several examples of the edgy punk poetry that emerged in the 1990s toward the end of the book. I succeeded with Sesshu Foster and Patricia Smith but failed with one other young poet.

I never talked with the poet himself; instead I talked and corresponded with his lawyer. The reprint fee requested for his poem—nearly $90 per line—came to more than ten times the highest rate we were paying anyone else. I explained that this was impossible, that we couldn't set such a destructively high standard for this book and others. The fee I offered instead, I was told, wouldn't even pay his New York rent for a month. In response to my asking whether he was really so much better than Adrienne Rich or Michael Harper, the lawyer replied, "Yes. He's been on MTV; he's been on Broadway; they haven't." When I suggested that being included in the first comprehensive anthology of modern

American poetry to be published might help the poet's career, the lawyer replied that he was doing just fine selling his small press books by hand at performances. She then, however, volunteered that he might relent on the fee if Oxford gave him a contract (with a healthy advance) for his next book. I allowed as how I hadn't that authority and that book contracts were negotiated, not extorted. Then came the final madness. I was told that the poet might adopt a different attitude if he felt I was part of the family. "*La familia?*" I asked, feeling as if I were in the middle of *The Godfather.* What on earth did she have in mind? Well, if he were offered a high-paying visiting professorship from the University of Illinois he would probably reduce the reprint fee for the poem. I suggested we really were verging on extortion now and cut the poem from the book.

Not all the memorable exchanges, to be sure, were over money. It took a long time for Oxford to track down Joy Davidman's heirs so we could ask to reprint "For the Nazis." The rights, it turned out, were held by her two sons, products of her marriage with William Gresham, an American veteran of the Spanish Civil War, whom she left when she ran off with C. S. Lewis half a century ago. (You may recall that Debra Winger played her in the film *Shadowlands.*) One son lives in the U.S. and granted reprint rights immediately. The other could only be reached through his Swiss lawyer. Unable to forgive his mother and determined to suppress her memory, he refused us reprint rights. In fact the lawyer suggested we abandon our project entirely! Again we had to devise an individual strategy, so I faxed a reply to the lawyer, saying I'd either reprint Davidman's anti-Nazi poem or explain in the anthology that the son was determined to suppress his mother's work, so the issue wasn't going to go away. It was their choice. A fax approving the reprint arrived shortly thereafter.

We were also flatly refused one reprint for financial reasons. Editors of American literature anthologies know that some publishers deny (or limit) reprint rights so they can offer more works by a given author in their own collections. Hemingway stories are a well-known example. In our case it was Hart Crane's *The Bridge.* W. W. Norton—for many years perhaps the last family-owned major publisher and now owned by its senior editors—would not let us reprint the poem sequence in its entirety, arguing that to do so would undercut sales of Crane's *Collected Poems.* Yet they already use all of *The Bridge* in the *Norton Anthology of American Literature,* an introductory text with proven sales much larger than anything we might hope for. So the real reason Norton refused, I conclude, is that they want to retain *The Bridge* for themselves. That estimate of their real motivation was confirmed when the third edition of *The Norton Anthology of Modern and Contemporary Poetry,* originally edited by Ellmann and O'Claire and now revised by Jahan Ramazani, was published in 2003; the major competition for the Oxford, it touts inclusion of *The Bridge* in its entirety.

Norton also charges high reprint fees for the poems they do allow others to reprint. Had they granted permission for all of *The Bridge*, they might well have approached Arthur Miller territory of $15,000 to reprint it, a sum we could not have paid in any case. Their high charges serve a dual purpose—maximizing immediate profits and burdening competitors with nearly disabling costs. Much the same set of impulses, I suspect, underlies their poetry publishing program as well.

Norton is very canny about bringing authors with growing reputations on board, not necessarily because sales of their individual volumes generate major profits but because control of the reprint rights for poetry is a great advantage in the potentially lucrative textbook market. Norton's individual volumes of poetry are often indifferently designed and printed. Adrienne Rich's books, for example, deserve loving care in design and production, but they do not receive it. The results are almost industrial in appearance.

Norton's control of modern and contemporary American poets—the poets from Cummings to Rich for whom they own the rights and do not have to pay fees to other publishers—gives them about a $20,000 advantage in the permissions fees they have to pay to produce their own anthologies. That is part of what is virtually a monopoly publishing program for this imprint. A wide variety of anthologies from numerous publishers would be to readers' benefit, but reprint fees make that impossible. A large anthology can thus come only from a publisher with major resources. Direct costs of $200,000 to $300,000 and more are to be expected, which is why only larger commercial houses can publish introductory anthologies. Except for Oxford and Cambridge, then, university presses cannot compete to produce such books. And no one can produce them for a general audience alone. Course adoptions are the only basis of long-term sales. There is likely to be no other market that can enable a publisher to recoup costs, let alone earn a profit.

In sum, a major anthology is as much a financial project as a cultural one. Anyone who thinks this sort of book can flow unimpeded from intellectual reflection is simply unaware of the costs involved. Indeed the Ellmann and O'Clair *Norton Anthology of Modern American and British Poetry* remained unchanged and unchallenged for so long because no one could afford the permission fees they'd have to pay to challenge it. My own anthology became possible—just barely possible—because the seventy-five year copyright limit under the old copyright law had begun to expire for a number of the texts of high modernism.

T. S. Eliot's *The Waste Land* used to cost $7,500 to reprint in an anthology. Now it's free. Ditto with Robert Frost's early poems. Despite the high rates charged for some contemporary poets, then, we were able to assemble a potentially viable package, though the book will be in the red for some time.

Poets would be better served by a more competitive, less financially prohibitive and monopolistic environment, but late capitalism is unlikely to grant them one. Would Hart Crane support Norton's policies? Obviously he has no say in them. Nor are there a lot of Hart Crane heirs out there benefitting from the market value of his poetry. What poets could do—if they wished to do so and thought about it—is negotiate with their publishers to limit the size of the reprint fees they could charge at the time they sign their own book contracts. The young poet who wanted $90 per line may be unlikely to champion this proposal, but many poets would like to see their work more widely disseminated and read. As things stand now, the future of anthologies is very much in jeopardy. That in turn means American poetry will be less available and less widely read.

II

Whatever intellectual and cultural decisions inform publishing projects, they are increasingly constrained by financial pressures and financial negotiations. Readers rarely think of such matters, but editors think of them all the time. My publisher (Oxford) was very tolerant of the growing cost of doing business with me. Nevertheless, they could hardly give me so much latitude that I would actually cause them to lose money on the project. My original contract called for a book of 950 pages in print. I had little confidence I could do the job properly and well at that length, but I had no hard proof at the outset and no firm page estimate of my own. So I signed the contract on a hope and prayer that all would work out. In fact the complex mixture of poems, annotations, and headnotes— along with questions like whether to start each poet on a new page, what size type to use, and how many lines to place on each page—made estimating length very chancy. I did ask for (and received) an agreement that Oxford would increase the number of lines per page in the printed book from the initial estimate of 48 to 53 lines to give me a little leeway with which to work.

I also checked journal and magazine publishing histories as carefully as possible to maximize the number of poems that would fall into the category of public domain. Many anthologists pay for permission fees unnecessarily by using book (rather than magazine) publication dates.

As a student of the old copyright law, I also knew a few other obscure regulations of benefit to anthologists. If an author permitted first publication without a copyright notice—as a number of authors did during the depression or when publishing in political magazines or issuing broadsides—then the poem was in the public domain from the outset. Similarly, even if a poem without copyright notice was published without the author's permission, the poem is in the public domain unless the author took legal action against the publisher. Langston Hughes considered taking legal action against the publisher of "Goodbye Christ" (1932), but his lawyer dissuaded him, so the poem is in the public domain.

Detailed knowledge of this sort saved us thousands of dollars in fees, no small matter when we were confronting high priced publishers at every turn. Yet I also missed a few journal publications for poems, so we paid a few hundred dollars in fees that we could have avoided. We lost another thousand dollars when publication was delayed to the year 2,000; we had thus committed ourselves to paying for several poems that were actually in the public domain by the time the book appeared in January.

In the end, financial pressures made a difference in how some poets were represented. When I had to cut a few poems from the book to bring me back within a budget already expanded more than once, I turned, as I said, to relatively expensive poems. Elizabeth Bishop's "Manuelzinho" was one of the poems I cut, not happily. It was there in part to show a major poet writing in what would now be a politically unacceptable way. The poem violates so many contemporary taboos that it is almost unthinkable from a late twentieth century perspective. Yet it was, I felt, less critical to her career than the poems I did include. Sacrificing "Manuelzinho," however, made Bishop a bit more conventional, a result I still regret, though Farrar, Straus, & Giroux, her publishers, made the shorter Bishop selection inevitable because of their high reprint prices.

Only if price is no object could an editor include, say, as many Elizabeth Bishop or James Merrill or Adrienne Rich poems as he or she might choose. Early Frost poems, on the other hand, are in the public domain, and one may thus choose freely from them, though the question of balance with poets still under copyright will necessitate some constraint. One could not very well routinely have huge selections from public domain poets and tiny selections from expensive poets under copyright. My point is that throughout a project like this financial and intellectual or aesthetic questions are thoroughly entangled with one another.

III

At times the entanglements are straightforward. Granting space to one poet uses up some of the available printing budget and thus must entail exclusions elsewhere in the corpus of modern poems. From the outset I was determined for the first time in any anthology to give adequate representation to long poems and poem sequences. Without them I do not feel either the cultural ambitions or the real achievements of modern American poetry can be recognized. But long poems and poem sequences take up more space, and they can be quite expensive to reprint. So printing a series of sequences in their entirety sent a kind of tidal wave through the poets who might otherwise have been included, significantly limiting the available space and thus sweeping aside a number of poets I had hoped to include in the book.

Poem sequences also have a non-relational command over space. Printed in its entirety, Gertrude Stein's "Patriarchal Poetry" takes however many pages it takes. Ordinarily, anthology editors apparently ration space to approximate a hierarchy of importance. Eliot gets more space than Moore because he's more important. Edwin Rolfe cannot get as much space as Robert Lowell because he's less important. The page count cannot be impeccably administered in a canonical merit system, but one is to try one's best. I chose to set this strict accounting principle aside.

My aim was to make the experience of modern American poetry, as I saw it, available to readers in a single volume. The decision to do poem sequences in their entirety was enough on its own to dismantle any hierarchy of poets based on space allotments. A poet like Frost, who wrote mostly short poems, can be well represented in relatively few pages. His twenty-three poems take up twenty-one pages, despite the inclusion of two longer narrative poems, "The Hill Wife" and "The Witch of Coös." These count as long poems for Frost, and, more importantly, they show his interest in presenting female characters in his narrative verse, but they are still much shorter than many other long poems in the book.

The poet with the most pages in the book, a total of sixty, is Melvin Tolson. I wanted to include his *Libretto for the Republic of Liberia*. Not only that, moreover, but I wanted to provide it with full annotations for the first time, a task that Edward Brunner performed splendidly. Henry Louis Gates deserves credit for including *Libretto* in his *Norton Anthology of African American Literature*, but Gates does not add to Tolson's own annotations, which leave foreign language passages untranslated and a great number of obscure historical references unidentified. The decision to annotate *Libretto* fully would have been impossible had I been held hostage to a page-count hierarchy. Our *notes* to *Libretto* alone came to over a hundred pages of manuscript, a burden that Oxford took up without a word of protest. T. S. Eliot, by comparison, receives thirty-four pages in the anthology, not because he is half as important as Tolson but because I felt that was enough space to represent his major work. I include "The Love Song of J. Alfred Prufrock," "Gerontion," *The Waste Land*, "The Hollow Men," "Journey of the Magi," and "Burnt Norton." The two-volume Library of America modern American poetry anthology uses only a small sample of *Libretto* because it links page counts to cultural status. It is also, of course, an anthology edited by a committee. Reaching group consensus on a fully annotated *Libretto* might be difficult; a single editor with a committed and supportive publisher has as much freedom as finances permit.

Later in the book, Muriel Rukeyser gets thirty-five pages because I include her long poem sequence "The Book of the Dead." It is the most important poem sequence by a progressive poet in the first half of the century. Including it gives political and aesthetic counterbalance to Eliot and Pound. And it underlines the often forgotten fact that experimental modernism was taken up by poets with diverse cultural aims and political beliefs.

Presenting the story of modern American poetry fully, in my view, meant rejecting a strict pecking order for poets. At the same time I needed some notable generosity from poets' heirs and publishers to be able to include these long poems. Were Rukeyser and Tolson and Stein represented by Farrar Straus, Random House, or Norton, their long poems would not be in the book. I would not have been able to afford them. Instead, Stein was represented by Yale University Press, which treated us very fairly and made it financially possible to reprint the whole of "Patriarchal Poetry," the most rigorously deconstructive poem of American modernism and thus a poem in some ways decades ahead of its time philosophically. From Muriel Rukeyser's son and Melvin Tolson's son we also received generous treatment focused on helping their parents' legacies get wide distribution.

As a reader moves through this book, with numerous long poems and poem sequences—some of them unfamiliar—the legacy of twentieth century American poetry begins to be reshaped. I have always been surprised, for example, that Adrienne Rich's "Twenty-One Love Poems" is represented with excerpts rather than with the whole sequence; we print the sequence in its entirety, which gives a much more accurate portrait of the subtleties of Rich's thought and method. More unfamiliar still to readers of anthologies is William Carlos Williams's *The Descent of Winter*, a dadaist and politically speculative mix of poetry and prose, perhaps Williams's single most experimental sequence and one that balances his exquisite short lyrics with a more complex form.

Perhaps most unfamiliar of all the poem sequences we print is Welton Smith's "Malcolm," one of the most interesting poems of the Black Arts Movement but largely forgotten because Smith's literary career lasted only a few years. With no ongoing series of books appearing, we would typically only remember Smith if he continued to be anthologized. Smith did, as it happens, issue one pamphlet of poems in 1972, and "Malcolm" was included in the famous 1968 Larry Neal/Amiri Baraka anthology *Black Fire*. But his work, so far as I know, has not been reprinted since. I would not have thought about reprinting "Malcolm" but for Karen Ford's wonderful analysis of the poem in her 1998 book *Moments of Brocade*.

Critics can revive a poet's reputation, but the only sure way to keep a poem alive is to anthologize it. Much more, I suspect, than people realize, anthologies shape our memory of poetic history. They help establish not only whether a poet will be remembered but also *how* a poet will be remembered. When a poet is represented in anthologies with one sort of poem but not another, to a large degree even specialists in the field will remember the poet by way of the poems regularly anthologized and not others. Those will, after all, be the poems faculty members reread and teach year after year. Those are the poems students will read. Those are the poems most available in bookstores. If the poet has no collected volume of poems, moreover, then buying a series of his or her individual books requires a certain dogged effort over time.

The power of anthologies to shape cultural memory was brought home to me most dramatically early in this process. As part of its marketing research, Oxford sent out a detailed questionnaire to modern poetry specialists. The questionnaire took the form of a detailed table of contents for a proposed anthology of modern American poetry. People could vote on whether or not to include each poem. There followed a supplemental list of additional poets with space to recommend whether or not to add them to the book. Finally, there was an opportunity for more extended commentary.

The Oxford editor who compiled the prospective table of contents, Tony English, later told me that he had made it as conventional as possible in order to get people stirred up and guarantee responses. Anyone who completed and returned the questionnaire received a $100 honorarium. As it happened, I was so annoyed by the table of contents that I threw the envelope aside determined not to respond at all. I had no idea at the time that Oxford was contemplating inviting me to edit the book; if I had ignored the questionnaire, they would probably have gone elsewhere. In the end, I decided to write a response explaining how I would treat half a dozen of the poets included but suggesting that the contents needed a complete overhaul.

Once I had agreed to edit the book Oxford tabulated the results of the questionnaire and sent me both the compiled statistics and the individual forms with the names of respondents deleted. There were just over sixty complete questionnaires. Although I wasn't required to honor the results of the survey, Oxford did want me to think seriously about the financial consequences of dropping modern poems that people expect to be able to teach. Yet only a small number of poems received significant votes, and as they were all poems I wanted to include in any case, so on that issue we had no conflict.

What was more interesting to me was how the existing anthologies had shaped peoples' attitudes. Only one respondent suggested adding Edna St. Vincent Millay's witty, rhetorically polished, and decidedly anti-romantic sonnets to the book. These poems weren't on the list because they are not widely anthologized. No one seemed to notice the absence of her political poems. The only Edna St. Vincent Millay in readers' minds was the ecstatically romantic Millay regularly anthologized. In the anti-romantic category we reprint, among other poems, her entire "Sonnets from an Ungrafted Tree" and then end her section with three political poems, "Justice Denied in Massachusetts," "Say That We Saw Spain Die," and "I Forgot for a Moment." The effect, as with many of the selections, should be to change the way a poet is perceived and remembered.

Other absences from the Oxford survey were equally predictable. Sterling Brown was not on Oxford's list and no one thought of mentioning him. Langston Hughes was represented as he usually is in anthologies, without his most searing poems about race, like "Christ in Alabama," and without his poems of the left, like "Come to the Waldorf-Astoria." Only one respondent suggested, without being specific, that his section should be rethought. The lesser-known poets of the Harlem Renaissance remained unmentioned.

There were nonetheless many good suggestions in the comments section of the questionnaire. One writer made a good case for how to present John Ashbery. Another argued for Adrian Louis, whom I much admire, and who is well represented in the book. Often respondents were particularly knowledgeable about one or two authors, and they made detailed and interesting suggestions in those instances. So there was much of value in the results. Yet there was very little encouragement to make fundamental changes in how canonical poets should be treated. Most respondents saw little reason to alter the picture presented in existing anthologies, though it is also true that the list of respondents Oxford used emphasized established faculty who had been teaching modern poetry for some years. Few if any assistant professors were queried. This older group at least had cultural memories largely shaped by their textbooks.

Marianne Moore was thus substantially remembered as she is anthologized. A few people did, I was pleased to see, recommend including

"Marriage." What we did instead was reprint her two most philosophically ambitious long poems, "Marriage" and "An Octopus." These poems also display her most complex use of quotations and the depth of cultural analysis she is capable of, without which her role in modernism is severely slighted. I added two historically oriented poems, "Sojourn in the Whale" and "Spenser's Ireland" to complicate her image still further.

IV

One general issue that came up repeatedly in the survey responses, however, was the emphasis on multicultural poets toward the end of the Heath and Norton anthologies of American literature. A number of people considered these selections second-rate. Unfortunately, both in the questionnaire comments and in conversations with many colleagues around the country, I encounter the same conclusions: multicultural poets do not equal canonical poets in rhetorical skill. Their poems are narrowly and unreflectively autobiographical and often overly sentimental.

I believe the emergence of several vital traditions of minority writing is the single most exciting development in American literature in recent decades. Yet I do not see how you could reach that conclusion from the most widely adopted classroom anthologies, where the multicultural poems tend to be not only rhetorically slack but also uniformly respectful toward minority cultures. In many cases anthologies mute the element of protest in minority poems as well, with poets' strongest critiques of the dominant culture omitted. The result is sometimes a bland, unthreatening multicultural poetry that celebrates diversity but avoids all passionate and rhetorically inventive social commentary.

Then a certain inertia sets in. The competition includes Gary Soto and Cathy Song, so you have to include them as well. The editors may not even have read widely in contemporary minority poetry, or they may be uncomfortable with multicultural poems that are more frank and challenging. In the end many faculty conclude not only that political correctness alone has put these poets in anthologies but also that the poetry itself lacks both courage and quality.

I was determined to prove otherwise by including a series of rhetorically inventive and culturally potent poems by minority poets. These poems are often critical of both minority and majority cultures. Whether it is Adrian Louis or Sherman Alexi writing about Native American alcoholism, Yusef Komunyakaa interrogating black and white sexuality, Ray Young Bear indicting a history of white oppression, Martín Espada wittily celebrating the ironic triumphs possible within poverty, Jessica Hagedorn and Ana Castillo meditating on sexuality and popular culture, or Patricia Smith writing about the antagonisms flowing from racist history, there are minority poets creating poems notably different from anything we have seen in America before. Louis' "Petroglyphs of Serena," with its portrait of the hopelessness of reservation lust, Alexie's "The Native American Broadcasting System," with its remorseless satire of the contemporary Powwow, Patricia Smith's "Blond White Women," with its physical hostility, all these are poems with an unsettling edge. Unlike the multicultural poets so often anthologized, they have not signed on to a good neighbor policy.

Of course there is one requirement to be met for someone to recognize that these poems are rather different from what they have seen before—they have to *read* them. That requirement was not quite met by the January 2000 participants in an American poetry electronic discussion group who began debating the merits of the anthology before they had seen it. The discussion began when one senior faculty member who had not even seen the table of contents came to a confident and purely phantasmatic conclusion—that I had eliminated all the major male modernists from the book.

Reaching a state of conviction about an unseen table of contents, then broadcasting that false conviction on the internet, goes well beyond irresponsibility; it suggests madness, a commitment to one's own spleen and bluster and prestige that transcends any checks the material world might impose. What was even more remarkable, however, was that this one faculty member's irrationality provoked a nationwide moral poetry panic, as one person after another chimed in with regret or outrage that Eliot and Pound were absent from a book called *Anthology of Modern American Poetry*.

Did people really imagine that I do not teach Eliot and Pound? That Oxford would tolerate such a foolish (and financially catastrophic) agenda even if I proposed it? Were either Oxford or I interested in producing a book that could not possibly sell? What concept of literary history could encompass *eliminating* much of the poetry readers have valued for decades? Should any of these folks loosen their collars and reduce their body temperatures long enough to read the book, they will find that Eliot and Pound are not only there but also more thoroughly annotated than in any previous anthology.

My favorite posting was from a faculty member who has like me been working with noncanonical poets for some years. She testified with passion about how she teaches *both* the traditional and the expanded canon and about how useful it is to compare them in the classroom. Why can't we have an anthology that includes *both*? she asked plaintively. I hope that someone has distracted her from her performance of the wise and saddened teacher so that she can discover the anthology she wanted is more or less the one I edited.

Once this chorus actually saw the table of contents, some of its members began to dissent from the moral panic. Then the most committed complainers shifted ground: the anthology was declared "a PC travesty." Look at all these slack multicultural poets at the end. Slack? Try Thylias Moss's wildly inscaped language. Read Anita Endrezze's inventive linguistic equivalents of Native American understandings of nature. Try Sesshu Foster's hard edged postmodern prose poems or Mark Doty's fierce denunciation of homophobia. Read Michael Harper's gritty renditions of deaths in his family. And if you decide death holds no fear for you, turn to Sharon Olds and C. D. Wright.

The complaints about the presence of so many minority poets in the book are in fact part of a general backlash by more conservative members of the profession. In an essay review ("Twentieth-Century American Poetry, Abbreviated") in the spring 2001 issue of *Parnassus* William Logan complains that "The Harlem Renaissance has received far more critical attention than its achievements deserve" (467), opines that Tolson's *Libretto* is "a ludicrous pastiche of modernist practice," and concludes that "It takes an editor without fear of God to favor Muriel Rukeyser over T. S. Eliot" (470–71). Rukeyser, he notes, receives thirty-five pages in my anthology, whereas Eliot receives but thirty-four. While I would be willing to take credit for this gesture of lese majesty, the truth is I had no idea what the final page count would be. Perhaps Logan has no experience editing large, heavily annotated anthologies. Such books are still set from hard copy, typically photocopies of reliable editions of the poems and computer printouts of headnotes and annotations. With over 500 different published sources with varying type sizes and line lengths and no way of knowing how the extensive notes would compress when type set, it was impossible to calculate either the length of the published book or how many pages each poet would receive. As it happened, my 2,000-page manuscript gave Rukeyser forty-two pages and Eliot sixty-one; Eliot ended up with one fewer page in the book because the elaborate notes to his poems took up less space. I suppose a properly respectful editor would go back and cut poems to preserve the expected hierarchy.

The most well known exemplar of the racist backlash against multicultural poetry is Harold Bloom's introduction to *The Best of the Best American Poetry: 1988–1997*, where he castigates Adrienne Rich for her inclusion of "enemies of the aesthetic who are in the act of overwhelming us" (1998, 16) in her own anthology, *The Best American Poetry 1996*. Bloom has in mind, among others, such Native American poets as Sherman Alexie and Adrian Louis, poets more recently attacked by Marjorie Perloff on the modern poetry listserve mentioned above and in an essay "Janus-Faced Blockbuster." Perloff, notably, makes an exception among poets of color for those who write in the narrow, linguistically experimental tradition she values. Bloom chooses as the epigraph for his piece a line from Thucydides—"They have the numbers; we, the heights"—intended to evoke a horde of multiculturalists about to overwhelm those few white cultural stalwarts in possession of the truth. Always convinced he has one hand securely grasping the eternal verities, Bloom regrettably has the other hand embedded in temptations he might better have resisted. Perloff meanwhile is ending her career in an aesthetic reprise of the last films of Shelley Winters—blowsy, potted on power, and forever trumpeting warnings against the poetic equivalents of "Earthquake!" and "Fire!"

There are many other poems I could cite against the claim—voiced by folks who cannot or will not read the book—that it is a politically correct collection. Let me cite just one: if this were a PC book, would Vachel Lindsay's "The Congo" be in it? Throughout the editing process I felt I was resisting the aesthetic of political correctness, which valorizes tame poems that sacralize minorities. I wanted instead a broad range of poems taking up American and world history and interrogating the difficulties of social life. There are private poems, poems about love and family life as well, but overall there are far more poems devoted to public life than one usually finds in recent anthologies. In my view, that unifies a century of poetry and some of its predecessors, from Walt Whitman's devotion to the social meaning of democracy to the Japanese American citizens who wrote exquisite haikus about their World War II experience in America's concentration camps.

CN

11. Transforming Teaching and Reaching the Public on the Internet

THE TITLE OF THIS CHAPTER IS AN ADMISSION of and testimony to those moments, if you will, in which many of us have succumbed to utopian ecstasy in the presence of the World Wide Web. Or, more accurately, it is an expression of the possibilities I and my collaborators have glimpsed as we worked on the very large modern American poetry Web site we maintain at the University of Illinois. There are times, to be sure, when the Internet seems mainly a new way to spend money. At other times, the low quality of so much of the material online makes even a bad book seem a better buy. And there are dark commercial clouds on every horizon suggesting that economic opportunism and bullying will preempt every anarchist Internet impulse. Yet at least one humanities discipline, history, has amassed impressive and sometimes overwhelming online resources. The resources in literary studies are more uneven, but a group of collaborators at the University of Illinois and elsewhere manages what may be one of its brighter lights, and it is that project we want to describe.

MAPS—http://www.english.uiuc.edu/maps—began as a companion to *Anthology of Modern American Poetry*, published by Oxford early in 2000 and described in the previous chapter. The Web site still serves that purpose, since the authors we focus on are the 180 poets in the book, but the project has also opened out and evolved in ways we could not have easily anticipated. We did not, for example, realize how isolated scholars who work on American literature abroad can feel, especially those who publish in European journals, and how often they despair of reaching an American audience. They have thus been especially eager to publish work on MAPS and have it available all across the world. We did not anticipate that people would want to use MAPS to publish revised versions of earlier book chapters and essays, though our Advisory Board member Ed Folsom did point out that the Internet is the prime territory of second chances—a place where you can revise and update that argument you cannot easily market a second time to a traditional publisher. Nor did we expect to be publishing so many original essays, but we now have over one hundred online. When we began putting thousands of pages of excerpts from scholarly essays online we did not think through the reality of what we were offering here and abroad to people who lack first-rate library resources. Early on teachers in Belgium and Thailand wrote to say that for the first time their classes had access to a wide range of modern poetry scholarship. An American teaching in Sarajevo and his class used MAPS at a time—when the city was under assault—when not only books but also libraries were unavailable. And the truth is that the overwhelming majority of the 3,500 college libraries in the U.S. are not models of comprehensiveness either.

After several years, MAPS has over twenty thousand pages on line, and we regularly add more material. It is designed to be a resource people use repeatedly, not a one-visit site. Because of that, and because the quantity of material is substantial, our designer Matthew Hurt, who has his PhD in American literature, and I decided on a very straightforward structure. We both also took a web design course from the novelist Richard Powers, which was like having a philosopher king as your tech person, and he too urged elegant, transparent design principles. There's a tremendous amount of visual material on MAPS, but there are no bells and whistles, no gimmicks.

The main body of the site is organized as an alphabetical list of poets. You click on a poet's name and arrive at the poet's main page. There you'll find a list of poems and a series of other links. If you click, say, on Anthony Hecht, then on the title of one of his poems, "More Light, More Light," you'll find first a series of excerpts from published interpretations of the poem and finally a previously unpublished analysis by Joshua Charlson. MAPS thus gives key access to existing scholarship and then adds to it. But since "More Light, More Light" is a Holocaust poem, you can also click on one of MAPS' historical sites, in this case "About the Holocaust," which will take you to a page with links to a whole series of Holocaust resources. There is a factual overview by Martin Gilbert, a more impassioned essay by Elie Wiesel, and extensive exhibits of Holocaust photographs and Holocaust art works. There is in addition a Holocaust glossary, a Holocaust timeline, and a group of excerpts from theoretical writings about the Holocaust. There are dozens of such historical and cultural background sites on MAPS, from "About World War I" to "About Marilyn Monroe" to "About the Sonnet," and we add to these regularly as well. The idea is to provide what we call "a comprehensive learning environment for the study of modern American poetry." Each poet's site has from one to three editors, and MAPS as a whole has a Board of Advisors.

It was one of our site editors, Ken Roemer, who teaches in Texas, who first decided to use MAPS as a creative forum for one of his graduate seminars. Following class discussions, each seminar member wrote and revised an analysis of a Scott Momaday poem, and those revised analyses were published on the site. I made the process a bit more elaborate. Each of my grad students writes a detailed poem analysis and commentary on MAPS critics each week and posts it to the other seminar members before class. This is quite different from the internet bulletin boards and threaded dialogue some classes use. First of all, I ask for only one carefully written post per week, not a continual flood of emails. That practice has a way of taking over your life, whereas this more modest use of an electronic classroom does not. Part of the purpose of the weekly posts is to jump-start the seminar meeting by getting the discussion under way before class begins. Even shy students are thus guaranteed to be in dialogue with everyone else. When posts make particularly challenging comments on a critic's work, I will forward the comment to the scholar and invite him or her to join the discussion. Some have been a little surprised at this and declined to participate; others have become involved and responded substantively, which is particularly exciting to the students.

Halfway through the semester everyone picks their best analysis for MAPS. I then assign four or five commentors for each analysis. I try to choose people with both similar and different perspectives. An analysis of a Sylvia Plath poem will get a commentor with long term interest in Plath if one is available, along with someone who works primarily in another period. A Marxist analysis will be assigned to a Marxist critic and to a psychoanalytic critic to provide both fraternal and deconstructive commentary.

It's not unusual for comments to be a full page in length, in response to a mini-essay that may only be two to five pages long, so people are getting very focused attention to their work from several different people. The seminar members revise one another's sentences and challenge one another's ideas. Everyone has several weeks to revise their posts before I consider them for MAPS. Some go up immediately; for others I request another round of revisions. The benefits to participants are several. To begin, they get exceptionally detailed commentary on their work. It's a writing lesson about intense sentence-by-sentence concentration on both conceptual and stylistic issues. And it gives everyone a model of focus and intellectual intensity they can apply to their dissertations.

One other requirement I make is that all critiques of each other's essays be shared with the whole class. The first benefit from that is a lesson in how to give and receive criticism. A public airing of commentary about their work does tend to get people over the disabling shock they often feel when first receiving tough criticism. Receiving honest commentary also makes people more inclined to provide it for others, something even many established scholars are reluctant to do. The mutual sharing of commentary also produces a second-level response, in which the class may collectively reinforce or discount a given suggestion. Writing workshop classes, of course, have been doing this sort of thing for years. Doing it by e-mail, as we do, means that people receive written, rather than oral, comments, which tends to produce more carefully thought-out remarks and gives people a chance to reflect on suggestions more carefully.

Then they revise and the hard work pays off. They get a publication they can list on their vitas. These poem analyses amount to concise writing samples. They give a hiring committee access to work that may be both somewhat less specialized than the dissertation and more obviously given to classroom applicability. Both for my graduate students and for faculty elsewhere it's also an opportunity to distribute sections of work in progress and potentially to obtain some feedback on it. And perhaps most importantly these essays are a way of communicating with and influencing readers and critics across the world. I do a modified version of this exercise with undergraduate seminars, which also send weekly email commentaries to each other. The undergrads are not required to revise for publication on MAPS, but when one of their essays merits the effort I work with them to that end, and several analyses by undergraduates are now on the site.

Therein lies my modestly utopian claim for the discipline. For there is another agenda at work here. T. S. Eliot, Robert Frost, Ezra Pound, Wallace Stevens and other canonical poets are well represented on MAPS. Marianne Moore's MAPS Web site is over 300 pages long. William Carlos Williams has over 200 pages, as does Frost. Poets with a long history of commentary thus have book-length sites on MAPS. But both the anthology and MAPS devote a great deal of space to noncanonical poets as well, including many for whom there were no detailed poem analyses published anywhere.

The task of writing the first full-length essay on a poet can be daunting. The research alone can be quite time consuming. Yet the need for this sort of critical work is very great, since simply disseminating unfamiliar poems may not be enough to ensure they will receive a thoughtful and informed reception. Especially, when new rhetorical and topical issues are at stake, people may read poems antagonistically out of cultural ignorance. For some of the poets in my anthology it will take a generation or two before a sufficient body of scholarly essays exists to assure sufficient complication to the ways we read. The poets of the Harlem Renaissance, for example, still lack adequate scholarly analysis. Needless to say, the new Native American poets of the 1980s and 1990s often have still less. It is only that lack of informed commentary that makes it possible for critics like Harold Bloom and Marjorie Perloff to claim their work has no literary merit.

In time we will have the books and essays we need. In the meantime there is an alternative way to reform and inform the profession—MAPS. I encourage my grad students to go where no one has gone before, to write about poets and poems so far ignored or neglected by the profession. Often enough these writers have notable audiences but as yet no scholarly commentators. The most canonical modern poets come effectively pre-packaged with extensive interpretive discourse; we read their work in the context of commentary disseminated directly and indirectly, commentary that inevitably both encumbers and facilitates whatever semiotic productivity these texts can have, but commentary that nonetheless produces value, meaning, and cultural capital. Silence may have its own productivity but it does not compete so well for our attention. Using H.D. as a benchmark, one may estimate it takes twenty years of recovery work to make a poet fully a part of the discipline's ongoing conversation. I'm not that patient when my interests extend to scores of neglected poets.

That's a process that a Web site like MAPS can clearly facilitate. Of course there have been a number of journals featuring close readings of individual poems—*Explicator, Modern Poetry Studies, American Poetry,* and others—but none has ever, or would ever, have the reach of the Internet. No subscription is necessary. MAPS is free; you can visit it wherever or whenever you have Internet access. And so people have. Just a few years ago our home page had 500 hits a week. Now we get well over 1,000 a day. But search engines typically take people directly to a poet's site, bypassing our main page. The main page itself will passed 1,000,000 hits in 2003. The site as a whole has had far more than that.

Since MAPS supplements a text that is regularly assigned to new classes, there is a built-in mechanism that will continually bring in both new and returning visitors. Indeed, every time someone buys the anthology in a bookstore or borrows it from a library they are encouraged to visit the site. Every time someone types one of our poet's names into a search engine, they'll be invited to MAPS. For any member of the reading public interested in modern poetry, MAPS displays the discipline at its most practical and useful—helping people read and value individual texts by interpreting them and supplying essential background information. Not that everyone will be able to understand every analysis, but even those analyses steeped in the language of theory are situated within an understandable interpretive context. That is why MAPS and other web sites offer a way of demonstrating the value of scholarship to members of the general public. Internet sites tend to break up scholarship into manageable units and to focus on segments that are of immediate use. It does not require scholars to write books and essays differently so much as it offers an opportunity to package segments of books and essays in ways the public will find practical and accessible. You carve out one or more portions of an essay, frame it somewhat differently if necessary, and place it online. It is an easy way to reach both a wider variety of academic disciplines and readers outside the academy.

It is thus one effective response to the critique so many have made of academic scholarship over the last several decades—that it has become inaccessible to the general reader and that faculty members have done a very poor job of explaining it to the public. Yet arguments for the value of humanities research are often both irritating and unpersuasive; they seem like interested pleading. Internet presentations of excerpts from scholarship have the virtue of persuading indirectly and by example. Moreover, although many scholars are unwilling to recast their whole writing style to make it accessible to nonspecialists, the sort of quick repackaging necessary for the internet is inoffensive for many. It amounts to adjusting to the demands of the medium, rather than abandoning your integrity.

As the discipline at the center of the culture wars, and thus the discipline most maligned over the last two decades, literary studies is clearly most in need of this kind of public outreach. Yet the public has little awareness of why the humanities as a whole is an enterprise of ongoing research, rather than just a container for eternal truths, so all humanities disciplines would eventually benefit from this gradual display of their relevance. At the moment universities are not inclined to staff or fund broad Internet projects of public education; it is time they saw it as central to their mission. Indeed, if resultant changes in public attitudes would be relatively slow, the impact on students' respect for scholarship is immediate.

The effect on classes of this kind of presentation of scholarship is particularly dramatic. Undergraduates who may not have the patience to read dozens of scholarly books and essays looking for interpretations of a Frost poem can click on the poem's title and get immediate access to exactly the material they most want. If they are required to do so, the results will be more consistent. Then the impact on a class can be considerable. Since students are better informed about the history of commentary, they are more able to agree or disagree with it and to participate actively in discussion. The effect, moreover, is democratizing and liberating because students are much closer to being a faculty member's equal if they have equal knowledge of a poem's critical reception.

Both teachers and students are more likely to deal with unfamiliar noncanonical poetry if they have even a few representative close readings and are provided with the relevant historical background. Except for MAPS there is so far as I know no place to find close readings of poems by Asian American poet Sesshu Foster, Native American poets Anita Endrezze and Adrian Louis, Puerto Rican poet Martín Espada, or radical poets John Beecher, Thomas McGrath, and Lucia Trent. You can find there as well a "Libretto Colloquy" with a dozen members of a graduate seminar opening Melvin Tolson's groundbreaking poem to more innovative critical perspectives than have been applied to it in the last fifty years.

It is this kind of cultural work—opening up an international dialogue about ignored or neglected writers, rapidly theorizing the margins of the canon, disseminating worldwide new views of familiar and unfamiliar texts and subcultures—that the Internet has the potential to do more powerfully than perhaps any other medium. But in the end it's not an independent role but a collaborative one. We expect some of the people who read excerpts of books online to seek out the rest of those books that excite them and ask their libraries to order them. We expect the close readings on MAPS to grow into or stimulate longer essays and book chapters. Certainly MAPS makes it significantly easier to engage with the history of criticism when working on a new interpretation. MAPS makes the cumulative, collaborative, collective, and disputatious history of interpretive discourse far more evident. It works against the tendency in recent years to ignore other critics and indulge in a fantasy of absolute originality.

In the infinite expandability of the Internet, MAPS can accommodate a variety of disciplinary and cultural projects. It has space to consolidate the high cultural consensus of the cold war canon and space to disseminate revolutionary readings of the suppressed poetry of the American Left. If it is for me partly a project of revolutionary change—disseminating readings of Langston Hughes's powerful poems against racism and Edwin Rolfe's searing attacks on McCarthyism—and partly a project of bringing together multiple celebrations, for example, of Allen Tate's and John Ransom's cultural conservatism. In the end, it mirrors and assists a contradictory discipline that is capable of doing both.

CN

12. What Would an Ethical Graduate Program Be?

"No responsible educator has ever claimed that the Ph.D. carries with it any implication, let alone guarantee, that one who has earned it will be a good teacher. The only claim which can be seriously made for it, and it is not a negligible one, is that without it . . . one is not well-equipped to teach at the college and university level, whatever other virtues and gifts he [sic] might possess."

—Moody E. Prior

"We could afford to give up the [Ph.D.] degree, or to abolish the dissertation, *only if everyone else agreed to do so.* Given the unusually decentralized nature of the American system, *there is simply no way for this to happen.*" [our emphasis]

—David Damrosch

THE FLOOD OF COMMENTARY on graduate education in the later 1990s suggested that either some faculty had succumbed to an unrelenting *fin-de-siècle* impulse for introspection—a kind of stocktaking and backward look common at the ends of centuries, never mind millennia—or that we were living, insofar as higher education is concerned, in desperate times which demanded change. The MLA's Committee on Professional Employment (CPE) intimated as much about the latter possibility when, in a kind of Dickensian funk in the early pages of its "Final Report," the Committee referred to the "worst of times amid the best of times": "As we began to formulate our report in the summer of 1997, the best of times at large contrasted eerily with the worst of times in academia" (6). If such conditions had not yet prompted cries for the installation of guillotines on quadrangles across the country, they at least motivated pointed discussions of both the most fundamental assumptions of graduate education and the material realities of graduate student life. Such analyses, in turn, have led to calls for the reformation of virtually every component of advanced degree programs as we know them, particularly of the PhD degree in the humanities. In fact, two such major national initiatives were highly visible in 2002 and 2003: The Carnegie Foundation's multi-year program "The Carnegie Initiative on the Doctorate" (CID), initiated in 2002 and whose first national meeting was convened in the summer of 2003; and the publication by the Council of Graduate Schools of the results of the Preparing Future Faculty (PFF) program: *Preparing Future Faculty in the Humanities and Social Sciences: A Guide for Change* (2003). These projects, as of 2003, were at quite different stages in their respective developments: the Carnegie Initiative identified partner institutions during the previous year and sponsored the authorship of essays by leading figures in such disciplines as English as inaugural steps. By contrast, the PFF program has existed since 1993, and a number of schools—Colorado, Florida State, Georgia, Howard, Indiana, New Mexico, Texas A &M, and others—have actively participated in such disciplines as English, Speech Communication, Sociology, Psychology, and Political Science, and their findings were published in 2003. The questions we want to raise in this essay, especially in relationship to doctoral programs in English and the humanities, are these: What professional or ethical principles have informed or contained such discussions? What ethical principles *ought* to guide the formulation of any revisions to doctoral programs in the humanities, English in particular, in these "worst of times," if indeed this characterization is accurate?

It is important, we believe, that these are regarded as very different questions, questions that require consideration before any revisions of doctoral programs are formulated and urged, which we shall do at the conclusion of this essay. And, although the provisional definition of ethics that follows might appear primitive–just as it will presume considerable agency on the part of individual faculty, a hangover, perhaps, from our own liberal-humanist education[1]—one distinction between these two

---

1. When, in a recent article on downsizing graduate programs, Watt expressed too much confidence in faculty ability to make sure reduced enrollments did not necessarily lead to less representation of minority and working class students, Jim Neilson and Gregory Meyerson pointed out that this optimism was "so steeped in the tradition of liberal individualism" that the extent to which individual faculty, departments, and "universities in general conform to institutional pressures and constraints" got ignored (281). Perhaps, and there is little question that they are right about the myriad pressures exerted upon individuals and departments. But no change is possible, finally, without the presumption of a subject endowed with at least a minimal agency. Faculty *do* possess, at the very least, some minimal power to improve graduate programs.

questions informs our use of the term "ethics": namely, Jean-François Lyotard's distinction between "must" and "ought," the latter of which, he claims, is a "'you must' already grafted onto an ontology, even if it be an anti-ontology" (44). This point in *Just Gaming*, Lyotard's dialogue with Jean-Loup Thébaud on Kant and the possibility of ethical action, emerges from Thébaud's conflation of "must" and "should," a conflation Lyotard takes seriously. For "ought" requires an interlocutor to "deduce obligation" and derive prescriptions (which, in this instance, Lyotard declines to do). As the derivation of prescriptions falls, according to Lyotard, within the domain of the intellectual–and even at the risk of legitimating these prescriptions in a manner similar to the way totalitarian regimes attempt to legitimate their exercise of power, i.e., by narrative—we won't similarly resist the opportunity to formulate recommendations for programmatic change. The legitimacy of these prescriptions depends, finally, on our ability to see them as compatible both with a narrative of the origin of the PhD *and* as part of the narrative of a better future for students who pursue advanced post-graduate work.[2] And, to be sure, they acquire greater urgency within the narrative of revolutionary crisis advanced by the MLA's Committee on Professional Employment in 1997, however fatalistic the Committee's vision at times seems.

More important, as we have suggested throughout this book, proposals that simply add dimensions to graduate curricula without *concrete* recommendations for their financial support and a calculation of what effects such accretions exert on the crucial matter of time to degree will not satisfy the *materialistic* ethics we want to propose here. Our chapter on "Disciplining Debt" explains this topic in more detail, but suffice it to say that several valuable suggestions offered by the PFF report—the establishment of teaching mentors at institutions other than the Research One schools that offer the doctorate, for example, to whom doctoral students would travel and "shadow" as teachers–might very well succeed in exposing students to the professional cultures they are likely to enter and in refining their teaching techniques. Such a program would also

---

2. In his "Memorandum on Legitimation" from *The Postmodern Explained*, Lyotard identifies two "primary procedures of language that come to mask the logical aporia of authorization: . . . one procedure directs this dispersion upstream, toward an origin, the other directs it downstream toward an end" (41). Our redaction of the point might be expressed this way: calls for the reformation of graduate education typically justify changes either on the basis of the history and traditional requirements of degrees or, conversely, on a largely pragmatic basis of what the future might demand. The CPE report, for example, bases its recommendations on a largely instrumentalized future for today's graduate students, one heavy on service to the corporate university and light on the time and means necessary for the production of cultural criticism. If fully implemented, the CPE recommendations might only ensure that such a future would occur.

address graduate students' "greatest concern" as revealed in a 2001 survey quoted in the PFF "Guide for Change": "a perceived mismatch between the training students receive and the expectations of their careers" (11). But who will pay for such multi-institutional mentoring? For how long? How will this suggestion further attenuate the seven to ten years most doctoral candidates spend in graduate school and thus exacerbate the debt burden graduate students carry?

At base, the term "ethics" denotes a nexus of values that underlie our conduct, our relationships, and—most relevant in the present context—our professional decisions. If these decisions were always easy to make, if they did not in the most extreme instances involve equally compelling, but inherently contradictory options, there would be little need for ethics. Or for humanity. For the most primitive computer could negotiate such decisions as, "It may rain. Should one take a raincoat or risk getting wet? Yes or no." But what about a question like "*Should* we require doctoral candidates to spend an additional semester or year acquiring further teaching and service experience?" a real possibility if programs were to follow the PFF suggestion. Or, as intimated by a number of critics of the present doctoral degree, "Should PhD programs retain the requirement of a dissertation and, in so doing, preserve the notion underlying the requirement that the conferral of the degree is contingent, finally, upon an 'original contribution to knowledge'?" This question, involving as it does such factors as time, the exacerbation of debt, a program's attrition rates, and a host of other factors, is a far more complicated matter, in large part because it pertains so directly to the aspirations of our students and to our own senses of identity as their teachers. Are we even responsible for such factors as the money students borrow? And what about high attrition rates? Local data in our departments indicate that more students drop out of our program *after* they are "ABD" than before. Is this an argument for abolishing dissertations? What sort of attrition rate is acceptable—or what rate is unconscionable—for a competitive doctoral program?

It is precisely because of these complexities that disciplines in the humanities *should* articulate bedrock or first principles before advocating any radical transformations of programs, degrees, and the educational values they represent. In this regard, as David Damrosch observes, merely "tinkering with requirements in the absence of a larger vision and a sustained commitment to change will have little effect" (1995, 158). "Tinkering" is also dangerous for precisely the reason we outlined earlier in "The Postdoc Paradox": because in a delicately balanced system like graduate education, any change is likely to impact other program elements in ways we cannot anticipate and may not find palatable. Finally, again following Damrosch's lead, we want to clarify that it seems inappropriate, even presumptuous, to try and "invent a template that should be applicable to the dramatically varying situations of different institutions and different disciplines" (157). For this reason, we are speaking in the main about graduate programs in English at Research One institutions that produce the majority of today's professorial faculty.[3]

A Very Brief Recent History:
From the 1960s to Today

Two principles, neither of them original, underlie everything that follows. Both are as foundational and unvarnished as bedrock gets, yet neither would meet with universal approbation these days. First, as Moody Prior affirmed over thirty-five years ago, the PhD degree is "the graduate school's chief educational product as well as its principal justification"; and second, "the reiterated demand to keep higher education in tune with the times . . . has been as much a part of our educational traditions as anything else" (1965, 31, 33). When Prior made these claims in the mid-1960s, the times were indeed "a' changin'" insofar as graduate education in general and the PhD in English in particular were concerned; not surprisingly, not everyone embraced them. One such change, for example, was a movement in English away from its heritage in philology, an evolution that by the 1960s had convinced some that the mastery of Latin and German was no longer essential to all field specialties within English graduate curricula.

Yet these revisions were hardly attributable solely to shifting disciplinary imperatives, as Marjorie Hope Nicolson, president of the Modern Language Association, lamented in her 1964 presidential address. She contended that reduced language requirements for the PhD constituted a significant "debasement" of the degree and was caused by a market economy exactly the opposite of today's brutal "job system": namely, one in which an intense demand for teachers of English existed. Trying to produce new PhDs to meet an inflated post-war demand for college faculty, graduate programs were refashioning curricula to better stay "in tune with the times," times somewhat different from those in 1920 when Nicolson completed her PhD in three years. Adverting to the title of her presentation, she recalled the "generous education" she received then,

---

3. We specify "professorial faculty" here only to indicate those faculty who hold terminal degrees in their field, the majority of which will be the PhD. Of course, too many doctoral holders have not found such positions or meaningful full-time employment, for that matter, conditions which have prompted most of the commentary cited then in this essay.

one quite different from the one advocated by the PFF, which involved minimal preparation as a teacher and even less experience as a professional. It was only after landing a job as an assistant professor at the University of Minnesota with several other junior faculty, Nicolson confessed, that her department chair "almost literally dragged us youngsters to MLA meetings and made us deliver the first scholarly papers written under our own steam" (1964, 6). In a nostalgic mood for her presidential address, Nicolson also recalled the "dim view" many academicians took toward the German-manufactured PhD degree itself two generations or so before completing her own, as well as her own previous ambivalence about its necessity: "Certainly I have no recollection of feeling or being told that a Ph.D. was essential for college teaching. On the contrary. . ." (1964, 5). Yet, reflecting on such matters in the mid 1960s, Nicolson's attitude had changed: then, there was little question that a PhD should be required for university teaching, although not necessarily the kind of revamped degree she was writing to oppose.

The revision of language requirements for the doctorate seems like so much small beer today when, prompted both by their own sense of ethics and by more formal calls for self-study from such organizations as the Carnegie Foundation, a number of critics of the PhD have abandoned the cloistered virtue of their scholarly pursuits and sallied forth with far more wide-reaching ideas about graduate education. (Actually, many of the more severe recommendations, as we shall see, are hardly new.) As the advocacy of curricular change is entirely consistent with the second principle above—indeed, the notion of "staying in tune with the times" demands continual self-meditation—we have no quibble whatsoever with the enterprise. Not all recommendations, however, are equally thoughtful or salutary; indeed, several are disastrous, particularly those that erode the first principle of graduate education, the foundation upon which any revisionist architecture must rest: the centrality of the PhD degree to graduate programs and to graduate schools as a whole. And this is why in the present climate, concerted debate about graduate education in the humanities, as welcome as it is, has reached a kind of danger point where we must ask ourselves what basic principles or values are being placed in jeopardy by various calls for reformation of our programs.

The "first principle" was placed in jeopardy in the later 1990s as influential humanists, one of them a past president of the Modern Language Association, called for such a radical evisceration of the doctorate that, were such advice heeded, little would remain of graduate education save for its function of credentialing service workers for the corporate university. At Indiana University, for example, such an academic laborer—one unqualified to make any serious claim as a researcher, hence as a producer of knowledge—might slog away in the expanded "Courses to Go" program, waiting on the other end of the telephone line for a per-plexed student to call and take advantage of one of the marketing "bul-lets" for this distance learning initiative: "Direct **one-on-one** contact with your instructor by telephone." (Is this higher education we're talking about or phone sex?) Such critics of the doctoral degree include Louis Menand and Elaine Showalter who, in separate and widely-circulated essays, called for the transformation of the PhD in the humanities, in-cluding in the former's case the elimination of the dissertation and with it, finally, any intimation that research in the humanities is important to either the university or society as a whole. In his much-cited article "How to Make a Ph.D. Matter," Menand's recommendation for the abolition—or drastic reduction—of doctoral dissertations is about as blunt as one could imagine: "If all PhD programs were three-year programs, with no teaching and no dissertation–if getting a doctorate were like getting a law degree–graduate education would immediately acquire focus and efficiency" (1996, 81).

Such a position runs directly in conflict with the 2003 report of the PFF and one of its fundamental premises: "Broadening the scope and raising the quality of faculty preparation—giving greater attention to teaching, to broader definitions of scholarship, and to professional ser-vice—are central to the future of their [English, Sociology, Psychology, Speech, Philosophy] disciplines" (Menand 1996, 4–5). That is to say, the PFF recommendations are clear: while continuing to foster disciplinary research, doctoral programs should also "include teaching experience that involves increasingly independent and varied responsibilities, sup-port, and feedback"; and "offer exposure to and experience with service to the department, campus, community, and discipline" (Menand 1996, 5). Thus, while in his *fin-de-siècle* ruminations Menand called for a dras-tically reduced research degree, the PFF "Guide for Change" endorses a more expansive training that embraces everything from teaching to com-munity service. Menand's degree has the virtue of being achievable in three years; the PFF's curriculum would require major reductions and transformations of typical degree requirements if it were to be completable in a decade. In which direction *should* we go?

Menand's position on dissertations provides a partial answer to the question. On the positive side, his abolition of the dissertation might help stanch the rising swell of debt among graduate students, a worthy reason for change, and one even more imperative now, as the average debt for those students who incurred substantial debt in 1996 when Menand made these observations has more than tripled on some cam-puses. The case against the dissertation requirement, as he acknowledges, is by now partly an old one emphasizing its unrelatedness to teaching and partly the newer one that "many scholarly books" originating in a leaky, often hastily or poorly written dissertation are "just scholarly articles on steroids" anyway" (81). We'd all be better off without them. But we wouldn't be, and this is not to cast a blind eye to factors like debt and attrition rates, nor is it a brief for the production of even more premature academic books at a time when university presses are struggling. For in this instance Menand attempts to solve one problem, the state of academic publishing, by creating an even bigger one. More of this in a moment.

Menand found something of a confederate in Elaine Showalter who, in her 1998 presidential address, attempted to rejoin several arguments against the promotion of "alternative careers" for PhD-holders that we outlined in *Academic Keywords: A Devil's Dictionary for Higher Education* (Nelson & Watt 1999). Of course, such careers as screenwriter or magazine editor scarcely require doctoral dissertations. Rather, writing a dissertation, as we argued in *Keywords*, "provides a model [for our students] of intellectually committed writing, writing as a serious and extended undertaking" (1999, 120–21). Additionally, proposals like Menand's advocating the elimination of the dissertation would, in effect, "dumb down" the degree, placing humanists on campus in an even more tenuous position than they already occupy vis-à-vis their colleagues in the sciences: "Since no one is suggesting that physics or chemistry professors do not need to do dissertation research to get a PhD, the possibility of a two-tier credentialing and prestige system arises, with humanities faculty even lower in the professorial pecking order than they are now" (Nelson & Watt 1999, 121). This would be the inevitable effect of proposals like Menand's, and the importance of the intellectual commitment represented by the dissertation would be squandered on the altar of a presumed efficacy.

But any response to Menand and Showalter, as the latter with considerable justification suggests, has to offer more than indictment and counterargument; it must ameliorate some of the most difficult aspects of today's graduate student culture:

> [M]eaningful change in humanities graduate education and employment has to go beyond questions of admissions and address the internal structure of doctoral programs, the ever-increasing length of training . . . , the requirements for the PhD, and the possibility of confronting these new graduate students with a variety of serious careers they might aspire to enter and with an education that will help them succeed. (Showalter 1999, 322)

Showalter's statement might be lightly redacted as follows: an ethical graduate program based on the two principles articulated above has to defend the requirement of a dissertation while, at the same time, addressing the very real, material concerns she and Menand identify: the length of time candidates spend pursuing the degree, the consequent debt many incur in the process, and the bleak job "system" that awaits. Add to these factors one of the more salient points made by the CPE report and reiterated loudly in *Preparing Future Faculty in the Humanities and Social Sciences*—that "the vast majority of PhD students today will have careers that do not replicate those of their graduate student professors" ("MLA Final Report" 1997, 32)—and we have a congeries of serious, in some cases conflicting, problems and imperatives that require careful negotiation undergirded by a foundation of firm ethico-professional principles.

Before offering specific suggestions on what shape these changes might take, however, we want to address two issues related to these complications: one Showalter mentions in the passage rendered above; the other a problem raised by Robert Paul Woolf in the final chapter of his uncanny 1969 book *The Ideal of the University*, a kind of Ur-text for this debate. What exactly does Showalter mean by "the possibility of confronting these new graduate students with a variety of serious careers they might aspire to enter?" "Confronting . . . with" is an odd gerund phrase in this context, one that presumably means something more than "exposing . . . to" or "informing . . . about." Indeed, both the context and language of the point imply that graduate programs have an ethical responsibility to do more than merely disseminate information about "alternative careers" to their students. But precisely what we *ought* to do in the name of alternative careers isn't made clear here—or anywhere else in her essay. As most everyone knows, several English departments—at Penn State, Iowa State, Purdue, Texas Tech, and others—have invested significant resources in preparing students for "alternative careers" in professional communication, business and technical writing, even desktop publishing and editing. Is this what Showalter is recommending for every doctoral program? If so, how would this additional responsibility affect such factors as time toward the degree—not to mention the PhD degree itself? Does this mean, for example, the *addition* of requirements in, say, business communication, or the *replacement* of a demonstrated proficiency in a first or second language with a required course in publishing? How might the offering of courses in these sub-fields, along with Showalter's emphasis on teacher training, affect the material concerns she raises earlier in her essay?

We'll never know the answers to these questions, as the point is left sufficiently ambiguous save for her suggestion that "We could also prepare

MAs for careers in management, government, the media, and university administration" (Showalter 1999, 323). No doubt we could and, as she points out, a number of schools have already tailored very specific MA programs to accomplish similarly narrowly-defined goals, including the preparation of students for careers in publishing, marketing and advertisement, medical and legal writing, and so on. But, equally obvious, this putative solution has nothing whatsoever to do with the PhD degree and the serious material realities both she and Menand identify. What about doctoral programs and the nature of the PhD degree?

On this topic, Showalter unwittingly advances a solution similar not only to Menand's three-year degree, but also to the revolution Robert Woolf hoped to incite over thirty years ago: the overthrow of the PhD and the consequent ascendance of an MPhil or some other intermediate degree shorn of anything that would intimate specialized research expertise and commitment. Showalter's MPhil degree, apparently, would be offered in a one- or two-year program like the MA in the Humanities offered at present by the University of Chicago—her analogy, not ours. It would "serve students," she hopes, not "provide cheap labor, hide a huge attrition rate, or fill seminars on Spenser or semiotics" (Showalter 1999, 324). In this program, she argues, students "could be allowed to take the first year to decide for themselves how to go on—whether to continue on a research-degree track or take advantage of other career opportunities" (1999, 324). How such a respite in the Showalterian MPhil differs from the same advantages MA degrees already provide isn't quite clear, save for the MPhil's commitment to training in pedagogy and "communication." Apparently, though, an intermediate degree obtainable in a year or two would afford students an opportunity to defer making any decision about the pursuit of the PhD, and quite possibly also lead them to "discover unsuspected talents for other kinds of work" (Showalter 1999, 324). But is this epiphany "devoutly to be wished for," as Hamlet might say, the product of a curriculum enriched by courses in communication and pedagogy, or merely a desperate hope that students once interested in literary study and cultural critique can be persuaded that technical writing is far more rewarding?

While Showalter's recommendation seems startlingly inchoate—students are expected to decide if they want to "continue on a research-degree track" by taking a curriculum in which research is significantly diminished?—it poses no threat to the two bedrock principles announced earlier. But her vision of a revised PhD degree does. In this way it also resembles Woolf's quite similar 1969 proposals to reform higher education. Showalter calls for "a true, and not a rhetorical, apprenticeship" in pedagogy for all doctoral students, one that allows for a "variety of teaching experiences" (1999, 324). Of course, today most graduate students in English teach more than enough, far more than Nicolson or scholars of Showalter's generation ever did, so in fact it is greater faculty involvement in teacher preparation, for the most part, that for her would lead to a "true" apprenticeship. Taken out of any context, this would appear to be a fine idea; however, it is unclear how this "apprenticeship" would ameliorate the very factors Showalter argued earlier must be improved for a change to be deemed "meaningful": namely, the length of time a PhD requires, the "internal structure" of graduate programs, and so on. In *The Ideal of the University*, Woolf, a Columbia philosopher writing at the precise moment anti-war protestors were storming the offices of university administrators, found himself similarly caught up in the revolution around him. Convinced that the "conflict between professional certification and intellectual initiation destroys the coherence of graduate education" (Woolf 1969, 23), Woolf's first salvo was aimed at the dissertation. How can a dissertation make an "original contribution to knowledge," he mused, when the dissertation writer is advised to place artificial boundaries around her project: "Take on a topic you can manage," "Don't make it too long," "Do something you can finish" (1969, 23)? The contradictory goals or "incoherence" of doctoral programs to train teachers *and* initiate scholars militate against their accomplishing either so well as they might; thus, he urged the elimination of the scholarly component from what would become solely an enterprise of teacher preparation.

For Woolf, as we have mentioned, the solution to the contradictions and cumbersome rituals of the PhD was simple: replace it with a three-year degree "designed to certify candidates as competent to teach their subjects at the college or graduate level" (1969, 153). Armed with this certificate, graduate students would obtain teaching positions, and those determined to become scholars could later apply to a national grant program established to provide recipients with a carefully mentored research training. Of course, Woolf conceded, "the elite jobs would still be won by those young men and women who either did—or showed promise of doing—original research" (1969, 154). Still, this restructuring of graduate education would achieve many of the objectives Menand and Showalter would advocate thirty years later; in particular, it would lead to a renewed focus on teaching without the distractions of research programs or projects. The only thing sacrificed in this scheme would be the dissertation, hence any semblance of expertise or intimation that research in the humanities matters.

But there is more. For this proposal rests on the notion that teaching is an activity that neither requires research nor bears any relationship to the production of specialized knowledge. One of our colleagues has a bumper sticker on his office door which expresses this relationship by way of a delicious analogy: "Research is to the classroom as sin is to the confessional. Without the former there is nothing to talk about in the latter." So, when Woolf argues that a three-year, more teacherly curriculum would empower one to offer meaningful courses in a graduate program, one might ask how many graduate programs would be improved by relieving all present faculty of teaching responsibility and replacing them with fourth-year graduate students? Advanced doctoral students are, in many cases, superior teachers of undergraduates, harnessing the enthusiasm and energy for the endeavor that tend to dissipate over the decades. But would a three-year degree largely devoted to pedagogy prepare one adequately for the seminar room? It isn't even clear that faculty so lacking in specialized training could direct the work of advanced undergraduates effectively.

The affinities between Woolf's 1969 proposal and those of Menand and Showalter are striking. All of them want to make graduate education more efficient, including Showalter, the only one of the three not to recommend the total elimination of the dissertation. In fact, all three implicitly or explicitly address the length of study in most doctoral programs, supporting reforms which would bring the graduate curriculum more in line with that of law schools or other more compact regimens of study. All three, especially Woolf and Menand, envision an advanced degree in which research is minimized and pedagogy is privileged. And Showalter would like to see graduate programs—somehow, some way—develop more extensive offerings in communication and alternative careers at the same time that they addressed the problems mentioned above.

David Damrosch might be added to this short list of critics of doctoral programs writing during the 1990s; and, although some of the premises of his opposition may seem eccentric, several of his solutions are worthy of consideration. Throughout *We Scholars* (1995) Damrosch works hard to accomplish what the subtitle of his book promises: "changing the culture of the university." What's wrong with this culture? In a word, specialization, which has led to the rise of the superstar and fractured any sense of a scholarly community within the walls of academe. Where does this sundering start? According to Damrosch, in the culture of graduate education and the ethos of humanities faculty, who, all too aware of what it takes to succeed in the contemporary university, discourage "most of the really intellectually sociable candidates" from completing their degrees, leaving only "that fraction of the population who are naturally less sociable" (1995, 147). Today's graduate programs, in Damrosch's somewhat jaundiced view, produce young faculty who are constitutionally ill-suited for faculty life, hence incapable of even a polite collegiality:

> To the extent that intellectually sociable people never go to graduate school or never complete it, we are similarly lessening the overall quality of the resulting pool of new Ph.D.s. Solitary scholars can be fully as interesting and valuable as more sociable scholars would be, but if those who enter and complete graduate programs tend to be solitary workers, then we are likely to end up with a higher proportion of merely competent perseverers entering the job market than we would if selection and training did not disfavor an entire kind of scholarly personality to begin with. (1995, 148)

Like Showalter's mystery curriculum in alternative education or the putative epiphanies of graduate students when exposed to the allurements of "alternative careers," Damrosch's "intellectually sociable" colleague isn't drawn in much detail. Yet his point is finally more lucid than Showalter's about the transformation of young scholars in training into gleeful, self-fulfilled insurance underwriters: solitary scholarship equals a reduced "ability to address problems that require collaborative solutions, or even that require close attention to the perspectives offered by approaches or disciplines other than one's own" (1995, 148). One result of this ethos of hypertrophic individualism in graduate school, therefore, is a brittle, dogmatic younger colleague addicted to her own work and dismissive of the values of her senior colleagues. Damrosch doesn't say it quite so vulgarly, but that's the kind of younger faculty member he is describing—or, rather, disparaging. Training as a solitary scholar means naturalizing the notion of academic productivity, which in turn concretizes and rationalizes the ethos of the critic as entrepreneur, which for Damrosch is ruinous to the "culture of the university." "Many professors," he maintains, "and particularly the most original and productive scholars among them, no longer behave like good citizens, or even like citizens at all. They are more like resident aliens" (1995, 41), ruthless and solipsistic aliens at that, who abandon their own graduate students in their quests for academic celebrity and the perquisites that come with it.

Well, maybe. Maybe these "intellectually unsociable" sorts *have* destroyed the communities once nurtured by a vanishing breed of more gentlemanly and gentlewomanly scholar-teachers. (And there is little doubt that collaborative interdisciplinary work might both revive a kind of intellectual torpor in which the humanities languishes today and facilitate the kinds of collegiality Damrosch misses.) Maybe graduate education and the psychological stuff it takes to write a dissertation are to blame for the fragmented condition of many humanities departments.

But maybe they aren't. Maybe utopian community is not founded upon scholarly inactivity or intellectual torpor, as Richard Russo's novel

Straight Man (1997), an inspired burlesque of academic life at a fourth-rate university, seems to confirm. Perhaps less isn't more, as Russo's department chair-protagonist Hank Devereaux tends to believe as he careens like a pinball from one personnel mess to another. None of Damrosch's entrepreneurs teach at West Central Pennsylvania University, where Devereaux chairs the English department and where promotion to professor is as dubious an achievement as winning a "shit-eating contest" (1995, 27). At West Central, a "colonial" outpost located on the edges of civilization and at the nadir of intellectual accomplishment, writing a slender book twenty years ago qualifies one as a "successful writer," the allegation a pitifully insecure colleague hurls at Devereaux before filing a grievance against him. Far from being flattered, he regards the accusation of his own success as both an ironic joke and a symptom of "how little we have in the way of expectation around here" (Damrosch 1995, 105). And, in fact, the entire English department he administers is littered with incompetents, embittered alcoholics, and underachievers, save for the Damroschian assistant professor who hates literature and the fact that he was hired instead of a woman. Nicknamed "Orshee" because he corrects his colleagues' overuse of the masculine pronoun, this caricature of a young academic adds absurd comedy to the novel and allows Russo to take a cheap shot at political correctness. His feminist sensibilities honed to an extreme, Orshee exhorts his colleagues to vote against his tenure and hire a woman in his place. Scholarly hyperproductivity and academic entrepreneurship, however, Damrosch's *bête noires*, are hardly responsible for the lack of community at West Central. In Russo's department, the most striking element of community is not, to redact Clark Kerr's famous line, the faculty's mutual interest in obtaining desirable parking spaces, but their daily practices of sniping at Devereaux and each other—and producing virtually nothing to be proud of.

In short, graduate training and solitary acts of scholarship aren't necessarily the key sources of departmental incivility and boorishness; numbingly routinized teaching and a faculty incapable of real achievement or professional advancement are more responsible for the exaggeratedly dysfunctional, yet all-too-familiar department Russo portrays. One could argue that such a disparaging characterization *is* actually rooted in the lengthy rituals of doctoral programs and the resultant failure of scholarly initiands to live up to the expectations of their "jet-setting" graduate advisors. James Sosnoski has coined the apt term "token professionals" for faculty teaching at remote campuses with no research facilities, no time to conduct research anyway, and no defense from malevolent administrators who, in a vicious and unprincipled Catch-22, use the faculty's minimal professional achievement against them at salary and promotion time. Yet many of Russo's malcontents lack doctoral degrees— as does Devereaux, for example—and still another obtained his PhD through the mail, thus never undergoing the (un)socialization process Damrosch deplores. Russo's remarkably undistinguished English department says as much about uncollegial and dysfunctional faculty as Damrosch's collection of over-achieving entrepreneurs at Columbia. As is the case in many debates today, Damrosch and Russo also portray extremes: the top-notch department peopled by egocentric academic celebrities, the bottom of the barrel department inhabited by delusional wannabes and self-described losers. The majority of English departments we are interested in, those with doctoral programs, and virtually every department that has been able to hire younger faculty in these lean times, are ill-described by either representation, for even the least distinguished of these can boast of numerous productive faculty who are as professional as they are "sociable."

Proposals for Change

Damrosch, however, does make one proposal well worth considering, and we want to conclude both with it and several specific recommendations of our own, all the while keeping in mind Showalter's observation that any "meaningful changes" in graduate education *must* improve the material conditions of doctoral students. Toward the end of his invective against graduate programs and their cultivation of unsociable boors, Damrosch calls for a "new understanding" of the aims of the doctoral dissertation:

> Why should the dissertation be presumed to be a protobook rather than a series of articles, each produced independently [and each, perhaps, directed by a different faculty advisor], sharing a common general theme or approach rather than developing a single argument?... Perhaps four or five 50-page projects would be manageable in a way that a single 250-page thesis may not. (1995, 162)

In this way, he speculates, the doctoral project would prove more consistent with the experience of writing seminar papers and thus, one hopes, would lead to the more expeditious production of a thesis. And, as an added longer term benefit, the process would help make collaboration more central to graduate students' training and thereby better equip them for collegial interaction as young faculty.

Whatever one thinks about Damrosch's emphasis on sociability, his reconceived dissertation might serve as a catalyst to spark at least two other very positive results. One involves the greater possibility that graduate students, after working closely with several research advisors, not a single director, will enjoy the positive relationship with at least one or two faculty on which their professional survival depends. For a relationship gone bad between a dissertation writer and her director almost always means a protracted, if not doomed, job search, as a number of the testimonials in *On the Market: Surviving the Academic Job Search* (Boufis & Olsen 1997) confirm. One physicist, "on the market" for a tenure-track position for well over a decade, confides that a "conflict between me and my dissertation director . . . took several years to put aside" (1997, 244); another young scientist learned, after nearly five years of post-doctoral fellowships and unsuccessful applications for tenure-track positions, that his dissertation supervisor had made one "just plain awful" comment about him in a letter of recommendation. After challenging his former director, the scientist learned that the aspersion was not made out of malevolence or personal animus, but rather out of the dissertation director's misguided notion that he was obliged as a recommender to make "the problem comment" in order to "provide a balanced judgment about me. . . . His uneducated opinion was that what he wrote would not adversely affect my employment chances" (1997, 57).

He was wrong.

The second advantage of Damrosch's redacted dissertation resides in its potential to make the reward structures in many English departments more varied and equitable. For if Damrosch is right, if values and professional identity become naturalized in graduate curricula and structures, then a dissertation regarded as a series of articles, not a "protobook," might have a considerable impact not only on institutional expectations and tenure deliberations, but on the daily praxis of scholars for whom, at present, "the book" is the only professional capital that matters. At a time when academic presses are forced to make decisions based not only on a manuscript's academic merit, but on its potential marketability, humanities departments do a great disservice to young faculty by holding over their heads the Damoclesian sword of a one- or two-book requirement for tenure. Such pressures often result in lousy books, Menand's complaint, and promulgate the misconception that everyone in the humanities, regardless of their field of specialization, enjoys an equal opportunity to publish their scholarship in book form. This simply isn't the case. Anyone who doubts this should compare the number of books published by top academic presses on, say, Augustan satire or Victorian melodrama with those on such mass cultural forms as action films or rock music (who, for example, would ever have predicted that Harvard University Press would publish two books in 1999 with Chuck Berry duckwalking with his electric guitar on the covers?) And what about those colleagues who spend considerable time writing a study that will make a significant intervention in their fields? Think, for example, of the two books Martin Meisel has written on Victorian culture—*Shaw and the Nineteenth-Century Theatre* (1963) and, twenty years later, *Realizations: Narrative, Pictorial, and Theatrical Arts in Nineteenth-Century England* (1983). Can such enormously learned books, especially the latter, be written in the present institutional climate without its author being penalized by negative salary reviews or reluctant promotion committees for failure to get the next book "out" more quickly—or for failing to be, say, a Terry Eagleton? Books like *Realizations* or, to take another example, John Bishop's wonderful *Joyce's Book of the Dark* (1986) on *Finnegans Wake*, aren't written in a year or two—or four or five years, for that matter.

Such singular scholarly achievements, in short, require time; and, again, if they happen to address only a small segment of the market that reads university press books, they may have difficulty ever being published in the first place. Academic publication isn't a level playing field. Yet English and other humanities departments typically behave as if it were, applying the same criteria for tenure and promotion to all colleagues, regardless of their areas of expertise and, in effect, discouraging scholars from undertaking the kinds of massive and important projects represented by Meisel and Bishop's books.

Such a practice is thus not only unfair and unwise, but also inherently antiquated as electronic journals are able to disseminate scholarship with an immediacy that makes traditional book publication appear an even more sluggish, Luddite practice than it already is. A dissertation conceived as a series of articles may help re-introduce the notion that articles and conference papers are more than activities preliminary to or useful only insofar as they facilitate book publication. This is not a brief for academic under-development, but rather a call for both the greater appreciation of the array of different media for publication available to today's scholar and for professionally thoughtful ways to de-fetishize the scholarly book as the only product worthy of our time—and of institutional rewards. If only in this way, Damrosch's redacted dissertation is therefore worth our collective consideration.

But, in addition to the years many spend writing of the dissertation qua protobook, graduate programs are also structured in such a way as to introduce other time-consuming hurdles along the way. Certainly, given the eight years plus many doctoral students spend in graduate school—the "median years to degree" in many humanities departments exceeds eight years—the time has come to re-examine these requirements, the length of time needed to satisfy them, and the debt into which many students fall along the way. Along with this reconsideration of the structure of doctoral programs, graduate faculty and directors of graduate study might also continue their meditations on ethical responsibilities. Here are several, listed in the chronological sequence that obtains in most PhD programs.

1. **Admissions.** All informational materials sent to prospective graduate students should contain statistics not only on the job placement record of the department to which they are applying, but also on the range of debt incurred by its doctoral candidates. If the most recent data on graduate student debt at Indiana University is indicative of a larger national trend–and there is no reason to believe that it isn't–too many doctoral candidates in the humanities are borrowing $50,000, $75,000, even $100,000 to complete their degrees.[4] Offices of Student Financial Aid need to make these facts known to departments, while still protecting the anonymity of the borrowers, and directors of graduate study in the new millennium will need to counsel beginning students about the long-term implications of carrying this level of debt. And why shouldn't they? Medical Schools don't presume their students fully understand the business aspects of establishing a private practice. Why should humanities faculty assume that a student whose intellectual attention is focused on Chaucer's England or Sartre's France is any more able than a first-year resident to understand fully the long-term ramifications of such borrowing?

Worried about this very matter and getting little help from their university in informing prospective students about this ever-growing cancer, the Graduate Student Association of the University of Georgia, like a number of similar organizations across the country, took it upon itself in 1998 to provide new students with crucial information on debt, insurance, and other important matters. In fact, nearly one-quarter of its eight-page "Guide to U.G.A. and Athens" concerns debt, complete with case studies of graduate students and hints at how to avoid racking up huge loans. Don't faculty, directors of graduate study in particular, also bear some ethical responsibility to provide new students with such information? Shouldn't directors of graduate study, with the support of graduate faculty, do everything in their power to make sure none of their students is induced into what, for some, will be certain bankruptcy?

In one of its first, finally disappointing contributions to the CID project, the Carnegie Foundation sponsored an essay by Andrea Abernethy Lunsford ("Re-Thinking the Ph.D. in English," 2003) that

---

4. See "Disciplining Debt," chapter 4 of this volume for a more expansive treatment of recent borrowing patterns among today's graduate students.

emphasized a slightly different point about graduate admissions, calling for procedures that diminished the "intense competition" created by test scores, essays, letters of recommendation, and the like.[5] She inveighed in particular against GRE scores, as they "always favor white students," and asserted that "an amazing student can easily emerge from a low-prestige school." Instead of test scores, and she apparently forgets that transcripts and GPAs might also help in such an assessment, as she never refers to the kind of undergraduate preparation a prospective student has had, she asks, "Why not consider, for example, evidence of excellence in forms of public service or teaching, or other work-related talents?" (4).

Such a position, however well-intended, would have dire consequences if actually enacted. Quite obviously, fine students can emerge from a variety of undergraduate institutions—as everyone knows—and by now everyone should be aware of the racial bias of many standardized tests. But imagine what might happen to a new graduate student with little preparation for the rigors of the seminar. Working at the local homeless shelter or serving as a copyeditor of a newspaper might provide valuable experience for a new student, but it will not prepare her for graduate school. Moreover, what happens to the quality of a doctoral seminar if the criteria Lunsford suggests are prioritized in the admission process? Any faculty member who has tried to counsel students considering leaving a graduate program must surely be familiar with the disillusionment ill-prepared students feel when they have little possibility of succeeding. The ethic of a doctoral program *cannot* be "leave no child behind." Nor can it foster an immediate partnership between faculty and new MA students, as Lunsford recommends. The paradoxical logic of her essay is stunning: how can ill-prepared students become instant "collaborators" with graduate faculty?

If the humanities are to survive at the corporate university, if faculty working in the humanities are to garner the respect they deserve, they must be trained rigorously from the start of the program, and we contend that working at the local soup kitchen or planting trees on Arbor Day provide no measure whatsoever of an applicant's ability to succeed in a seminar on Faulkner or French Feminist Theory. Teaching experience, as Lunsford also notes, might provide a better measure, but in no way can or should this experience replace an undergraduate transcript that details both a breadth of education and a significant measure of accomplishment. Moreover, writing samples have to be judged by criteria broader than just acquaintance with scholarly convention and evidence

---

5. Lunsford's essay is quoted by permission of the Carnegie Foundation for the Advancement of Teaching, Stanford, California.

of some theoretical sophistication (which is more a measure of the training a student has received than of writing ability). If dissertations are wrongly viewed as protobooks, then undergraduate papers ought not be judged solely or largely as proto-seminar papers. Vivid prose, the presentation of evidence and its lucid analysis, the ability to sustain a persuasive argument—all of these abilities must be in evidence in an applicant's writing sample. Too often we have seen admissions committee swayed by the presumption of sophistication in a writing sample that is merely serviceable in articulation and execution. Graduate curricula ought to provide the sophistication and knowledge of scholarly conventions crucial to the student's subsequent success.

2. **Curricular Efficiency.** Better funding and shorter programs—programs that can actually be completed in four or five years, not seven, eight or nine—are crucial to the goal of a more efficient doctoral program. Graduate curricula, in our view, need not involve more than four to six semesters of coursework, with the last one or two also devoted to the kind of pedagogical training that Showalter and the PFF endorse. Fellowship support during the first year—in which six to eight courses could be taken—is crucial to attaining this goal, as is a semester or more of fellowship support during the last year when the dissertation is nearing completion. Summer funding for doctoral students in the humanities is crucial as well, for unlike their peers in most science departments who are funded for twelve months, many students in the humanities are faced with an impossible choice: borrow more money so as to have time to work on their dissertations, or take summer employment and thereby minimize their chances of making significant headway on their thesis research and writing.

3. **Reductions as well as Accretions.** Perhaps the greatest single way to make doctoral programs more efficient—other than to reconsider the nature of the dissertation along the lines Damrosch suggests—is to eliminate the Qualifying Examination, which in our collective experience often creates more problems than it solves. To begin, it typically slows students down a year or more when both the time needed to prepare and the time needed to recuperate are added together. The problems range from the often feeble attempts to explain its purpose—"What does a qualifying examination qualify one to do?"—to unnecessary anxiety and panic, to pointed faculty disagreement over a student's performance. We have known several students who, paralyzed with fear, never attempted to take their exam; we know others who could never pass theirs. In many cases, these were students who had received nothing but grades of "A" or "A–" from as many as a dozen different faculty. What happened to so terrify a student with a 3.9 grade point average that she couldn't

summon the wherewithal to sit for the exam? And, perhaps a better question, how could such a student fail the exam miserably after twelve graduate faculty had independently judged her work to be outstanding?

Of course, qualifying exams also provide an opportunity for faculty to criticize their own colleagues' performances as well: their insipid questions, their bullying manner of interrogation, their ideological biases or sexism, their total lack of standards, or, conversely, their unwavering adherence to standards no one else much cares about. Disputes common to the discipline as a whole often get played out on the field of a qualifying examination, sometimes at the student's expense. In fact, some of the most damaging rifts in departments can be traced back to the examination room, not to mention the copious disagreement among faculty about what such an exam should entail in the first place: What areas should it cover? What form should the examination take? How should it be administered? When in a student's matriculation through the program should the exam be given?

But even if none of this were true, even if examinations always led in the idyllic tradition of romantic comedy to a celebration and a reinvigorated sense of intellectual community, what do such exams accomplish that the 12–16 courses most doctoral students take don't? An opportunity to "master" a canon or field? Hardly. A proto-version of the job interview that will occur, one hopes, some years later? If in fact graduate programs enhance their offerings in pedagogy, won't that reduce the need to have students prove they know a field or fields well enough to teach? And whatever a qualifying examination does to prepare a student to write a provocative dissertation can be just as easily achieved through the careful—and expanded—mentorship several advisors can provide. Most important, a year or more can be removed from the inflated time it takes PhD students to complete their degrees.

4. **Departmental "Communities."** All of the above, save perhaps for the courses a first- or second-year graduate student might take to remedy large deficiencies in literary background or theoretical preparation, should be achieved within well defined sections of the department, not the department as a whole. This is not a recommendation for further splintering and even less collegiality than Damrosch finds at Columbia, but rather a call for more collective instruction (in formal and informal settings) on the part of well-defined sub-groups within departments: Victorianists, medievalists, feminists, Americanists, and so on. Graduate faculty need to learn more about collaborative writing and learning, and departments need to find ways of rewarding such enterprises.

5. **The System.** Finally, before following the recommendations Lunsford and the authors of the PFF report advance, we need to pause

and assess the effects of such revisions. To be sure, departments *should* support all doctoral students in the search for jobs. Most English departments organize seminars that include advice on letter-writing, interviewing at various types of institutions, mock interviews, job talks, teaching presentations, and so on. That so many doctoral candidates complain about the lack of such support—nearly 75 percent in a poll reported by one of the document's authors, Jerry G. Gaff, expressed concern about this–is both regrettable and shocking. We should, of course, avoid elitism and other biases in the application process, as Lunsford recommends; collaborate more closely with doctoral students, and provide opportunities for them to serve on departmental and college committees. When they *are ready* we *should* encourage their participation in conference presentation, book reviewing, and other appropriate professional activities. (Note: This means that the first seminar papers produced by MA students ought *not* be revised for conference presentation—we've heard far too many of these.) But do students really need to be mentored in community service? Don't concerned individuals assume such responsibilities out of their own sense of communal obligation or interest? Similarly, don't the best doctoral students in the humanities already teach far more—and far more independently—than any generation of students ever did? Recall Marjorie Nicolson's doctoral training, which included no teaching at all and no professionalization of any kind. Again, an *accretive* model of revision—one that simply adds more content to degree programs—will hardly solve the most serious problems facing graduate education in the humanities.

The first of these serious problems, of course, originates not in the teaching versus research schizophrenia Robert Woolf identifies, but in the student/employee binary we have discussed throughout the book. This means that labor, a topic the Carnegie Initiative has refused to recognize as crucial to its project of re-imagining the doctorate, must be moved to the center of our considerations. Without such a relocation, how can any of us consider our revisionist projects to be ethical?

Thus, there is really only one educational goal ahead of us: graduating PhD students—with substantial dissertations, not necessarily protobooks--in four or five years. Period. If we cannot find ways to do this, then we have failed in our ethical responsibilities to our students, one of which is not to lead so many of them into financial ruination that may damage their lives for decades after graduation. Similarly, how ethical would it be to admit students with little or no evidence of the ability to complete a program successfully? Are the 50–75 percent attrition rates at many departments acceptable? This commitment to change both graduate student culture and PhD programs, moreover, is vitally connected to our commitment to transform the profession as a whole: its system of rewards and prestige, its modes of disseminating research, its expectations of young faculty, both when they are hired and when they are advanced for tenure. The bedrock underlying all of these possibilities is the PhD and the continued valorization of research and meaningful cultural criticism in the humanities. For without them, there is little reason for the degree to exist in the first place.

SW

Bibliography

American Association of University Professors (AAUP). "Protecting Human beings: Institutional Review Boards and Social Science Research." *Academe* (May–June 2001): 55–67.

Anderson, Paul V. "Ethics, Institutional Review Boards, and the Involvement of Human Participants in Composition Research." *Ethics and Representation in Qualitative Studies of Literacy*. Ed. Peter Mortensen and Gesa E. Kirsch. Urbana: NCTE, 1996. 260–85.

Aronowitz, Stanley. *The Knowledge Factory: Dismantling the Corporate University and Creating True Higher Learning*. Boston: Beacon Press, 2000.

Bartolovich, Crystal. "To Boldly Go Where No MLA Has Gone Before." *Day Late, Dollar Short: The Next Generation and the New Academy*.

Bérubé, Michael. *The Employment of English: Theory, Jobs, and the Future of Literary Study*. New York: New York UP, 1998.

———. "Epilogue." *Day Late, Dollar Short: The Next Generation and the New Academy*.

Bloom, Harold, ed., *The Best of the Best American Poetry: 1988–1997*. New York: Simon & Schuster, 1998.

Bloom, Lynn Z. "Living to Tell the Tale: The Complicated Ethics of Creative Nonfiction." *College English* 65.3 (January 2003): 276–89.

Boufis, Christina, and Victoria C. Olsen, eds. *On the Market: Surviving the Academic Job Search*. New York: Riverhead Books, 1997.

Bousquet, Mark, "The Waste Product of Graduate Education: Toward a Dictatorship of the Flexible." *Social Text* (Spring 2002): 81–104.

Byrne, J. Peter, "Academic Freedom Without Tenure?" American Association for Higher Education New Pathways Working Paper Series, Washington, D.C., 1997.

Calvino, Italo. *If on a winter's night a traveler*. Trans. William Weaver. New York: Harcourt Brace Jovanovich, 1979.

Carroll, Peter N. *Keeping Time: Memory, Nostalgia, and the Art of History*. Athens, GA: University of Georgia Press, 1990.

Chossudovsky, Michael. *The Globalization of Poverty*. New York: Zed/Pluto, 1997.

Cole, Jonathan R. "Balancing Acts: Dilemmas of Choice Facing Research Universities." *Daedalus* 122 (Fall 1993): 1–36.

"The College Boom," *Time*, November 15, 1999: 22.

Damrosch, David. *We Scholars: Changing the Culture of the University*. Cambridge: Harvard University Press, 1995.

Dubson, Michael, ed. *Ghosts in the Classroom: Stories of College Adjunct Faculty—and the Price We All Pay.* Boston: Camel's Back Books, 2001.

Edmundson, Mark. "On the Uses of a Liberal Education." *Harpers Magazine,* Spring 1997, pp. 39–49.

Evans, G. Blakemore, ed., *The Riverside Shakespeare,* 2nd ed. Boston: Houghton Mifflin, 1997.

Gaff, Jerry G., Anne S. Pruitt-Logan, Leslie B. Sims, and Daniel D. Denecke. *Preparing Future Faculty in the Humanities and Social Sciences: A Guide for Change.* Washington: Council of Graduate Schools, 2003.

Gilman, Sander L. *The Fortunes of the Humanities: Thoughts for After the Year 2000.* Stanford: Stanford University Press, 2000.

Gunsalus, C. K. "Rethinking Protections for Human Subjects." *The Chronicle of Higher Education* (November 15, 2002).

Herman, Peter C., ed. *Day Late, Dollar Short: The Next Generation and the New Academy.* Albany: State University of New York Press, 2000.

Indiana University Distance Education. "Adding a Course? Take It To-Go!" Fall, 1999.

Judy, Ronald A. T. "Some Notes on the Status of Global English in Tunisia," *Boundary 2* (Summer 1999): 3–29.

Karabell, Zachary. *What's College For? The Struggle to Define American Higher Education.* New York: Basic Books, 1998.

Kerr, Clark. *The Use of the University.* New York: Harper and Row, 1972.

Knight, Jonathan, Margaret A. Blanchard, Jonathan T. Church, and Linda Shopes. "Should All Disciplines Be Subject to the Common Rule?." AAUP Report to the National Human Research Protections Advisory Committee, June 17, 2002.

Kohl, Kay, and Jules LaPidus, eds. *Postbaccalaureate Futures: New Markets, Resources, Credentials.* Phoenix, Arizona: The American Council of Higher Education and the Oryx Press, 2000.

Kumar, Amitava, ed. *Class Issues: Pedagogy, Cultural Studies, and the Public Sphere.* New York: New York University Press, 1997.

Laurence, David, and Elizabeth B. Welles. "Job Market Remains Competitive." *MLA Newsletter* 32.1 (Spring 2000): 6–7.

———. "More Data from the October 1998 *Job Information List." MLA Newsletter* 31.2 (Summer 1999): 2.

Lively, Kit. "Indiana University's Golf-Course Proposal Lands in Sand Trap." *The Chronicle of Higher Education,* January 21, 2000: A36.

Lovitts, Barbara E. *Leaving the Ivory Tower: The Causes and Consequences of Departure from Graduate Study.* Rowan and Littlefield, 2001.

Lunsford, Andrea Abernethy. "Rethinking the Ph.D. in English." *Carnegie Essays on the Doctorate.* Stanford: The Carnegie Foundation, 2003.

Lyotard, Jean-François. *The Postmodern Explained.* Trans. Julian Pefanis and Morgan Thomas. Minneapolis: University of Minnesota Press, 1993.

Lyotard, Jean-François, and Jean-Loup Thébaud. *Just Gaming.* Trans. Wlad Godzich. Minneapolis: University of Minnesota Press, 1985.

Manning, Robert D. *Credit Cards on Campus: Costs and Consequences of Student Debt.* Washington: Consumer federation of America, 2000.

Menand, Louis. "How to Make a Ph.D. Matter." *The New York Times Magazine,* September 22, 1996: 78–81.

Michael, John. *Anxious Intellects: Academic Professionals, Public Intellectuals, and Enlightenment Values.* Durham: Duke University Press, 2000.

MLA Committee on Professional Employment. *Final Report.* New York: Modern Language Association, 1997.

Morgan, Dan. "Ethical Issues Raised by Students' Personal Writing." *College English* 60:3 (March 1998): 318–25.

Neilson, Jim, and Gregory Meyerson. "Mr. Levin's World." *minnesota review* 48–49 (December 1998): 277–86.

Nelson, Cary, and Barbara E. Lovitts. "10 Ways to Keep Graduate Students from Quitting." *The Chronicle of Higher Education*, June 29, 2001: B20.

Nelson, Cary, and Stephen Watt. *Academic Keywords: A Devil's Dictionary for Higher Education*. New York: Routledge, 1999.

Nicolson, Marjorie Hope. "A Generous Education." *PMLA* 79 (March 1964): 3–12.

Oakes, Michael J. "Risks and Wrongs in Social Science Research: An Evaluator's Guide to the IRB." *Evaluation Review* 26:5 (October 2002): 443–78.

Perloff, Marjorie, "Janus-Faced Blockbuster," *Symploke* 8:1–2 (2000): 205-13.

Powers, Richard. *Galatea 2.2*. New York: Farrar, Straus and Giroux, 1995.

Prior, Moody E. "The Doctor of Philosophy Degree." In *Graduate Education Today*, ed. Everett Walters. Washington, DC: American Council on Education, 1965. 30–61.

Rich, Adrienne, ed. *The Best American Poetry 1996*. New York: Simon & Schuster, 1997.

Russo, Richard. *Straight Man*. New York: Random House, 1997.

Sassen, Saskia. *Globalization and Its Discontents*. New York: New Press, 1998.

Scholes, Robert. *The Rise and Fall of English: Reconstructing English as a Discipline*. New Haven: Yale University Press, 1998.

Shaw, Kenneth A. "Memorandum to Members of the University Community." 4 September 1998.

———. *The Successful President: "Buzz-Words" on Leadership*. Phoenix: American Council on Education/Oryx Press, 1999.

Showalter, Elaine. "Presidential Address 1998: Regeneration." *PMLA* 114 (May 1999): 318–28.

Sieber, Joan E., Stuart Plattner, and Philip Rubin. "How Not to Regulate Social and Behavioral Research." *Professional Ethics Report* 15:2 (Spring 2002): 1–4.

Smallwood, Scott. "Stipends Are Key in Competition to Land Top Graduate Students." *The Chronicle of Higher Education*, September 28, 2001: A24–5.

Smith, Mark F. "Graduate Programs: Getting Some Help but Needing More." *Academe: Bulletin of the American Association of University Professors* 85. 3 (May/June 1999): 77.

Wallach, Lori, and Michelle Sforza. *The WTO: Five Years of Reasons to Resist Corporate Globalization*. New York: Seven Stories Press, 1999.

Watt, Stephen. "Faculty, Academic Freedom, and the Strike at Syracuse." *M/MLA: The Journal of the Midwest Modern Language Association*, 32 (Spring 1999): 40–50.

———. "The Human Costs of Graduate Education; or, The Need to Get Practical." *Academe: Bulletin of the American Association of University Professors*, 81.6 (November/December 1995): 30–36.

Woolf, Robert Paul. *The Ideal of the University*. Boston: Beacon Press, 1969.

Wright, David. "Writing the Real World." *Kenyon Review* 24: 3–4 (2002): 34–38.

Zaidi, Ali Shezhad. "Powerful Compassion: The Strike at Syracuse." *The Monthly Review*, September 1999: 27–38.

Zavarzadeh, Mas'ud. "The Dead Center: *The Chronicle of Higher Education* and the 'Radical' in the Academy." *The Alternative Orange* 5 (Summer/Fall 1997): 57–60.

Žižek, Slavoj, ed. *Mapping Ideology*. London: Verso, 1994.

Authors' Notes

Cary Nelson is Jubilee Professor of Liberal Arts and Sciences at the University of Illinois at Urbana-Champaign. He is also Vice-President of the American Association of University Professors. His previous book with Stephen Watt is *Academic Keywords: A Devil's Dictionary For Higher Education*. Among his 24 authored or edited books are *Repression and Recovery: Modern American Poetry and the Politics of Cultural Memory; Revolutionary Memory: Recovering the Poetry of the American Left; Madrid 1937: Letters of the Abraham Lincoln Brigade from the Spanish Civil War; Cutlural Studies, Marxism and the Interpretation of Culture;* and *Higher Education Under Fire.*

Stephen Watt is Professor of English and Chair of the Department of English at Indiana University. In addition to his earlier collaboration with Cary Nelson, *Academic Keywords: A Devil's Dictionary For Higher Education* (1999), he is the author of *Joyce, O'Casey, and the Irish Popular Theater* (1991), *Postmodern/Drama: Reading the Contemporary Stage* (1998), and—with Walter Kalaidjian and Judith Roof—*Understanding Literature: An Introduction to Reading and Writing* (2004). He is the editor of several books, including *A Century of Irish Drama: Widening the Stage* (2000); and the forthcoming volume, *Ian Fleming and James Bond: The Cultural Politics of 007.*

Index